The Politics of Recession

R. W. Johnson

MACMILLAN

© R. W. Johnson 1985

First published 1985 by
Higher and Further Education Division
MACMILLAN PUBLISHERS LTD
London and Basingstoke
Companies and representatives
throughout the world

Printed in Hong Kong

British Library Cataloguing in Publication Data
Johnson, R. W.
The politics of recession.
1. Great Britain—Politics and government—
1964–1979
2. Great Britain—Politics and government—
1979–
I. Title
941.085′8   DA589.7
ISBN 0–333–36786–3
ISBN 0–333–36787–1 Pbk

To Anne, Annette and Joan

Contents

Preface

When I was growing up people always referred to the times through which we were living as 'the post-war period'. After many years of this I became discontented: when would a new period start? Didn't history ever change and move on? We know the answer to this now. The post-war period ended in 1973 and a new era began. Clearly, I should not have been so impatient. For all the difficulties of those times the period from 1945 to 1973 is likely to be remembered as something of a golden age: no world wars, sweeping emancipation from colonial rule, growing detente between East and West, continuous and headlong economic growth. The period which began in 1973 looks altogether less hopeful and at worst it looks positively frightening.

Everything I have written in the last decade has been influenced, in one way or another, by the belief that the most urgent intellectual task before us today is to understand and analyse this new, post-1973 world. To be sure, history will never be an irrelevance. But the situation is quite new. Very little that we learnt about the world of 1945–73 has prepared us for an era of world recession, high inflation, mass unemployment, the chaos over currency and gold which has followed the collapse of Bretton Woods, the growing divide between Europe and the USA, the resurgence of the Cold War, the oil crisis, the world debt crisis and the rise of new economic powers in the world. Every one of these phenomena – and many more besides – first emerged in 1973. The politics of the new period are different too. In place of the the comfortable and optimistic world of social democratic liberalism a new, sharp-edged conservatism is much in evidence. Moreover, change and oscillation have hardly subsided. Even if – as seems likely – the present recession continues for another decade or more, there is no sign of equilibrium at this new level.

It is already clear that almost everything hangs on the question of how long and how deep the present recession will be. All of the new problems mentioned above would be made more tolerable by a true recovery from recession and some might disappear altogether. The trouble is that in the past the world has only got itself out of a trough like this by means of war. Rationally and humanely such a solution would seem to be precluded this time and already, it is true, we have weathered a number of crises in the post-1973 period which in earlier times would almost certainly have led to war. None the less, the tightening of international tension is evident on every side and there is no certainty that rationality and humanity will continue, even in their present, limited way, to prevail. On the other hand, if prevail they do, the present recession may have no end in sight at all. We are stuck with this frightening and unstable equilibrium. Our only, minimal hope of security lies in at least understanding this new world in which we live. If we fail in that then even hope dies, after which it will not be long before a lot of other things die too.

In selecting essays for this book it was thus not difficult to decide that those dealing with the international political economy should come first. Part Two, which follows, deals solely with British themes. There is, I hope, a more than parochially British rationale to this. For in thinking about the politics of recession Britain occupies a special position. It was the world's first industrial nation and now again it seems to be leading the way: if one wants to see the face of the future it may well be that it is to Britain that one should look. In no other developed economy has the post-1973 recession bitten so deeply. Nowhere else have production and investment fallen by so much and for so long. Nowhere else has unemployment (if honestly counted) risen so far and stayed so high. And nowhere else has the process of de-industrialisation gone so far or the disparity between industrial decline and the booming high-tech financial services sector been so extreme.

In large part Britain's failings now are the result of past success. Her early industrial strength, the enormous benefits of Empire and her freedom from dislocation by war or revolution all helped create uniquely powerful relations of social domination. The British bourgeoisie fused with the older ruling class and thus took over many of its attitudes and prerogatives while the British working class – the world's oldest – learnt to internalise its own subordination. Thus while the British class structure is statistically similar enough to that found in other developed capitalist states, it still has a unique rigidity of manner and attitude, the ossified clarity of an ideal type.

This fact permeates every aspect of British society. Where else – to take but one example – could one expect to find a whole house of the national legislature which is a mixture of the hereditary and the appointive, with no democratic element at all? Nowhere else have the democratic and egalitarian impulses of the capitalist free market been so stifled in their social and political expression. Undoubtedly this has been a major cause – perhaps *the* major cause – of British decline. The sanctity of every form of vested interest in Britain – trade union as well as bourgeois – has produced a classic form of immobilism which has robbed the country of the flexibility needed to face up to its post-imperial challenges, even, it sometimes seems, to face up to its problems honestly at all.

This immobilism, as in Italy or Fourth Republican France, has as its counterpart a government which, despite outward appearances, is woefully weak. At least since 1951 no British government has been bold enough to confront this problem of ossified privilege head on, to complete the democratic revolution in Britain. The result has been a lasting political paralysis. Governments of differing stripes have come and gone, sometimes making quite sweeping attempts at economic reform. They have never persisted for long and the failure to attack the class root of the problem has reduced these reforms to fore-doomed ripples on the surface. This in turn has meant that Britain's decline, despite the appearance of frenzied effort to halt it, has been pretty much a matter of free fall.

This almost idealised form of class society entered the recession, typically enough, locked in a social struggle of surpassing intensity – the miners' strike of 1973–4. This was followed by 'business as usual' – that is to say, five more years of weak, temporising government. These Labour years stood for nothing so much as the exhaustion of the spirit of reform. The 1945–51 Labour government, despite many lost opportunities, had carried through a major reform package. The 1964–70 government had at least begun with reforming intentions. The 1974–79 Labour government had clearly given up the ghost almost from the start. Its ambition was just to survive, treading water in the Micawberish hope that an international recovery would somehow 'turn up'. It didn't, of course.

This was followed by the Conservative counter-revolution of Thatcherism – which, again, has an important international dimension.

Nowhere else has there been a government more consistently and tough-mindedly intent on reducing inflation through the age-old remedy of the balanced budget and regardless of the human cost. And nowhere else among the Western democracies has such a government had such a free hand – the time, the legislative majority, the undivided executive authority – to work its will. J. K. Galbraith was only one of many foreign observers to grasp that Thatcherism would provide a virtual laboratory test of monetarist doctrine.

Such a government held a certain promise. It was bold, it was strong, and it was utterly committed to free market capitalism. Logically this ought to have led it to attack at least the grosser feudal anachronisms in British society. Instead it was soon clear that the government was concerned only to defer to and even to reinforce such institutions. At the end of the Thatcher experiment it seems certain that the pro-modern and anti-democratic encrustations on British society will have been measurably strengthened, not weakened.

On both counts then – Britain as the paradigm class society and Britain as the eye of the storm in the world recession – it seems clear that the 'model' the country poses to the world will become even more extreme. On the one hand, Britain's relative economic decline, merely relative until 1979, has since then become absolute: by 1983 industrial production was below not only the 1979 level but even the 1970 level. No other developed country has known anything like this. On the other hand, at least as fast as government policy has shrunk the size of the overall cake it has also redistributed what remains quite sharply away from the have-nots towards the haves. This remarkable – and hideous – process again makes Britain a virtual laboratory test case of retrogressive social change in the world of recession. No one can live through this in Britain without recalling the old Chinese saying 'may you live in interesting times' – or remembering that this saying was a curse.

The essays in this book were all written for an audience which is, I hope, both popular and serious. Anyone who tries to write about politics in this vein is bound to be conscious of the giant shadow cast by Orwell. On the one hand, Orwell was determined to avoid the triviality of the popular press and the clubby, collusive atmosphere of 'the posh papers'. 'What I have most wanted to do throughout the past ten years', he wrote in *Why I Write*, 'is to make political writing into an art.' On the other hand, the cautious, neutered tone of the academic journals was not for him: 'my starting point', he wrote, 'is always a feeling of partisanship, a sense of injustice'. He wrote, moreover, with a wonderful directness and in a beautifully plain English – the key to getting across serious subjects to a wide audience – which makes him seem an accessible model. Appearances are deceptive though: this sort of thing is far harder than he made it look.

I have tried to take all this to heart. A publisher friend once described my essays as 'a sort of reverse Dale Carnegie: how to influence people by losing friends'. I can't say about influencing people, but I have tried to be direct. This is not always easy in Britain where public debate is hemmed in not only by legislative restriction, but by the high premium placed on not causing undue upset or embarrassment. It says a great deal for Paul Barker, the editor of *New Society* (where a number of the essays in this book first appeared), that in his pages I was always able to write what I wanted the way I wanted.

He must often have disagreed with me, but even when I wrote in a way which was likely to be unpopular or which departed quite sharply from the general tenor of his magazine, he raised no demur. Paul deserves my thanks, but he deserves more than that. His creative indulgence – to many others besides myself – has helped maintain an honourable, if often isolated, tradition of real openness and independence. Most, perhaps, of those who write for *New Society*, are, like myself, liberals or socialists of one stripe or another, but you can find Conservatives and Communists in its pages too. This is a rare and precious thing. Perhaps the best way of expressing Paul's achievement is to ask, were Orwell still writing today, who would publish him? Not *Tribune* any more, alas. If one runs through the list of possibilities one realises fairly soon that only *New Society* would allow him the space, independence and catholicity he required. I can think of no higher accolade for Paul than that.

My opinions are my own, but I do have other debts to acknowledge all the same. I am grateful to Steven Kennedy at Macmillan for his persistence in getting me to do this book, and I am also grateful to two of my Magdalen colleagues, Frank Parkin and Andreas Boltho, who have both influenced me more than they probably realise. Frank's intellectual influence was particularly important to the long essay on the Conservatives, while Andreas has frequently made me re-examine my views about international economic questions. During three of the years when many of my *New Society* articles were written I was also Senior Bursar of Magdalen and I should, too, note my gratitude to the Bursary staff, particularly Joan Forrest and Annette Richardson, for putting up with my Bohemian ways, which provided the only way of doing that job and meeting my deadlines. Finally, and most of all, I owe a further debt to Anne Summers, always my first and toughest critic even though she was usually heavily involved with writing of her own.

December 1983   R. W. JOHNSON

Part One
The New World Order

Part One
The New World Order

1

The Oil Crisis Revisited*

The outbreak of peace between Egypt and Israel seems to have prevented anyone from commemorating the fifth anniversary of the Yom Kippur war. But the news of the shut-off of supplies from the strife-torn Iranian oil fields reminds one fairly sharply that we stand too on the fifth anniversary of the Great Oil Crisis of 1973. It is an era fairly burnt (if that is the word) into one's memory. Looking back, the event that sticks most clearly in my mind is going out into Oxford High Street at 8 pm on a Saturday evening and finding so little traffic that one could have played a rubber of bridge in the middle of the road without serious risk of disturbance. Other images of the crisis were less pacific – the hysteria of the filling-station queues and the furious resentment at the Arabs 'holding the west to ransom' by acting in the most traditional western way and getting the best price they could for their product.

In fact OPEC's self-assertion ran up hard against some deeply ingrained imperial notions. The major oil producers, it seemed clear, would now all become super-rich and powerful states, their potency quite unrestrained by links binding them to either of the two great blocs. This destabilisation of the political balance would be paralleled by the creation of a major structural imbalance in the international economy. Many of the new rich would simply be unable to spend their wealth, their economies lacking the prodigious absorptive capacity that would be required. As a result they would build up enormous cash surpluses. This would put the international financial system at their mercy, for they would be able to capsize any currency, even the mighty dollar, simply by moving their elephantine assets from counter

* First published in *New Society*, 16 November 1978.

to counter. Armed with such funds, the Arabs and Iranians would descend on us to buy up our major enterprises.

There was a strong sense of affront at this large alteration in the balance of power. It wasn't long, in many case, since we had commandeered the resources of many of these states by *force majeure* or 'bought' them for a few old rifles and broken promises. This sudden and unwelcome reversal wasn't, well, quite fair. I remember one BBC interviewer solemnly putting it to the Shah that Iran hadn't really earned this wealth, it was just luck they had all this oil under the ground. So wasn't it a little indecent to take such advantage of the situation? The Shah replied that he'd gladly swap the oil for Britain's rainfall, which did not, after all, seem likely to run out after 1990.

On the home front, equally strong expectations were held. We had clearly heard the death-knell of the motor car – at the very least, we'd all drive minis from now on. Pedestrianisation would now go ahead in all our major cities, which would, incidentally, be saved from further decline now that rising commuter costs would stop or even reverse the outward flood of population from them. The age of rail, of bus and bike, had returned, as also the age of coal. We would all save a lot of energy by turning down the heating, insulating lofts, and organising car pools for travel to work.

Again, one could detect some deeper notes among the reactions. One of the few clear remnants of the Puritan spirit in England is the considerable constituency eager to believe that any crisis or difficulty for modern industrial society (= 'selfish materialism') is a good thing. Not a few voices were, accordingly, now heard intoning sombrely, but with quite audible satisfaction, that the crisis meant the end for western civilisation 'as we know it', and that we would now have to do things *their way*. There was, though, great variety in the prescriptions offered, for the crisis not merely convinced many ecology enthusiasts that their hour had struck at last, but also brought to the fore that richly English figure, the amateur inventor.

Alternative schemes

The media found time and space to interview all manner of such enthusiasts. We would, it appeared, have to build a lot of windmills. Huge mirrors would be erected on hilltops to turn our paltry sunshine into incandescent energy. Dams and barrages would be built across our major estuaries, most notably that of the Severn. Vast lines of floating contraptions to collect wave power would be laid in the North and Irish Seas, the sea-lanes having presumably been vacated by tankers anyway. Old steam locomotives would be dusted off and brought back to service.

By no means all of these schemes were mad, but it is those touched with eccentric genius that linger in one's mind. My own favourite came in a radio interview with a man eager that we grasp to the full the ghastly possibilities of producing methane gas from human manure. His scheme envisaged the siting of methane plants in all public lavatories – the new powerhouses of Britain – linked by a vast network of pipes into the national grid. The scheme, Victorian in its scope and grandeur, unfolded like some great mechanised Freudian dream. Not just anal compulsion, but anal propulsion. Incremental power from excremental energy. With rising delight I heard the inventor conclude that while he had not yet obtained a patent on his scheme he was ready, none the less, to put it immediately at the nation's service because 'everyone must do his bit'.

Five years later . . . well, the results of the crisis have nowhere been as dramatic as first envisaged. The OPEC states have, like any ordinary pools winner, astonished themselves and others by the speed and ease with which they've been able to spend money. An unknowable, though certainly large proportion of their wealth has been wasted on luxury consumption and unproductive investment. Enormous sums have been spent on arms and aeroplanes, often far beyond the capacity of OPEC armed forces to use or man them. Throughout the Gulf area there has been a ludicrous replication of massive port construction schemes and other capital-intensive prestige projects. The Nigerians spent enormous sums on buying cement they could not even land, let alone use. Huge amounts have been expended on setting up or expanding national airlines, on filling them with passengers bound for the world's fleshpots, and on paying for all the drink, women and gambling when they get there.

Then again the price of oil has fallen like a stone. That is, its price has remained relatively steady in money terms while world inflation has roared away and, at least as important, the oil price is denominated in dollars and has thus fallen in real terms along with the dollar. Thus over the past two and a half years the oil price has fallen 20 per cent in sterling terms, over 60 per cent in terms of the yen, deutschmark and Swiss franc, and by proportions somewhere in between those two figures in most other major currencies.

The reason for this development is partly that new sources of oil have come on stream (in Mexico, the North Sea, Alaska, Egypt and so on); partly that consumption has dropped somewhat due to recession and conservation; and partly because everyone can see that vast new supplies now lie within easy enough reach. Meanwhile, despite successive production cut-backs by the Saudis and others, there is a world crude oil surplus of around two million barrels a day.

The result of the oil-producers' spending binge and the falling oil price is, in turn, a dramatic fall in the OPEC cash surplus from $65 billion in 1974 to around $10 billion in 1978. Such figures conceal the fact that many of the biggest producers are not in surplus at all, but deep in debt. Some of them, such as Nigeria and Indonesia, are even having grave difficulties in persuading the banks that they are good credit risks for further loans. The Shah, to whom we have toadied so obsequiously in recent years, is looking the very opposite of a good credit risk.

Paradoxically, the result both of the few years of massive surplus and of its shrinkage now has been the extraordinarily rapid integration of the major OPEC states into the western economic order. As the surpluses built up and assets were bought abroad these states acquired a powerful interest in maintaining western prosperity. A big fall on Wall Street or a collapse in London property values would now inflict losses on many Arabs.

Secondly, because they receive payment for their oil in dollars, the OPEC states have become the staunchest and most conservative defenders of the present international monetary system. Saudi Arabia, in particular, has emerged as almost the strongest supporting pillar the US Treasury has. Not only have the Saudis persistently refused all schemes to demand payment for their oil in baskets of currencies, SDRS or gold (preferring simply to revalue the riyal against the dollar in an almost endless succession of upward movements), but they have exerted strong and successful pressure on all the other Gulf states to follow their lead.

And thirdly, as some of the less affluent oil-producers have gone into debt they have found their dependence on big western banks increasing commensurately. As a result of all these developments the notion of the OPEC states threatening the stability of the world capitalist economy by gestures of 'irresponsible independence' has become almost laughable.

No hasty action

Thus the impact of the oil crisis on our parochial home front has also been rather smaller than expected. None of our major enterprises have (publicly, at least) passed into OPEC hands. Happily or not, British Leyland is still ours. The British firm that is absorbing the most Arab money is very probably Marks & Spencers, presumably enabling Lord Sieff to be more generous than ever in his various benefactions to the zionist cause.

Meanwhile the price of petrol in real terms is back at its 1973 level and – an added bonus – price wars rage delightfully at our filling stations. Because we are so hopelessly slow to react to anything, we also avoided making hasty and irreversible mistakes. The French, for example, went for broke with a massive nuclear power construction programme and now find themselves stuck with high, fixed energy costs and a large number of angry ecologists.

So, were all the erroneous expectations of five years ago merely part of a wild folk-panic? Not entirely. It remains the case that our economy and social lives depend overwhelmingly on oil and that even with many of the North Sea wells on stream we import half our needs. Other industrialised states rely just as heavily on oil and their import-dependence is higher too. Our collective needs are certain to grow even if recession continues to dampen demand and conservation efforts are maintained. And, despite new discoveries, there is a finite amount of the stuff.

So the news of the cut-off of Iranian oil production is no joke. We may even be able to celebrate the anniversary of the oil crisis with renewed queues at the petrol pumps. One thing I do know is that on any future such occasion I shall feel a lot more philosophical than in 1973. Indeed, as the lights dim my spirits will soar. For it won't be long then until the BBC manages to re-interview the man with the plan for our public lavatories. I'm dying to know how he's been getting on.

2

Far from Vietnam*

My daughter was just three when she came home (from nursery school) talking, confusedly, about something she'd heard about 'the Vietnams'. Last week – she is eight now – she came home from school talking about 'the Vietnamese boat people'. This time she knows more clearly what she is talking about – and wants to discuss it with me.

It reminds me of how during the spring of 1954 (at the age of ten) I listened, utterly gripped, to the unfolding drama of Dien Bien Phu on the radio news. Thus – in somewhat garbled form – two generations brought up against the endless background tragedies of Indochina. It would be possible, of course, to go much further back and (though heaven forbid) it may be possible to go further forward, too. Whether or not we like it, we all seem to be actors in our own long-running versions of Godard's *Far From Vietnam*.

The scale of the thing is overwhelming, not just in the length of time for which the agony has endured, but in the sheer quantity of human suffering. The new rulers of Phnom Penh say that the preceding Pol Pot regime killed or allowed to die some three million of Cambodia's nine million people. There seems, give or take a million, little reason to doubt their word. Before that our friends, the Americans, killed Vietnamese and Laotians on a scale of barbarism previously equalled only by Hitler's pogroms against the Jews. Henry Kissinger, who was responsible for a good share of these deaths, is Jewish. But this didn't seem to make much difference.

The Indochina war has come to assume two quite separate realities. It is, on the one hand, 'a quarrel in a far-away country between people of whom we know nothing', and, on the other, it is the continuing

---

* First published in *New Society*, 15 February 1979.

moral cockpit of our consciences. It elicits all our feelings, all our judgements. It has been our Spanish civil war – except that it is also our Thirty Years' War (longer really – hostilities have been more or less continuous since Japan moved into northern Indochina in 1940). It has, as a result, rung all the notes and all the changes on the scale of our moral response.

During my childhood the basic themes were fairly simple. The BBC and the *News Chronicle* taught me to have a romanticised sympathy with the French, personified by the dashing, moustachioed figures of foreign legionnaires in tropical battledress. They, one understood, were fighting the good fight against the Communist hordes. The Communists were robotic fanatics who employed terrifying 'human wave' tactics. One had no feeling that it was really their country. They seemed to be there just incidentally, though in very large numbers. One was awfully sorry when the French began losing, but not very surprised. Frenchmen were all gallant, but not very good soldiers, being too talkative and romantic.

A few years later, the same legionnaires and the dreaded 'paras' had become synonymous with retaliatory executions of whole Algerian villages and the mass torture of civilians, employing for the first time that bestial toy of our age, the electrode.

By then a new set of images of Indochina had taken over in one's mind. This area was, it appeared, the *locus classicus* of the new 'bush-fire wars', of which the charismatic young JFK so impressively warned us. These were to be dealt with by a glamorous mixture of tough idealism and technical efficiency: the Green Berets. Combining the virtues of the PT 109 with those of the peace corps, these would clinically seal off such dangers with executive efficiency and technological flair. One was vaguely uneasy about all this but it sounded tough-mindedly exciting and, anyway, JFK could do no wrong. He had been gunned down in Dallas by the time that Lieutenant Calley, gunning down large numbers of women and children in My Lai, rather changed one's view of the Green Berets.

Moral torpor

By the time I arrived at Oxford (in 1964) I was following developments in Vietnam closely. I devoured the inch-sized snippets in the papers every day, always fearing the worst. This, almost invariably, was the right thing to do. Barring one American friend, Mike, no one else felt the same. We were appalled to find that no section of British opinion seemed to have any sense or to be even morally awake on the issue.

When the US bombing of North Vietnam began in 1965, I was actually shaken awake by a furious Mike, brandishing that week's *New Statesman*. There was not a thing in it about the bombings. As I rubbed sleep from my eyes Mike stalked my room, declaring that 'This mag is not left-wing, it's not intellectual, but by God it's British', tearing the offending NS to shreds on my floor as he spoke. As week followed week and still the NS remained silent on the issue, we cancelled our subscriptions.

Then its editor, John Freeman, was made ambassador to India and the new editor, unconstrained by any foreknowledge of an impending appointment to a major post in south Asia, began a furious campaign against the bombing. We regarded the event as a perfect paradigm of the whole mealy-mouthed attitude of the Wilson government towards Vietnam.

Within a year or two one had the justified feeling of opinion coming around to one's side *en masse*. There were marches, demonstrations, teach-ins galore – a great gale of protest which blew and blew without slackening. This was only partly pleasant, for one was uncomfortable about many of one's new bedfellows. Many wanted peace, without thought for its terms. We felt it would be bitterly unfair if the Vietnamese ended up with less than their whole country. That is, in practical terms, we wanted the north to win.

On the other side, we were aghast at the cult of personality of Ho Chi Minh, the glossing over the harshness of his land reforms of the late fifties and, most of all, the terrifyingly unreal enthusiasm and special pleading. It became gospel that the North Vietnamese army was not operating in the south or from across the Cambodian border – which, in both cases, it clearly was. The 'domino' theory was wicked and must be wrong, it was said; to us it seemed wholly plausible. The bombing was wicked, too, but it was almost a good thing because it made the Vietnamese fight harder than ever. The more American arms sent in, almost the better too because, didn't you know, the Vietnamese would capture them in the end and thus be all the stronger.

In a word, entirely different moral and even human standards than those applying elsewhere were held to prevail in Indochina. As was once said of Kingsley Martin, for him 'East of Suez, somehow or other, God was Left-wing, and once you got west of Suez, He was a Right-wing reactionary.'

Then there was the draft question. One could not but sympathise with one's American contemporaries, and later one's pupils, who faced this awful dilemma. Having become a teacher, I found that the draft question devoured hours of one's day, years of one's time. Imperceptibly, one's sympathy declined. By the seventies it was an old issue, after all.

Finally, one colleague turned to an American student who diverted all his tutorials into such discussions and told him that it probably didn't much matter what he did. He could either be pointlessly bored doing a desk job in Saigon or he could desert and be pointlessly bored doing odd jobs in Malmö. Listening, I was surprised to find I approved.

The fact was that, struggle as one might, moral exhaustion had set in. The war just dragged on and on. Nixon bombed, invaded Cambodia, got out, evicted Sihanouk and imposed Lon Nol, Vietnamised the war, retreated. It all registered only dully. One was simply punch-drunk. Even the final collapse of South Vietnam, an event at which I would have been appalled in 1954 and elated in 1965, seemed, when it came in 1975, merely like the end of a Western. The classical bad guys, Ky and Thieu, had met their just deserts. The bombast of 'never surrender' was over. No more children would be napalmed in defence of the Free World. The fall of Lon Nol soon after seemed an equally just and merciful event.

Wearily, one knew in one's bones that this was merely a new beginning. The North Vietnamese, the world's best soldiers since the Japanese, looked, in the later stages of thier victory, more like Prussians. Their country was utterly ruined and the only thing in it that worked was their army. The Americans had left the south awash with human flotsam and jetsam – torturous policemen, half a million prostitutes, every possible variety of pimp and drug-peddlar, and a bourgeoisie that had done well out of the war. Such elements, combined with a triumphant northern army and a countryside scientifically treated with defoliants to produce likely mass starvation, seemed a mixture able only to generate more woe.

Cambodia and Laos presented a similar picture. One could not have predicted that the Khemer Rouge regime would be so abominable, that the Vietnamese would turn on their Chinese minority, that there would soon be another war in Indochina, this time between neighbouring communist regimes. But now this has all come to pass, none of it seems surprising.

I feel – or try to feel – horrified by these events, and also by my own fatalism. Where is the line drawn between moral exhaustion and moral corruption? Is there, indeed, a line? I truly don't know. None of this is, in any case, much use for answering my daughter's questions about the Vietnamese boat people – and, being young and un-fatalistic, she *does* want to know. I could tell her that refugees are inevitable in such a situation. Or that, since the refugees include many former beneficiaries and supporters of the insupportable Ky–Thieu regime, they may have only a limited claim on our sympathy.

I could tell her that our present Oxfamish concern for them is a little suspect, in any case. We didn't do enough to stop the war that produced them. When that war ended, we carried out a grotesque mass kidnapping of thousands of Vietnamese orphans who might have been able to adjust to a new life in their country, leaving behind their elders who actually wanted to emigrate and couldn't possibly adjust.

There's always the next time

All such responses, it will be seen, point to constructing answers which prevent her from feeling too much sympathy for suffering people at their last extremity of desperation and misery. If that's what moral exhaustion does, then surely it is corrupt. The trouble is that to induct a whole new generation into emotional engagement with such problems means just allowing more wounds to feeling in the end. If she starts pouring her sympathies into the same bottomless pit, she can only end up morally exhausted, too.

One wishes to protect one's children from becoming oneself. But one can't protect them from exposure to such tragedy any more than I could have been prevented from imbibing my Technicolor childhood version of Dien Bien Phu. And if she is not allowed, even encouraged, to sympathise with real misery when she actually sees it, maybe she starts off morally exhausted in the first place. So one is condemned to repeat the cycle, hoping only that she won't be facing similar dilemmas with her children in thirty years from now. There's always next time, the time after that, the time after . . .

3

Dear Peter . . .*

Lord Carrington,   Magdalen College,
Foreign and Commonwealth Office,   Oxford.
King Charles St,   21 June 1979
London S.W.1.

Dear Peter,

Of course I don't mind setting forth my views for you on Sir
Nicholas Henderson's valedictory dispatch on Britain's Decline; its
Causes and Consequences. As for doing it without a fee, well that's all
right – I know how hard up we are. I haven't been deflected by the
media storm over the leak of Henderson's memo to *The Economist*,
but I hope you won't mind if I offer my reply to the weekly press as
well. It's not that I lack confidence in the ability of the FCO's resident
Deep Throat to place it there for me, but I have found that reliance on
such channels sometimes leads to unfortunate delays in publication.

I can understand your testiness over the Henderson thing – a
nuisance for you in your first month as Foreign Secretary. You say,
too, that as a sixth baron and Old Etonian you are 'not easily to be
impressed by the scribblings of a mere baronet who went to Stowe'.
Such prejudices are, as usual, extremely sound – but I hope to
persuade you to disregard Henderson's woolly nonsense on other
grounds too. How *The Economist*, heavily staffed as it is with my own
former pupils, can have been impressed by it ('unusually forthright
and timely', they called it) is a source of puzzlement and some chagrin
to me. I would suggest, rather, that it provides a perfect example of
how poorly served we are by our FO professionals.

---

* First published in *New Society*, 21 June 1979.

Henderson starts, you will recall, by putting the bald economic facts of Britain's decline relative to the French and Germans – comparative economic growth rates and the like. From this he moves (jumps, really) to our spiritual malaise. He notes, sadly, 'how poor and unproud the British have become. . . . It shows in the look of our towns . . . and in local amenities; it is painfully apparent in much of our railway system. . . . In France, for instance, it is evident in spending on household equipment and in the growth of second homes.' (Two jumps here: the first 'it' is *our* lack of pride, a subject which cannot possibly be transposed onto *their* spending habits; secondly, there is the smooth but entirely non-sequential jump from our public squalor to their private affluence. Any relationship that may exist between the growth of second homes and the upkeep of local amenities is almost certainly an inverse one.)

At this point Henderson pauses (as well he might): 'This is not the place', he says, to discuss the causes of our decline. He then proceeds to discuss them. The usual list: more movement needed between industry, government and academe (more Lord Goodmans?); our managers are no good *and* are paid too little; the unions. ('No French manager thinks twice about changing people's duties or their timetables . . . , nor does he hesitate to install new machinery and instruct people that from Monday onwards they will be working at x instead of y.') He seems to forget that the French have the great advantage that their largest trade union is Communist. This means they can get away with treating their workers like second-hand robots without any liberal guilt problems and without more than occasional riots (three so far this year). Our workers are far more conservative – as you know, that's why you're back in office – and consequently much harder to deal with. It's swings and roundabouts, Peter.

Henderson then reaches his main point: our economic weakness is sapping our foreign policy; Bevin wanting higher coal production to give him more weight at the conference table, etc. Then, a right-angle turn into a long excursus on how we mucked about and didn't get into the EEC on the ground floor because of Eden's blinkered stupidity. He jumps to the view (for him the point is axiomatic, not logical) that our salvation has always lain and still lies now in the fullest possible integration into the EEC. (In general he feels about the EEC much as women's magazines do about motherhood; no matter how many children you have or how ghastly it can be, you can't have too much of it because it's a Good Thing.)

And so to conclusions. First, 'We should be able to put at the service of the (European) community the imagination, tolerance and commonsense that have formed our own national institutions.' (Imagine, if you will, Peter, a visitor to your home informing you benignly that he feels his contribution to your household will be 'imagination, tolerance and commonsense'. You would, I have no doubt, regard him as ill-mannered, arrogant or mad – perhaps all three. You would, quite rightly, throw him out.)

Second, as far as our prodigious subsidies to our richer neighbours in the EEC go, 'there is only one way to go about it . . . and that is to have a heart-to-heart talk with the leaders of the other eight countries'. This is a bit like having a heart-to-heart talk with a bank robber over the problems of the money supply. Third, 'there would appear to be a need at the present time to do something to stimulate a sense of national purpose'. (One passes with embarrassment over the appalling vacuity of that 'something'.) In particular, more flag-waving is, it seems, required. Giscard, he tells us, is good at this: 'In a speech that he made recently that lasted only eight minutes he used the word 'France' over 23 times and the word 'win' seven times.' The basic idea would seem to be that our politicians should try to ape football managers giving their teams hurried half-time pep talks. On this argument the case for Brian Clough as prime minister seems overwhelming. I think he would regard eight minutes as a bit short, though.

Leaving aside the fact that this memo should have been addressed to the Treasury, not the FO, and that none of his conclusions have the remotest bearing on his original subject (our economic decline), the general analysis is quite extraordinarily wrong-headed.

Perhaps the weirdest idea, however commonplace it may be at the FO, is that we need a strong economy *so as to be able* to have an influential foreign policy. This is cart-before-horse with a vengeance. A strong economy makes us all rich and happy and is a good in itself; an influential foreign policy is at best a luxury and probably a liability. I would draw your attention to Schmidt's recent *Time* interview: 'The German economy is strong, it is solid. . . . It does not mean that the Germans can buy the whole world. The Americans could buy, more or less, the whole world. Germany is not a world power; it does not wish to become a world power.' The Japanese feel much the same, so do the even wealthier Swiss, so does anyone with anyone sense. . . .

Second, the most important point about Britain's economic decline is that it hasn't happened. As Henderson's figures show, our gross domestic product grew by a staggering 75 per cent between 1954 and 1977. There has been no period in our history when we have got stronger and richer at such a rate. If this produces a spiritual malaise in us, more fool us.

It is true, of course, that the EEC states, particularly Germany, have grown richer and stronger more quickly than us. But this has been happening, or trying to happen, for over a century. By 1914 Germany had heavily surpassed us on every possible index and had begun to dominate Europe. We didn't like it and spent several million lives and hideous amounts of money to make the Germans weaker, poorer and smaller. By 1939 Germany had almost drawn level again, so we had another fight and, having beaten them, inflicted another dose of the same medicine on them. By 1971 Germany had yet again far outstripped us. This time we decided to give up and join the German condominium over Europe (the EEC). Never mind about missing the boat in 1957 – if this was what we wanted we could, with considerable advantage, have done it in 1914 or even 1900.

Of course, it *isn't* what we wanted. Historically we have always wanted to keep Europe as disunited as possible. On the previous occasions when it has been united (under Napoleon and Hitler) we have fought like the devil against it – for we have always known that Europe can only be united under France or Germany (or, just possibly, the two together). It can't be done under us. For us European unity is a clear historical defeat and if we want to join it, it can only be as underdogs. Of *course* we will get a lousy deal from it, and of *course* it will get worse if we stay in.

This is what makes Henderson's fixation with our 'making a success' of our EEC membership so strange. The apparently ineluctable drift of Europe in an industrial age is towards the hegemony of Germany. It is this, not the EEC, which is the true fundamental. (Germany grew much faster in the 1950s before the EEC was formed; after she joined her growth rate slowed down to the EEC average; the EEC was not the cause of the German economic miracle, it was the *price* she was willing to pay for renewed dominance in Europe.) Please note that the three richest countries in Europe – Sweden, Switzerland and Norway – have used their strength to keep *out* of the EEC. If we felt strong or even had the heightened national purpose Henderson aspires to, the surest sign of it would be that we stayed out (or got out) too.

A final point. Henderson makes much of Eden's blindness in the 1950s when all the statistics pointed clearly to the strength of European growth. He might have added that this blindness was wholly shared by all other FO men of the time, almost certainly including himself. Now the conventional FO wisdom lies on the other extreme – and all the best statistics (Wynne Godley's from Cambridge) point inexorably to our breaking with the EEC. I greatly fear that Henderson's successors in ten years' time will be writing memos on the extraordinary blindness of the FO in ignoring *these* facts and figures.

I see, by the way, that you are sending Henderson off to Washington. I shouldn't think any harm need come of that. Indeed, he should be a great success. Americans love it when we play up to their notions of Olde Fashioned England. It's like our having to keep the monarchy and the Horse Guards so as not to disappoint their tourists. He'll certainly cut a good figure at the Embassy garden parties – and that's important. Mind you, memos like this last one are more or less inevitable if you send off men to countries notably more unequal than our own with instructions to 'go native'. They will interpret this as meaning they must mix with the richest 1 per cent of that country and you will get some very strange memos indeed out of that. Almost all the French 'virtues' noted by Henderson derive from their being easily the most unequal country in the western world. America's not quite so bad, but don't be too surprised if *The Economist* is soon carrying another leaked memo on how sadly we have fallen behind the Americans economically and castigating our politicians for having managed the War of Independence so badly.

Still, Peter, your predecessors displayed a commendably old-fashioned attitude when they filled the Washington post and were properly firm in rejecting the absurd charges of nepotism levelled against the PM's son-in-law. So if Henderson doesn't work out I think you should consider very seriously the possibility of sending your son, Rupert, in his place. You could do a lot worse, you really could.

Yours,
Bill

4

The Politics of Gold*

'If you can keep your head while all about you are losing theirs and blaming it on you', said Danny Blanchflower on quitting the managership of a woebegone Chelsea F.C. last week, 'then the odds are that you're out of touch with reality.' Anyone trying to keep a cool head amidst the speculative mania of the gold markets in the last few months will know how he felt. The recent surge has been so strong (taking gold from about $200 to $380 an ounce) that even the tabloid press has been advising readers on how to cash in, excitedly discussing the relative merits of gold jewellery, Krugerrands and South African mining shares.

The chorus of gold-worship has, as is usual on such occasions been both deafening and diverse. There is, quite simply, no mania like gold mania. No other commodity excites the hearts of French bankers *and* Indian peasants, South Africa House *and* Moscow Narodny Bank, *Pravda and* the *Daily Telegraph*. The chorus line stretches on from there – Indonesian gold smugglers, Hong Kong merchants, the great mining corporations, the Communist Chinese and right-wing kooks of every kind – all sing the same hymns in praise of gold. 'The only real commodity . . . better than oil . . . the hedge of hedges . . . timeless beauty . . . the intrinsic worth . . . the eternal store of value. . . .' The litany only gains in rhapsody from its endless repetition. And, of course, it's all complete nonsense.

For gold is not like oil. Not even like iron or aluminium. It has precious few uses and thus little real 'intrinsic' worth. By far its greatest 'use' still lies in sheer ornamentation. In the end the mainstay of the gold price is merely the appetite of pretty women for the stuff

---

* First published in *New Society*, 11 October 1979.

and their ability to persuade their consorts to buy it for them. When, as recently, the price surges the jewellers simply vacate the market *en masse*; from there on in it is simply a matter of speculation – and politics. This is not what you will read in *Pravda* or the *Telegraph* but it is true.

I must, at this point, declare an interest. Several years ago I became fascinated by the way in which the gold market acted as a barometer of complex forces within the international political economy. During the summer of 1976 I observed with growing excitement the vertiginous drop in the gold price towards $100 (in 1974 it had reached $197). The price fell under persistent American pressure (IMF and US Treasury gold sales, continual bearish rumours originated in Washington, etc.) – just as Henry Kissinger positioned himself to attempt a final pre-election diplomatic coup in Southern Africa. The price-fall hurt the Russians (the second-biggest producers) and the French (the biggest hoarders) but it almost capsized South Africa, by far the biggest producer, whose entire economy still depends crucially on gold. The American squeeze thus afforded Kissinger enormous leverage on South Africa – which he used to force it to force Ian Smith to give way. As soon as Smith made his historic concession of majority rule, Washington's pressure was released and the gold price began to soar. It has never really looked back. The soaring gold price has made South Africa all but invulnerable to pressure from the Carter Administration.

This history I then attempted to set forth in a book (*How Long Will South Africa Survive?* (Macmillan, 1977)) in which I traced in what detail I could the complex interplay of manipulation and inter-national pressures which, partly via the gold market, had played such a decisive role in southern African affairs. The book has already had an interesting life. It has been withdrawn briefly and then re-released. It was first banned and then unbanned in South Africa. It was praised in the Trotskyite press and the *Daily Telegraph*, denounced by the *Morning Star* and translated by the Yugoslavs. An anonymous letter of left-wing hue (and easily traceable origins) was mass-mailed to me and many of my friends, denouncing both author and book and mentioning, at several points, my imminent demise.

In terms of pure stamina, though, the response from the gold hawks surpassed all others. I still get wacky letters of denunciation from gold fiends in Sweden, California and points in between. Visiting South Africa last year I found my name still recurring fairly regularly in the press as an object of attack by (always unnamed) 'economic experts'

employed by the mining companies. I am endlessly badgered by the
editors of gold investment newsletters, many of them tough-minded
lunatics operating one-man-band financial services from places like
Buffalo or Milwaukee.

All this flattering attention derives from the belief gold hawks have
in their own propaganda about an 'intrinsic and eternal store of
value'. Oddly, I've had some flak too from Marxists, apparently torn
between a labour theory of value and some shadowy notion of a 'real'
value of gold. What both sides disliked was my contention that the
gold price was, above its basic 'jewellery level', politically determined.
It was bad enough for believers in either labour or eternal value trying
to explain why the price of this metal of such stable, intrinsic worth
could dance up and down like a yo-yo. Once it was conceded that the
price was essentially political neither Marx nor eternity were going to
get much of a look in.

But of course the price of gold *is* political. Apart from brief and
unsustainable periods (such as now) when 'pure' speculators take
over, the price is determined by the complex struggles and co-
operation of governments and central banks. Above all the gold price
has, in recent time, been an inverted image of us power within the
world economy. In the early 1930s Franklin Roosevelt, following
some rather weird monetarist advice, deliberately bid the price up day
by day (the idea being to start a reflationary recovery via a general rise
in prices). FDR took some pleasure in his daily price-fixings of what the
us Treasury would pay for gold. He generally conducted the business
over breakfast and, for example, in one day put up the price by 21
cents because, being three times seven, it seemed a lucky number. The
price was bid up from $20 to $35 before he gave it up as a bad job. The
$35 price was then frozen by American political fiat for the next
thrity-four years.

In the intervening period – essentially at Bretton Woods – the us
used its overwhelming power to nudge the capitalist world economy
on to a dollar standard. This conferred considerable advantages on
the Americans for, since it was unthinkable that the dollar could be
devalued (it was *the* standard), the us could run continual trade
deficits without their having the slightest effect on the value of their
currency. Simultaneously, they could keep the dollar's value artificially high against other currencies, enabling them to buy up
companies abroad or station imperial garrisons around the world all
at bargain-basement rates. Inevitably, this policy was hotly resented

by its victims in Europe, particularly the French who, under de Gaulle, began pushing hard to dethrone the dollar. Since no other currency could conceivably act as an alternative standard, the only other option was . . . gold. This Gaullist view was supported luke-warmly by other Europeans and eagerly – for obvious reasons – by the Russians and the South Africans.

The Americans, equally naturally, fought like tigers to retain their advantage, keeping the gold price down at $35, and tried hard to press on towards the complete 'de-monetization' of gold. The decline of American empire relative to the growing power of other capitalist states – particularly Japan and the EEC – meant that this was bound to be a losing battle. American defences gave way in 1968 – with the concession of a free market in gold – and then again in 1971, with the devaluation of the dollar. Thereafter only the more or less naked use of American political and economic power could prevent gold from rising against the dollar. Gold really took off in 1973–4 when Watergate undermined the credibility of US executive power. The price fell hard after the resumption of a stable presidency under Ford, has wavered upwards as Carter has staggered, and has now again 'taken off' into speculative mania as the markets perceive that there is a whole year and more of a lame-duck president in prospect ahead. Every next time OPEC slaps the US in the face and gets away with it the gold price is likely to rise. Equally, the emergence of a probable strong US president – Kennedy, Connally, even a reinvigorated Carter – will lead to an anticipatory fall in the price. At the end of the day it will still be true that the US has such prodigious gold reserves stored in Fort Knox that it can – if it has a government which really wants to – flood the market so heavily that the gold price would recede to $200 or, for that matter, $20.

This said, such an eventuality is extremely unlikely. So naked an exercise of US power would now be more unpopular than ever and the recent scramble for gold by central banks has greatly increased the vested interests liable to be hurt. Moreover, there are several new factors in the market – all of them political. Many central banks have recently been bidding the price up in an effort to 'burn' speculators planning to sell short: the banks want the speculators out of a market which has such disruptive effects on their own reserves and on international money markets in general. On the other hand, there is growing, if still mainly hidden, panic over the effects of the speculation on the Eurodollar market where many small and some big investment banks are now holding hideously large inventories of Eurodollar bonds which, amidst the rush to gold, they cannot sell. Some of the banks concerned are too important for governments to allow them to fail.

But whether the central banks and their governments can kill the present speculation is unclear. For the first time Arab money is beginning to pour into the gold market in substantial amounts. At the same time the Russians have been playing fast and loose with the market, restricting their (crucial) supplies to it to get a better price. And, third, countries which previously disdained gold – such as the Japanese – have begun to feel they must not get left behind: last year Tokyo soaked up a whopping 162 tons of bullion. If any combination of these forces were to continue for at all long, the market could explode upwards towards a gold price of thousands of dollars an ounce – before collapsing back amidst the calamitous international financial crisis which would ensue. Since *everybody* in the market fears that outcome, the political pressures to prevent it are very great.

Meanwhile, the present mania has already had important political repercussions. South Africa is in such booming economic health that the idea of anyone being able to apply financial pressure on Pretoria to produce a new Rhodesian solution is almost laughable. Pretoria has, moreover, won some potentially important new Arab partners-in-gold as a byproduct of the present mania. De Gaulle is laughing happily in his grave. The Russians are sighing with relief that they will be able to afford their next grain purchases so much more easily. This in turn is good news for American farmers, for it will push their prices up. Which will increase US inflation. Which will hurt Carter that much more. Which will tend to depress the dollar. Which will push up the gold price . . .

Thus the circle is complete. The logical beauty of speculative mania is that it reproduces in such fashion the reasons for its own indefinite continuation. Which is, of course, nonsense – the chain has to break somewhere. Meanwhile the higher gold goes the less 'intrinsic' worth it has, for its present price is taking it further and further out of reach of all those pretty women who are the main 'users'. My sympathies are entirely with them. Just at the moment, though, they would do well to develop an interest in, say, antiques.

5

The New Cold War*

A bare six weeks into the 1980s, the new decade already wears a
disturbing, Rip Van Winkle air. Repeatedly, since the New Year, we
have heard the proclamation of a new Cold War. Already Salt II has,
effectively, been abandoned and huge new programme of rearmament have been announced. There has been a radical cut-back in the
East–West trade which was the chiefest fruit of détente and the search
is on for other weapons of displeasure – Olympic boycotts and the
like. The two super-powers stand ranged against one another in the
same icy fury as of old and conflicts at the far corners of the earth
(Afghanistan today as Korea once before) are charged with planetary
significance by the simple methodological trick of reference to a
scheme of global bipolarisation; we are, at a stroke, back to the world
of the 1940s and '50s. As Rip Van Winkle wakes it is the 1960s and
'70s, which begin to seem unreal.

This surrealism has overlapped on to much of the press comment
on this alarming turn of events, where two contradictory responses
may be seen. The primary note has been one of panic, expressed either
as fear of an alleged Soviet military superiority and bellicosity or,
more simply, as a dread that the present diplomatic holocaust might
be followed by the real (nuclear) thing. A secondary note has,
however, been one of plain relief, the relief that only bred-in-the-bone
familiarity can bring. The multi-polar world of the '60s and '70s was,
after all, a confusing and frustrating place, shot through with
ambiguity and complexity. One had to decide who was 'right'
between, say, Israelis and Arabs or Cambodians and Vietnamese. One

---

* First published as 'Rip Van Winkle's New World', *New Society*, 14
February 1980.

had to decide who or what to blame for one's difficult relations with OPEC, the IMF or EEC and how on earth to cope with the commercial provocations of the French and Japanese. After all this it is not uncomfortable to be back on the old tramlines, facing an old and recognisable enemy who can be viewed in full-hearted Manichean terms. Four legs good, two legs bad. The old songs are not always the best but they do have the easiest lines.

Perhaps unsurprisingly, such reactions take little note of the revisionist school of diplomatic historians whose researches in the '60s and '70s have so altered older views of the nature and origins of the Cold War. The revisionists – Fleming, Mayer, Williams, Kolko, Levin, Alperovitz and others – were a various bunch but were united in their rejection of the Manichean view which traced all developments from the evil of Soviet expansionism. The USSR, they argued, was an almost pathologically defensive power. Even when it was willing to look beyond the narrow confines of its own territorial security, it remained so fixated by the idea of 'capitalist encirclement' that it was still merely concerned with the creation of a ring of protective buffer states. There was no real evidence for serious Soviet designs on Western Europe – even after 1945 the Red Army had vacated two states (Austria and Finland) where it could easily have chosen to stay on.

America, on the other hand, they argued, had reached its imperial zenith in 1945. Its armies were flung across the globe from Seoul to Berlin and almost everywhere they *had* stayed on. But it was an empire with a difference. America, which then accounted for over half of the capitalist world's production, was too powerful to want to set any limits on where her writ might run – it would be an empire without frontiers. As once the US had demanded an 'Open Door' to China, so now she demanded an open door to the world. The old closed systems of Western empire soon buckled beneath this pressure, leaving only the Communist world as the sole area to remain provokingly off-limits to the open system of American power. The Cold War was essentially the result of this confrontation between this irresistible American force and the immovable Communist object.

At this point the revisionists tended to divide, some imputing that the fault for the Cold War lay with the US for greedily demanding world political and commercial hegemony while the Communists simply wanted to keep their bit of it inviolate. Others concluded, more neutrally, that it was nobody's fault, merely the inevitable clash between two mutually incompatible systems. Where both agreed was in acknowledging that the Cold War's continuation was of quite unequal significance to the two blocs. For the Communist states it was simply a miserable, frightening and humiliating experience. They lived under threat from a vastly more powerful alliance, were denied access to goods they wanted to buy, and were treated as lepers and outcasts. The only consolation it brought was the virtually enforced unity of their disparate family of states.

For the US, on the other hand, the Cold War, though frightening and commercially expensive, brought many clear benefits. It served to consolidate not merely *de facto* US hegemony over the whole Western camp but the self-confident American claim to no less than 'the moral leadership of this planet'. The mundane realities – the establishment of the dollar as the world currency, a worldwide military role, and the headlong expansion of US multinationals – became at once synonymous with and usefully obscured by the cause of 'the Free World'.

Most important of all, the Cold War solved the urgent dilemma of a modern capitalism which had escaped from the Thirties' Depression only by recourse to massive, deficit-financed expenditure on war. After 1945 the arrival of nuclear weaponry made war unthinkable, but made the need for large-scale spending on arms no less urgent as a prophylactic against recession. The Cold War was the perfect answer, guaranteeing a permanent arms economy while always – and this was its real point – stopping short of actual nuclear war. As such it was extremely functional to the health of the Western, especially the US, economy.

It is not difficult to mount a revisionist interpretation of today's renewed Cold War, which has clearly been on the cards ever since the onset of the 1973 recession. The period since then has been marked by a continuous series of East–West crises – over Ethiopia (1974), Vietnam (1975), Angola (1976), Cambodia (1977), Zaïre (1978), North Yemen and Cuba (1979) and Afghanistan (1980), with the escalation of tension increasingly marked once the 1976 world economic recovery petered out into renewed recession.

The years since 1976 have been marked throughout the West by a swelling chorus of alarm over the (alleged) existence of a new Soviet threat in Europe and growing demands for a stepped-up Western response. This campaign found little favour at first with a Carter Administration eager to maintain détente while it tackled the pressing question of relations with the OPEC bloc and the North–South divide.

The Administration quickly found itself under heavy attack as a result of this 'lack of leadership'.

Under these pressures the Carter Administration has given way slowly, reluctantly, but in the end – as the next presidential election nears – quite surely. The result has been a gradual stutter towards confrontation. First Carter announced the deployment of the neutron bomb in Europe – but then, faced with the certain collapse of Salt II if he went ahead, drew back. Next, by mid-1979, the Administration had discovered that a grave East–West crisis existed over the presence of Soviet troops in Cuba – before again backing off and deciding that no such crisis existed. A few months later the Administration astounded the Russians – and effectively torpedoed Salt II – by its sudden decision to deploy the new Pershing and Cruise missiles in Europe.

Thus by the end of 1979 all that was needed for Carter to complete a staggering reversal of policy was one false move by the increasingly jumpy Russians. This, in the shape of Afghanistan, they have now provided. Within weeks Carter had announced a huge new $156 billion defence budget, with plans for a further increase in real terms of another $100 billion by 1985. With one enormous jump we were back to the permanent arms economy.

Thus the 'real' meaning of Afghanistan: the West, led by the US, has opted to spend its way out of world recession by the only means that has ever worked before. Although this option spells the end of monetarist conservatism, US business has warmly welcomed the news, doubting only whether Carter is going far and fast enough. (The American Enterprise Institute, a faithful spokesman of the business community, is demanding a sixfold defence budget increase to ($1 trillion a year.)

The numbers are larger now than in 1947 when the Truman Doctrine launched the first Cold War arms race, heading a troubled US economy towards an inflationary boom, but the script is essentially the same. Carter now, like Truman then, has suddenly been discovered to possess 'leadership' qualities after all. 1948 saw Truman save his incumbent Democrat Administration from an electoral defeat which had long seemed a forgone conclusion. Carter is straining for a similar political miracle in 1980.

But can the clock be so simply put back to 1947? For several reasons the answer is, almost certainly, that it cannot. Any attempt to reassert American hegemony must face the fact that whereas the US accounted for over half the world capitalist economy in 1945, today the proportion is under one-third and by the year 2000 will be around one-fifth. To be sure, empires in decay are prone to rely increasingly on their over-developed military muscle – but, as the British example has recently shown, this can only mask but not delay the consequences of relative economic decline. In the end the wasteful diversion of resources towards non-productive military purposes actually hastens the process of decline. In any case, the other Western states are now too strong – and their stake in détente too large – for them to be swept easily under the American banner again.

Second, a new Cold War will not make the real problems go away. The OPEC price rise of 1973 did more damage to US interests in one day than the USSR had done in all the previous post-war period. OPEC, the energy crisis, and the North–South divide all still exist and being nasty to the Russians will not change that.

Finally – and most important – it is doubtful whether a new Cold War can perform its essential function, that of curing a world recession via a deficit-financed arms race which stops short of actual war. Such a strategy, after all, is – partly by deliberate design – highly inflationary. But to pile the equivalent of a second Korean War inflationary boom on top of the double-digit inflation we already have is to run towards the danger of hyper-inflationary economic collapse.

None of this makes disaster inevitable – yet. Cold War is unpleasant and wasteful, but while its limited purpose, of stopping short of actual war, is firmly held in mind, it is only moderately frightening. Perhaps we can learn to live with higher inflation, climb out of recession, and begin a new period of détente. Perhaps we can even experience hyper-inflation without recourse to real war as a solution. Perhaps America can learn to accept that she counts for less now and must count for less still in the future. The 'ifs' are, admittedly, both numerous and large. But our situation is such that that we must remain thankful that there remain any 'ifs' at all.

6

The Way the World has Split*

During the steady prosperity of the 1950s and 1960s a heated controversy raged over the question of whether affluence produced a trend towards greater political conservatism. Victory went in the end to those who were able to show that it didn't. Now, after several years of a palpable drift to the right, the whole debate seems light years away. It now seems more apposite to stand the original hypothesis on its head – that is to ask why the recession of the 1970s has made people more conservative.

If we take the British (or any other isolated national case) it is not difficult to sketch out a rudimentary sociology of why this should occur. There is, of course, no direct correlation between immiseration and conservatism, any more than there was between affluence and conservatism. The experience of high unemployment and general hard times has a more complex, billiard-ball effect on social groups.

The middle classes, feelings squeezed, begin to feel they can less well afford paternal benevolence towards the have-nots, whose querulous resistance and dismay is easily mistaken for the cause, rather than the result, of the crisis. The haves in general are, indeed, greatly strengthened in their views by the arrival of hard times. The tough measures 'required' by the crisis are those they have been advocating all along – so the crisis is actually embraced as a self-confirmatory 'return to realism'. Hence the desire, frequently overheard in business circles at present, to see at least one really stunning bankruptcy to 'bring people to their senses'. The examples offered are, comfortingly for those who propose them, within the public sector. British Leyland is easily top of the list.

---

* First published in *New Society*, 20 March 1980.

These strange and self-flagellatory moods are quickly picked up and relayed by opinion leaders in the parties and the mass media. Hence the present weird spectacle of public money being spent to put Milton Friedman on television to tell us that our manufacturing industry should be allowed to fall to bits, and that public expenditure is a sin.

Among the workers, the effects of recession are rather different. A large underclass of the unemployed and downwardly mobile is created. This group alone suffers clear and large-scale immiseration – for it is perfectly possible that the real incomes of all other groups may remain steady, or even rise, during the crisis. The workers who remain employed endure the overriding fear that they may drop into this underclass. Accordingly – and mirroring the declining paternalism of their middle-class superiors – their desire for security undermines their traditional solidarity with the *misérables* of the dole queues.

The spread of this *sauve qui peut* atmosphere is fanned, once again, by the media. One could have no clearer example than the active celebration by the press by the decision by BL workers not to strike in support of 'Red Robbo'. Robbo had, of course, been an infernal nuisance to BL managers for years. (This is not intended as a partisan statement. Presumably he was proud of his record.) The fact remains that he was sacked, quite explicitly, for exercising his constitutional right of free expression, and his workmates refused to support him out of fear: a sad and ugly affair in all respects. Amazingly, though, it was greeted as a sort of moral triumph by nearly all sections of the media – even as they simultaneously denounced the Soviet authorities for treating Sakharov in almost identical manner.

Thus, recession breeds a powerful conservative mood even at the hard core of the working class. No group swung more strongly to Mrs Thatcher in May 1979 than did male skilled workers – the very heart of the labour movement. But it seems likely that there was *also* a net movement towards her among the underclass. More or less by definition, this group includes many of the politically most marginal and apathetic. They appear to be easily swept along by the mood prevailing higher up the labour movement, even if it may not be in their best interests.

Recession creates diffuse social influences towards conservatism, too, which are felt right across the board. Businessmen – previously viewed, mundanely, as mere managers – are now seen as leaders and possible saviours. Again, BL provides a case in point, with the near hero-worship of Edwardes and his Plan. This cast of mind exists quite irrespective of the merits of his Plan which, on all present evidence, seems unlikely to work without further huge redundancies.

There is even a reinvention of deference as recession and public spending cuts increase the social power of the rich. Perhaps the clearest sign of this is the veritable stampede to secure charitable donations and 'sponsorship' from the well-to-do for almost every variety of cause and activity – many of them hitherto subsidised by the state. Hospitals, universities and churches have all joined in the hunt. An Oxfordshire village school near me has even got local business sponsorship of one of its teachers.

Now, as an explanation for our present rightward drift, this all works tolerably well. With modifications, it could doubtless be used to describe the contemporary situation in many other developed capitalist states. It almost begins to appear deceptively obvious – even natural – that hard times should make us all feel more conservative. The problem is that it *can't* be 'natural'. The last great recession, the Depression of the 1930s, had very different political results.

Broadly speaking the interwar years were marked by two conflicting political trends. In a small minority of developed states, radical fascist regimes seized power and 'solved' their economic problems by resort to a sort of police-state Keynsianism: repression, giant public works and a military build-up. But these were aberrant cases – and nowhere did the fascists gain an electoral majority.

Far, far more common was the growth of the reformist and social democratic left – very frequently backed by record electoral majorities. These were the years which saw the electoral triumph of Popular Fronts in France and Spain, which saw Labour gain its record interwar vote in Britain, which brought the New Deal landslide in the US and the esconcement of Scandinavian social democracy in power for a whole generation.

The same reaction towards the reformist left was visible in many parts of the underdeveloped world. Populist reform movements such as those of Vargas in Brazil, the Congress Party in India and even the Kuomintang in China had things fairly much their own way. Alternatives on the revolutionary left either never emerged, were easily crushed, or tagged along hopelessly behind their more powerful reformist brothers. Mao was almost the only left-wing revolutionary to survive. And his movement remained small, obscure and geographically isolated.

The post-1973 recession has had very different results. Far from producing new fascist states, the crisis has laid them low wherever they existed (Greece, Portugal and Spain). The beneficiaries in these countries – as well as almost everywhere else in the developed capitalist states – have been fairly routine conservatives. In the few cases where the reformist left has held on (Carter in America, Callaghan for a while here, Schmidt in Germany, Kreisky in Austria), it has done so narrowly and only at the cost of itself becoming impeccably conservative. Even the great Scandinavian redoubts of social democracy have fallen this time. Nowhere is there a New Deal or Popular Front in sight.

In the third world, however, the 1970s recession has seen a fairly generalised collapse of feudal or racial oligarchies and a long series of triumphs for the far left. In Laos, Cambodia, Ethiopia and Afghanistan, the kings have departed and in every case radical regimes have grasped power. The radicals have fared equally well in South Vietnam, Guiné, Angola, Mozambique, Benin, Zimbabwe and such far-flung isles as Grenada and the Seychelles. In a host of other cases, existing regimes are under threat, almost invariably from the revolutionary left (in Chad, Spanish Sahara, Mauritius, Zaïre, Namibia and North Yemen, for example). Movements of populist reformism are nowhere very much in evidence.

To make comparisons such as these, therefore, is to undermine any notion of the 'natural' political effects of recession. To put it in a nutshell, the economic crisis of the 1930s saw a remarkably even progression of the social democratic left (with a few fascist exceptions) in both the developed and under-developed world, while the post-1973 recession has produced a far more radical polarisation between a conservative developed world and radical Third World. The key to this conundrum lies, almost certainly, in the increasing integration of the world market, which has proceeded at such a remarkable pace between the two recessions.

In the 1930s it was possible for fascists and social democrats alike to see the solutions to their problems in the attainment of national economic autonomy and the application of (one variety or another of) Keynesian policy at national level. In the 1970s, this was almost nowhere seen as a solution. In the developed world there has been an almost complete collapse of confidence in Keynesian remedies. How can one advocate inflationary increases in public expenditure in the face of the dangerous stagflation which already exists? The fact that conservative policies of monetary restraint and public spending cuts have never yet in history pulled a country out of recession is simply ignored. (In Britain we have been following such policies for five years now without any visible positive effect on either the rate of growth or the rate of inflation.) The conservative mood is too strong to be ignored, and anyway what is the alternative?

A similar impatience with traditional Keynesian remedies exists in the third world. The all-important fact is seen to be not the problem of the management of internal demand but the deteriorating terms of trade and credit between the poor countries and the hard-faced west. (Already this deterioration has been responsible for creating the conditions for the extreme left to come to power in so many of these countries.) The solution here has been to grasp, rather desperately, at a mixture of mass mobilisation and self-help, cartelisation against the west, and pleading for credit from either the Soviet bloc or western banks and multinationals. There are precious few signs that this strategy is working either.

It is at this point that the significance of the increased integration of the world economy becomes clear. In the 1930s it was still possible to seek national Keynesian solutions. In the 1970s these have become transparently inadequate, and so we are all seeking national non-keynesian solutions. They are turning out to be solutions at all. The answer lies, almost certainly, in an *international* Keynesianism.

That is, the rich countries should be incurring large deficit expenditure in the form of loans or grants to the poor nations. These, being spent outside the rich states, would have no direct inflationary effect upon them, but would generate a welcome increase in third world demand for rich world exports, thus mopping up unemployment in the developed states. The TVAs of this New Deal ought to be built not in Tennessee but in Cambodia or Mozambique – preferably in both. They would bring the same happy combination of economic and humanitarian benefit that the first TVA did.

Unfortunately, you have, to sketch the barest outline of this solution to feel that it is rather unlikely. The rich nations would have to stop seeing third world demands upon them as just one more claim they can ill afford, and see them instead as an opportunity for their own salvation. The third world, for its part, would have to stop bothering about whether the extension of rich world aid was a matter of charity or rights, and simply take it on any terms it could get. This might well mean a *de facto* surrender of national sovereignty, often immediately after it had just been fully attained.

One way and another, this seems a pretty tall order. But, as in the 1930s, the alternatives hardly bear thinking about.

7

The End of the American Era*

The intelligent reader will not have needed William Rees-Mogg's sensitive appreciation of the delights of Californian breakfast-time television to know that Britain has much to offer the American election campaign. In 1976 we figured prominently, with Gerald Ford campaigning under the slogan 'Don't follow England down the drain!' This year the Republicans have decided they have other sorts of lessons to learn from us. Hard-nosed men with horn-rimmed eyes (let alone glasses) have crossed the Atlantic to make admiring studies of how the battle of Britain of May '79 was won. They return home, one is told, to apply the gospel according to Saatchi, Saatchi and Thatcher with a terrible and scientific rigour. The wonderful humour-lessness of their efforts is excusable, no doubt, by the stern nobility of their cause: to bring about a conservative resurrection of strong leadership, thereby to restore the full bloom of American greatness. To be fair, it's not a party matter. If Teddy, Jimmy, Ronald and all the rest have one thing in common it is an overriding obsession with 'leadership' and 'greatness'.

Their time would be better spent in a little quiet reflection on that key moment in Anglo-American relations back in 1962 when Dean Acheson, the former Secretary of State, delivered himself of his famous West Point speech. 'Great Britain', he said, 'has lost an empire and has not yet found a role. The attempt to play a separate power role – that is, a role apart from Europe, a role based on a "special relationship" with the US, a role based on being the head of a "commonwealth" which has no political structure, or unity, or strength . . . – this role is about played out.'

---

* First published in *New Society*, 24 April 1980.

The speech caused an enormous furore. The *Daily Express* called it a 'stab in the back'. The *Sunday Times* concluded that Acheson's pleasure in the US triumph in the Cuban missile crisis had clearly 'gone to his head'. The *Daily Telegraph* commented that Acheson's dress had always been more immaculate than his judgement and that he was 'extremely unlikely ever again' to hold high office. President Kennedy spent much time on the hot-line trying to console and reassure Macmillan. The climate of public outrage was, however, too great for this to suffice and Macmillan delivered a bitter speech condemning Acheson for falling 'into an error which has been made by quite a lot of people in the course of the last four hundred years, including Philip of Spain, Louis XIV, Napoleon, the Kaiser and Hitler'. (Quite how one could champion the importance of the 'special relationship' while making public comparisons between former US Secretaries of State and Adolf Hitler was not explained.)

The uproar was transient but the incident had a lasting significance. First, of course, what Acheson said was perfectly true but hardly new. Britain was, by 1962, far advanced in its imperial decline, a process which had become irreversible at least fifteen years before with the loss of India. The full extent of the erosion both of power and of the 'special relationship' had been made clear six years before at Suez when we had come off a bad second-best in a clash with a tin-pot Arab state. Britain had waved her sword, found herself confronted with a terrifying oil shortage and a major currency crisis – and retreated, bitterly upbraiding her allies for letting her down. Thereafter the process had merely gathered pace so that soon it seemed that almost anyone – Makarios, Nkrumah or Mintoff – could pull the lion's tail and get away with it.

What Acheson had done, in effect, was to play the role of the mirror on the wall in the story of Snow White. Like the wicked step-mother we were angry not because we thought the mirror was lying about who was the fairest of them all but, quite precisely, because we did not doubt its objective veracity. Ageing imperial powers and personages alike do not take kindly to having their wrinkles pointed out.

So while Acheson's not unfriendly speech was heard, it was certainly not listened to. British voters and politicians alike had wrapped themselves in a many-layered cloud of imperial delusion. Acheson's shaft had caused enough pain by penetrating the cloud – lifting it altogether was out of the question. The truth was that what lay ahead was a long period in which the essential job of British political elites would be to manage the continuation of imperial decline and 'sell' its often uncomfortable consequences to the electorate. There was no way they could escape this task but they balked utterly at recognising it for what it was. Instead they sought refuge in a desperate rhetoric about the need for 'leadership' to restore national 'greatness'.

The result was a comprehensive and utterly destructive conservatism. Once the main national task was defined as the restoration of past glories (in Wilson's phrase, 'putting the 'Great' back into Great Britain') the country engaged upon a long and hopeless struggle to defend each separate rampart of the doomed imperial citadel. We would not devalue the pound, retreat from East or Suez, abandon the TSR2 or the independent deterrent, admit that Concorde was hopeless or accept that we were too weak to compete successfully within the EEC. In the end, of course, we had to accept all of these things. All that our long (and still continuing) resistance achieved was to prolong the agony and undermine the defensive positions on which we could once have fallen back. This costly rearguard action and the mood of all-encompassing conservatism it engendered, spelt doom, of course, to any serious hopes of internal social reform. Labour governments have held power for eleven of the eighteen years since 1962 but have achieved far less in the whole of that period that did Attlee's government in half the time, although it worked under infinitely harder conditions.

Instead, madly, we have dreamt the dream of Arthur. At each downward lurch the belief held that, if and when things got bad enough, the shade of Mallory's hero would somehow arise in modern form and, by dint of his dramatic 'leadership', would restore the realm of Logres. This myth had been fatally strengthened by the feeling that the spirit had already awoken once – in 1940, assuming Churchill's form. What we actually got was a cheekie chappie, a musical yachtsman, an avuncular tax-collector and a suburban housewife.

All this has a relevance for America rather different from anything Saatchi and Saatchi may have to offer. The US has been set in a process of imperial decline for at least fifteen years now (the large-scale debarkation into the Vietnamese quagmire in 1965 provides their possible point of no return). The full extent of the erosion of US imperial power became evident some six years ago, when it too came off second-best in a clash with a series of tin-pot Arab regimes. During the OPEC crisis of 1973–4 Kissinger waved the American sword too – refusing to rule out military action in the Gulf and talking darkly of the 'food weapon'. He too had to retreat under the double pressure of an oil shortage and a currency crisis, upbraiding his allies for letting the us down. Since then the process has gathered pace, so that Americans too have found that almost any number of puny opponents – Panama, Ethiopia, Afghanistan or the Ayatollah – can pull their tail and get away with it.

The result in America have been very much the same as they were here: an ever more desperate resort to rhetoric about 'leadership' and the restoration of 'greatness', an all-encompassing climate of conservatism which foredooms social reform whichever party wins the elections, and escapism into their own variant of the dream of Arthur. (Their equivalent is generally 'Remember the Alamo!') What they will get instead, of course, are crooked lawyers, men who play football without their helmets, bumbling peanut farmers or clapped-out film actors.

The real task ahead of the American political elite is exactly the same as our rulers faced in 1962. They must, above all, face facts. The us made up half the capitalist world economy in 1945 but only one-third of it now. By the year 2000 it will constitute only a fifth. These figures alone spell out quite definitively the end of the 'American century'. Nothing is more certain than the collapse of the dollar as the world reserve currency or the gradual abolition of all the other economic privileges which the period of hegemony brought. (To take only the most obvious: American industry must look forward to the day when it must compete against foreign exporters in markets at home and abroad without the benefit of a huge subsidy in the form of the world's cheapest energy.) They must expect, moreover, to have to do this while undergoing a variety of political harassments around the world, as former client states vent their long-pent-up resentments against the weakening giant. A lot more embassies will get burnt down and, probably, a lot more hostages seized. They must, finally, not expect their allies to rally round them as they undergo this slow crucifixion. They will all have better things to do, particularly since the rewards of the alliance for them will be diminishing all the time.

Having faced all of these somewhat uncomfortable facts, the really major task will be to manage the imperial run-down as smoothly as possible and 'sell' its consequences to the American electorate. This will involve a large-scale lowering of public expectations (Saatchi and Saatchi might be of real help *here*) and something approaching an admission of historical guilt. It will be necessary to explain that these trying situations at the Tehran embassy and elsewhere have much deeper causes than are to be found in any immediate situation. Just as at Suez the British were picking up a late bill for a hundred years of colonialism, for Omdurman and Nablus and much else besides, so the Tehran hostages now are paying for CIA support of SAVAK, for the deposing of Mossadeq and much more. (This is another reason why your allies won't be much help. What they are really feeling is that, well, you sort of had it coming to you for a long time, didn't you, old chap?)

All of this will be much harder in the American case than it was for the British, for two reasons. First, the bonds of American empire were always largely invisible to the public at large. This means that there is no formal process of decolonisation to conduct, through which your electorate gradually gets the point by seeing the flag hauled down in one colony after another. Second, no successor imperial power is in sight. It was a great help to the British elite in its age of decline to be able to lean on the strong supporting arm of the 'special relationship' with the new giant who – what luck – even spoke English and was willing to make occasional respectful gestures to the old lady. The US won't have this – merely a lot of Germans, Japanese, South Koreans and others, all competing fiercely with it on ever more equal terms.

It will be seen that if ever the time existed when the British might play their cherished role of Greeks to the American Romans, now is that time. The counsel we should give is plain. For heaven's sake avoid our mistakes. Cut your losses as hard and quickly as you can. Don't do the equivalent of decolonising India in 1947 and still find yourself mucking around with Rhodesia in 1980 – nothing is gained and much is lost in thus prolonging the agony. Forget the Alamo and avoid, at all costs, any talk about 'greatness'. Don't fall into the trap of thinking that a conservative reaction can save you. Your empire declined faster under Nixon and Ford than under anyone else and Reagan will be no different. You will need 'leadership' of a sort but it would be best to avoid talking about it in heroic terms.

It seems unlikely that we are going to produce a Dean Acheson to say all this. Those most suitable to the role (Sir Alec Douglas-Home, pre-eminently) don't yet fully accept our *own* imperial decline and are, anyway, far too polite. Still, we are sending the editor of *The Times* across and that's something. He has already mastered the subject of breakfast-time television in California. It's not exactly the heart of the matter but at least it's start.

8

The Buck Must Go On*

There is a curious international interchangeability to political speeches these days. Mrs Thatcher tells us that the main priority is the fight against inflation. An identical message is delivered by Ronald Reagan and Jimmy Carter to their voters, and by Helmut Schmidt to his. Raymond Barre tells the French the same thing. Whoever happens to be in power in Italy, from one day to the next, says the same. I have no doubt that if Prince Rainier manages to get a few hours away from the ski slopes he tells Monacans the same thing, too. So drearily universal is the refrain that it hardly seems worth reading foreign newspapers these days – it's pure Cole Porter:

Birds do it
Bees do it
Even cuckoos in the privacy of clocks do it.

Now the oddity about all these dozens of little national wars against inflation is not just that there are so many going on all at once. More striking is the fact that, with only the rarest exceptions – West Germany and Switzerland, to be precise – these wars are all being lost or, at any rate, not won. In some cases – Israel, with a current inflation rate of 100 per cent, for example   it is a rout the other way. Only when failure is clear, however, do politicians seek refuge in the excuse that inflation is an international phenomenon. They do not generally continue – as well they might – by asking whether their attempt to find a national solution to an international phenomenon wasn't a fairly futile game in the first place.

The question has to be asked, though. Any country which relies to

---

* First published in *New Society*, 16 October 1980.

any extent on imports (and all do) is liable to find the price of those imports inflating steadily upwards, simply because most countries exporting to it will be suffering from inflation. If the recipient country is not simply to import inflation it must either stop importing, continuously revalue its own currency upwards, or achieve such miracles of productive growth that it is able to keep releasing resources to pay those higher prices. In the real world only the Swiss, Germans and Japanese have achieved anything like this, and then only for some of the time. For the rest of us – and even for them a lot of the time – the problems of inflation and recession are quite largely a matter of international buck-passing.

A glance back at the history of the inter-war recession helps to broaden out this picture. The first world war – like most wars – had contradictory economic effects, annihilating prodigious amounts of capital on the one hand and generating a huge boom on the other, with vast numbers of people sucked into the industrial economy for the first time. If, at the war's end, the economic expectations engendered by this frenetic level of activity were to be sustained, and if those large capital losses were to be made up, something had to give. This buck was passed off in several directions: on to the Germans in the shape of war debts and on to the working classes of even the victorious countries in the shape of large-scale unemployment.

For a while it seemed this might do the trick. But politicians were nervous of pushing too great a burden on to the workers through fear of bolshevism. And the Germans passed the buck on their war debts by being simply unable to pay them. (The French and British, also with enormous war debts, were thus provided with a golden excuse to pass the buck on theirs.) The result was an endless series of debt-rescheduling conferences – that is, of formally institutionalised buck-passing – until the whole precarious structure came crashing down in 1929–31.

The Crash saw a new and ferocious round of buck-passing. The brunt fell on the workers, with unemployment everywhere far surpassing its old post-war peaks. In Germany and America (though seldom elsewhere) ruin was visited on large sections of the middle class, too. Those who had empires hastily turned the screw on their colonial subjects, whose lot deteriorated often far below starvation level. Finally, with the failure of the 1933 London economic conference, nations settled down to trying to beggar each other with tariff barriers, competitive devaluations and so on.

Economic and real war

After 1933 there were no further attempts to rescue the situation via international agreements on trade or money. Instead, every country devoted itself to (hopeless) little national wars against recession and to nationally based economic warfare in the international sphere. Jealously observing that the recession was mildest in Britain, France and other states gifted with empires, Japan, Italy and Germany set about acquiring colonies for themselves in Asia, Africa and eastern Europe. With this the world slid from economic war into real war.

The post-1973 recession has rather different roots, originating largely from the integration of a world market economy after 1945, and the colossal growth in world trade which resulted. This was the fundamental motor behind the almost universal boom of the 1950s and 1960s, which sucked millions of new workers and consumers into the market and generated almost limitless expectations of ever-increasing affluence. But this boom could not continue for ever. As integration ran its course, the growth of world trade was bound to slow in the end.

Moreover, integration brought about a gradual levelling-out process in the economic capacities of the major powers, with the result that the world market became ever more competitive – exercising a downward pressure on profits, and thus on future investment. Finally, the boom was based quite heavily in a steady deterioration of the terms of trade for the poorest countries: that is, in steadily falling commodity prices (in real terms) for the industrial world. With every passing year in the 1950s and 1960s, with only rare exceptions, the same volume of manufactured goods bought more copper, or iron ore, or oil than it had the year before. This could hardly go on for ever.

Integration had a further – and ultimately decisive – effect. Originally the national economies of the world had been like a host of unsynchronised clocks, some beating out a deflationary, others a reflationary tune. Gradually, integration corrected these disharmonies so that all the clocks began to beat as one. Hence the great synchronised reflation of 1969–71 and the equally synchronised world boom of 1971–3. With all the major economies roaring ahead together, demand at last pulled commodity prices up. The price of sugar, paper, copper, wool and so forth, shot up, one rocket after another.

This sudden and very dramatic reversal of one of the most

fundamental causes of the boom helped change the always predictable downturn of the business cycle into a virtual collapse. With this collapse already well under way, the price of oil – the Last Great Commodity – took off. The combined effect was catastrophic. In less than a year capitalist world production fell by 10 per cent, world trade fell by 13 per cent, and unemployment rose by over seven million in the developed world alone. A whole 11 per cent of the capitalist world's fixed capital was put out of use.

We are still living with the shock waves of this calamity – that is, with the new round of international and intra-national buck-passing it triggered off. The commodity boom saw the primary producers stake a large claim to the resources of the developed world – which promptly passed the buck in the shape of inflated prices for manufactured goods. Then the oil-producers did the same. The bite they took out of our resources was so great that the same tactic could not wholly succeed with them, so some measure of the burden was off-loaded onto industrial workers in the developed world.

Meanwhile other commodity prices collapsed, so that the non-oil-producing countries were cast into an outer darkness in which they suffered high prices both for oil and manufactured goods. They were saved, temporarily, by the recycling of OPEC funds. That is, OPEC lent its money at a good rate of return to the West, which lent it on at an even better rate of return to the really poor.

In effect the years since 1974 have seen a constant repetition of this ever-deepening cycle. Each time OPEC puts up the oil price we pass the buck on higher manufactured goods prices, which erodes the real price of oil, which leads to a fresh oil price rise. The buck, in other words, is still travelling – and as between these two parties, there is no real reason why it should ever stop. The problem lies elsewhere, for each time these ritual exchanges take place a further burden is off-loaded on to industrial workers at home and the non-oil poor abroad. Simultaneously, of course, there is a progressively greater tendency for industrial countries to off-load onto one another with the time-honoured weapons of economic war-tariffs and currency manipulation.

The crunch lies in the plight of the non-oil poor. (In the 1930s, when they were all colonies, they suffered in silence. Now they shout – ineffectually.) Very many of these countries have, in a true sense, been bankrupt for some time now. In many cases their annual interest payments on their debts amount to almost the whole of their total annual exports. The only way out – as in the 1920s – is a series of more or less openly dishonest debt-rescheduling arrangements which serve to disguise their bankruptcy a little longer under a new tidal wave of loans. The buck travels on.

The fall-guys

The trouble is, the non-oil poor must default massively in the end. When they do, the buck stops – in the leaden hands of the Western states lending to them. Hence the increasing desperation with which these states are trying to get OPEC to make direct loans to the non-oil poor, rather than recycle their funds safely and profitably through the West. This, very largely, is what international financial politics is now all about. All the old notions about the strongest Western economies acting as locomotives to pull the world out of recession have been quietly abandoned. Nowadays the IMF solemnly warns us all to avoid the perils of reflation *and* the evils of deflation. In effect this simply legitimates the high current rate of world inflation.

This is actually wiser than it seems. If inflation stops it will be because the buck has stopped. The 1930s suggest that this is the point when economic war gives way to the real thing. If the buck stopped right now, at least a score of poor countries would quickly be wiped out by famine, dozens of the world's biggest banks would take a hiding, and there would be a further calamitous fall in world trade. Not surprisingly, companies and countries alike will fight to the death to avoid the fate of being the fall-guys at the end of this line.

As yet we are still some distance away from that eventuality. Oddly, the only imperial 'grabs' to date have been made by the Communists (the Chinese in Vietnam, the Russians in Afghanistan). Mercifully, we have lots of nuclear weapons and are very properly frightened of them. Even more mercifully, we have budding antinuclear arms campaigns to keep us frightened of them.

Meanwhile, one can only pay that 'the fight against inflation' continues – and, of course, that inflation continues, too. The buck must go on.

9

Japanese Take-away*

'New axis for new axles' ran one headline, announcing the recent news of a reciprocal manufacturing and distribution deal between Volkswagen of Germany and Nissan (Datsun) of Japan. In most newspapers the subsequent story took up about twenty lines on something like page 8. In one sense this blasé reaction was pardonable enough. Attempts at defensive integration with the advancing columns of Japanese commerce are after all, almost ten a penny these days, especially in the car world.

We already know that BL has made a deal with Honda, General Motors with Isuzu, Ford with Mazda, and that Mitsubishi has taken over Chrysler-Australia. Beyond that, we have even become used to seeing the Liverpool football team charging around in Hitachi shirts. If the top soccer team in Europe can see Japanese capital as its natural ally, then where, really, is the limit? Why not the Mitsui Monte Carlo Rally, the Nippon Electric Blackpool Tower or the Fuji Bank Tour de France?

The Volkswagen–Datsun deal *is* different, though. Symbolically, at least – as that first headline suggests – it is of real historical significance. One of the clearest indications of this is that some of the echoes raised by that headline have a decidedly uncomfortable ring: their reverberation is too long. This alone may inhibit proper discussion. One only has to wonder aloud what Hitler, the proud progenitor of 'the people's car', would think of this un-Aryan genuflection to the zaibatsu, to realise that some old ghosts are still hovering in the shadows. Every sensible person can only rejoice that we are now all such good friends with the former Axis powers, and

---

* First published in *New Society*, 5 February 1981.

they will one another. It is, however, a grave mistake to identify these friendships with the need for complete historical amnesia. Exorcism is the enemy of understanding.

No one looking at a map of the globe would easily guess that a peculiar symmetry would come to link the fortunes of two such far-flung states as Germany and Japan, or that this relationship would have such fateful importance in world history. This symmetry, born simply from the fact that these were the two great losers of the post-Versailles world, began to find real expression just fifty years ago as that world – then as now – slipped into the icy depths of economic depression. Of all the capitalist states, these two were least able to bear the new climate.

They lacked raw materials, colonies, captive markets – and friends. Isolated and beleaguered, their very survival as industrial states was quickly seen to be at stake. Both were the heirs of fierce nationalist traditions (and grievances) which led them to refuse utterly the role of international beggars. Instead both had recourse to a sort of desperate spartan dynamism, cloaked by a ruthless militaristic nationalism. By dint of ferocious domestic belt-tightening and repression, they galvanised themselves into a brutal effort of expansion. They seized neighbouring countries and raw materials and hurled themselves energetically into export drives on the stagnant markets of the world.

In all of this they achieved an astonishing degree of success. (It should not be forgotten – but usually is – that the most dynamic trend in the international trade of the inter-war period was a prodigious expansion of Japanese exports.) It was not really surprising that by 1937 they had formally acknowledged their affinity in the Anti-Comintern Pact. (For all intents and purposes one may ignore Italy, whose strengths so palely reflected theirs, and which was really only tagging along for the ride.)

It was only with the commencement of war that the formulation of German and Japanese ambitions became clear. Of the two, Japan's aims were the more modest. Her strategic war plan, with its wonderfully Conradian title, the Great East Asia Co-prosperity Sphere, foresaw the conquest by Japan of the Philippines. Indochina, Siam, Malaya, Burma, Borneo, Indonesia, Australia and New Zealand, together, of course, with Korea and most of China, including Hong Kong and Taiwan. The only problem was India.

The major question mark over whether Hitler or the Japanese were to take this plum was never finally settled, so that its fate was effectively left hanging on the ultimate fortunes of war. All of this was pretty ambitious but it was, in the end, a plan for a gigantic regional hegemony, not world conquest. The Japanese were keenly aware of the need to leave room for other super-powers. They were careful never to attack Russia, for all Hitler's urging, and Hawaii and all points east of it were left to America. There was no idea of interfering with German ambitions in the Middle East – India was the outer limit of Tokyo's appetite.

Germany's ambition, on the other hand, was almost without limit. Europe had for centuries seen the whole world as its oyster and the Germans, who saw themselves as the most dynamic, indeed the master, race of Europe, naturally thought big. The essential first phase was the unification of Europe under German rule and the establishment of German mastery over most of eastern Europe, enabling the Reich to draw on a vast reservoir of *untermensch* slave labour.

All of this was achieved, with startling rapidity, by 1940 – whereupon the cry was raised, 'Today Europe, tomorrow the world.' By 1941 Germany was embarked on the conquest of the USSR and of north Africa, with the Middle East also clearly in her sights. It is difficult to see what might not have fallen into German hands had this second phase succeeded – the rest of Africa, certainly; Iran and much of central Asia; perhaps even Latin America. The only sense of limitation stemmed from an uncertainty as to whether the Reich would leave the USA alone – though by the end of the war plans existed for the bombardment of America with long-range v-weapons, using, no doubt, the German atomic bomb once it was ready.

The collapse of the Axis removed these plans irrevocably from the agenda – they are, happily, as distant as the nightmares of childhood. Happily, one may assert with some confidence that Russian propaganda about the revanchist designs of Germany and Japan is simply twaddle. On the other hand, as one surveys the staggering post-war economic expansion of Japan and Germany, one cannot but be struck by the extent to which they have fulfilled in peace the visions which took them to war forty years ago: one is reminded irresistibly of those games of Diplomacy which always end up refighting the first world war, as if such alignments are integral to the structure of the game.

Within a generation of the war's end, after all, Western Europe had again been reunited under effective German dominance – a new order greatly assisted, incidentally, by the creation of a new *untermensch* class of super-exploited and voteless migrant workers. Via the *Ostpolitik* German influence has again surged deep into eastern Europe, and there is no corner of the world where the mighty trading power of Germany is not felt. Hitler never succeeded in making Germany the principal trading partner of South Africa, or in building Volkswagen factories in Brazil – but both these things have come to pass under the benign eye of West German social democracy.

Japan's achievements have been even more startling. The ring of East Asian states which formed the old Co-Prosperity Sphere have fallen deep within the Japanese economic orbit. This time it is not a matter of Japan having to impose puppet regimes either, for several of them – Taiwan, South Korea, Hong Kong and Singapore – have enthusiastically opted to become 'little Japans'. Australasia becomes each year more and more part of the Japanese economic hinterland. The whole Pacific region has again become a Japanese lake.

This time, however – and this is really the whole point – Japan has succeeded in achieving a massive economic penetration far beyond the confines of the old Co-Prosperity Sphere. Her tanks never poured into America but now her cars certainly do. Nor is Russia off-limits any more. The Russians have repeatedly tried to entice Japanese capital into the Siberain oil fields – but Tokyo can now afford the supreme luxury of holding out for better terms. And this time India is far from being the Western limit of her reach. Japan is now the biggest foreign investor in Iran and is massively present throughout the Middle East. Beyond that, her goods pour into the furthest realms of Western Europe – including Germany.

Here, indeed, is the crunch, Germany, for so long the most dynamic economy of the Western world, now finds the roles of the 1930s reversed. This time Japan's ambitions and reach exceed hers, forcing her, not Japan, into a more narrowly regional role. Nothing demonstrates the position better than the car market. Japanese cars have all but evicted the Germans from the US market and are pouring into such 'natural' German markets as Britain and Scandinavia.

Most dramatic of all, in the last year they have doubled their share of the German market itself (to 11 per cent) and look likely to increase that stake massively. By contrast, *all* foreign cars took only 0.9 per cent of the Japanese car market in 1980. . . . It is hardly surprising that Volkswagen has quickly opted for a defensive pact with Datsun, though it seems in the highest degree unlikely that this will save the day. At best Volkswagen can hope for the generous offer made by Cyclops to Ulysses of 'I'll eat you last'.

And, of course, it's not just cars. Suddenly the whole German economy looks quite surprisingly vulnerable. The Deutschmark has fallen, unemployment is rising, investment is down, growth has all but ceased and there is a runaway trading deficit. The Germans have belatedly realised, moreover, that their strength is unhealthily concentrated in old, declining industries. In critical high-technology areas, such as computers and office machinery, Germany now actually imports more than it exports.

A crisis for Germany is, almost definitionally, a crisis for Europe. For the series of European 'economic miracles', so endlessly celebrated in the 1950s and 1960s, were all quite largely just the reflections of a single original miracle – the German one. The German economy grew most rapidly of all in the period before the EEC was born. Then, after 1957, the surrounding economies of Europe were allowed free access to the booming German market, producing a marked acceleration in their growth rates which soon approximated the now somewhat lower German rate.

While these later-day booms were taking place in the satellite economies of Switzerland, Austria, Holland, Benelux (and even France), Germany went questing abroad for fresh fields and pastures new. Thus the great growth area for German trade in the 1960s was not the EEC but the Soviet bloc: in the 1970s it was the Third World, especially the Middle East. By the middle 1970s, indeed, this leap-frogging process had gone so far as to cause many German economists to wonder whether the EEC was not becoming a costly and dispensable strait-jacket. Perhaps Germany would be better off in a truly free international market, instead of paying the lion's share of EEC subsidies to the greater enrichment of French farmers?

All such thoughts are well and truly banished now that Germany is at last beginning to feel the heat from the rising sun of Japan – a warmth her weaker European partners have felt, with growing discomfort, for some time now. The result is a growing consciousness throughout the EEC that all the worried talk of the 1960s of the *défi Americain* was a blind alley. It is the *défi Japonais* that really counts.

It is on the German reaction to this challenge that the whole question of a possible EEC inward turn towards protectionism now hangs. Such a move would almost certainly trigger a rippling wave of protectionism in the US and elsewhere, with enormous and potentially catastrophic consequences for the open international economy. But the alternative could ultimately be that we all become citizens of the Great West Europe Co-Prosperity Sphere.

Such choices are hardly comfortable, but they are real. They will not yield to chauvinistic reactions (or accusations of them). In any case, for third parties like Britain chauvinism is a peculiarly inappropriate reaction if the choice lies between Germany and Japan – between selling Kevin Keegan to Hamburg and the rest of one's team to Hitachi. But nor will the issues go away simply by dint of putting one's head in the sand and relegating the really important news to page 8.

10

Mitterrand Ousts a Monarch*

'Provided we don't make stupid mistakes, we ought to be in power until the year 2000.' Thus Alain Peyrefitte, a Minister in the French conservative Majority in the late 1960s. With the election of François Mitterrand to the French presidency this famous phrase – along with much else besides – will be hurled back into the teeth of French conservatism. The unthinkable has happened. For the first time in a quarter of a century – the first time ever in the Fifth Republic – the Left has triumphed and the Majority has been evicted from power.

At the time it seemed that M. Peyrefitte was hardly exaggerating. While de Gaulle was President it was possible to believe that the Right owed its dominance largely to his personal popularity. But de Gaulle went and the Majority continued to win one election after another. In effect it held three enormous trump cards which it simply played over and over again. First, with a disunited Left and united Majority, the choice at every election could be presented as one between stability and chaos. Second, given the strength of the Communists (the PCF) within the Left, the Majority could rely on the efficacy of 'red scare' tactics. And third, it could rely on the organisational power of the Gaullist party machine – the greatest mass movement of the Right France has ever known, reinforced at every point by the enormous advantages of governmental patronage.

The question now being asked in hysterical tones by the place-men and beneficiaries of the Right who have grown so fat under the protective umbrella of the Fifth Republic, is how on earth it could have happened. It is a question worth an answer. With advantages as

* First published in *New Society*, 14 May 1981.

huge as the Right has for so long enjoyed, its defeat immediately assumes historic, even miraculous, proportions in the eyes of many Frenchmen. Even the British media, which have been so lamentably ill-informed about this election, must have noticed the vast demonstrations of popular joy in the streets of France at Giscard's defeat, must have realised that this is no ordinary victory. (Were even Labour's victory celebrations in 1945 like this . . . ?)

To understand what has now come to pass in France one must go back to 1974 when Pompidou's sudden death created a momentary leadership void on the French Right. The fact that the succession within the dominant Gaullist party had not been prepared created an opening for Giscard – the perennial Minister of Finance whose own little Republican party of backwoods notables had prospered happily in junior alliance with the mighty Gaullists. In 1969, seizing another brief opening, Giscard had thrown his weight against de Gaulle in the decisive referendum which evicted the General from power – an act for which true-blue old Gaullists have never forgiven him. Now, while the Gaullists dithered over choosing a candidate (finally picking Chaban-Delmas), Giscard stepped masterfully forward.

At the same time Giscard contracted a crucial deal with Jacques Chirac, the thrusting young Minister of the Interior. Chirac destroyed Chaban's candidacy by swinging a crucial bloc of Gaullists across to Giscard and, via his control of the departmental prefects, ensured that the Gaullist party machine was never properly mobilised behind Chaban. Giscard squeaked in ahead of Mitterrand and immediately made Chirac Prime Minister. For Chirac, too, had taken his chance – he had vaulted to power right over the heads of the old Gaullist 'barons' – Chaban, Debré, Messmer, Couve de Murville and the like. Using his considerable prime ministerial patronage he swiftly took over the Gaullist party, thus concretising his claim to the Gaullist line of descent, the true heir of de Gaulle and Pompidou.

The events of 1974 had, however, created a split within the Majority which was never quite to heal. For Chirac, in common with most other Gaullists, assumed that Giscard would have to allow them a preponderant – or at least equal – voice in power: after all, they still made up the overwhelming proportion of the conservative parliamentary majority. Giscard had quite other ideas. He had had to play second fiddle to the Gaullists for quite long enough and had every intention of enjoying to the full the enormous powers bestowed upon a Fifth Republican President.

Chirac soon found he was much less than the equal partner he had intended to be and reacted with increasing bitterness to Giscard's lofty disregard. In August 1976 – perhaps the real turning-point of the Fifth Republic – Chirac furiously resigned from office and launched his renovated Gaullist mass party, the RPR, with the clear intention of cutting Giscard down to size. Giscard responded by seducing away from Chirac as many Gaullist deputies as he could and by launching his own new conservative alliance, the UDF, with the equally clear intention of cutting the Gaullists down to size.

This split in the Majority quietly knocked away one of the main props of conservative power. It did so, moreover, in the face of a united Left within which Mitterrand's new Socialist Party, the PS, had begun to enjoy a preponderant weight. Thus, for the first time, two of the Majority's three trump cards had been discarded: there was a united Opposition able to offer a stable alternative government, and the new-found strength of the PS meant that such a government would be less subject to Communist influence. What remained to the Majority was the organisational strength of the Gaullist machine (which Chirac had) and, above all, power (which Giscard had).

With the approach of the 1978 elections it seemed that this might well not be enough. In the event Giscard was saved from looming defeat by two factors – neither of his own making. On the one hand, for its own internal reasons, the Left split badly on the eve of the elections, and on the other, faced with the alarming threat of a Left victory, the RPR machine rallied behind the Majority, helping to push home Giscard's UDF candidates in one marginal constituency after another.

Buoyed by this triumph, and freed from any immediate threat from the Left, Giscard now turned the full fire-power of the state against the RPR. In every level of French life – in the state Administration, the prefecture, the media, nationalised industries and far into the world of private business – RPR supporters found themselves squeezed out in favour of Giscard's eager young placemen. At the same time Giscard moved to consolidate his hold over the media. His friend, Robert Hersant, was allowed to buy up a whole chain of newspapers, despite a French law forbidding the ownership of more than one paper by any single individual. Elsewhere other Giscardian supporters moved in – Jimmy Goldsmith to pick up *L'Express*, the Matra armaments group to buy up the huge Hachette publishing empire – while simultaneously the government sought to bring to heel with law suits papers such as *Le Canard Enchaîné* and *Le Monde* which resisted the Élysée's embrace.

More and more French life came to resemble that of the Second Empire. Everywhere the families and friends of the President and his friends scrambled into lucrative and powerful positions. The RPR, bitterly, cried 'foul': when it had directed the Majority it had shared out its patronage among Giscardians as well as Gaullists, and the whole ensemble had at least been grouped around a set of underlying Gaullist political principles. The new system, lacking any clear ideological basis or popular roots, was far more straightforwardly monarchical – the new placemen were courtiers to a king and his family, not militants for a cause.

In a way it was Giscard's only option. The UDF had no popular roots or real organisation. In those terms it could never remotely rival the RPR. What it had – in abundance – was money, pollsters, patronage, money, advertising executives, media control, money, placemen – and money. With this combine Giscard calculated he could reduce the RPR – but still be able to rely on it in a crunch to keep the Left out. It was a fatal miscalculation.

In 1979 it worked. In the European elections the Giscardian machine rolled to such effect that the UDF list outscored the RPR by almost 2 : 1. Annoyingly, the Left had won 41 seats to the Right's 40. No matter: Giscard's election commissioners obligingly declared null a number of PS, PCF and RPR votes but discovered an extra 80 000 UDF votes in the week after the poll, giving the UDF the extra seat it wanted. Mitterrand protested bitterly – and immediately found himself faced with a law suit by the State Procurator for having appeared on a pirate broadcasting station.

Accordingly, and despite the growing problems of recession, unemployment and the disaffection of the young, Giscard approached the 1981 election in confident mood. The UDF had no militants to put up posters? No matter, off-duty policemen were found to do the job for £50 a day. When Chirac appeared on TV the other two channels put on their most popular programmes simultaneously. When video cassettes of Giscard and Mitterrand had to be sent off for French voters viewing in the overseas territories, Giscard's went by air, Mitterrand's by boat. When leading Gaullists backed Mitterrand for the second round, the radio and TV found it not worth a mention. And so on, and so on. *Le Canard Enchaîné* brought out a special election dossier on the Giscard 'monarchy' – but although it was not banned, its supplies to the news-stands were mysteriously interrupted. (I found that many newspaper kiosque-owners had copies but were simply too frightened to sell them: 'M'sieu, vous savez, c'est l'élection . . . c'est très difficile avec la police. . . . ')

The first round of the election dealt Giscard a crippling blow in the shape of a sharply reduced PCF vote, which greatly reduced the credibility of the 'red scare' tactics all ready for use on the second round. But an even worse blow followed: Giscard's happy assumption that the RPR machine would come out in force for him when the chips were down simply proved to be false. Chirac carefully declared he personally could not vote for the Left, but then sat on his hands. The RPR machine lay silent. As Giscard's poll advisers dissected the results of the first round, utter panic set in at the Élysée. Great bouquets of flowers were dispatched to Madame Chirac, ministers were sent to Chirac to promise him five or even eight ministries in the new government, frantic pressure was exercised via the patronat on Chirac's team of advisers. It was no good. Chirac and his henchmen had decided that they simply could not survive another seven years under Giscard – and knew that no promise from him was worth the paper it written on. (Charles Pasqua, the RPR's chief organisation man, told the Élysée that he was terribly sorry but that his doctor had ordered two weeks' complete rest after the rigours of the campaign.)

Giscard, unable to rely on the RPR machine, could only fall back even harder on his control of the media. The Hersant press reached new heights in hysteria. As well it might: Hersant is losing money and has only been kept going by large loans from Credit Lyonnais. In the event of a Giscard victory Jimmy Goldsmith had apparently agreed to buy the Hersant group. But if Giscard lost, Goldsmith would cry off and Crédit Lyonnais would be nationalised. But Hersant was only one frightened man among many. All over France prefects were making plans for new careers. In the television studios and polling organisations there was utter panic, with Giscardian string-pullers rushing to join the PS and to cultivate the friendship of Socialist journalists and producers whom they had kept out in the cold for long years before. Even UDF deputies joined in the Gadarene rush. In offices up and down the country dossiers were quietly taken home 'for safe-keeping'. (Once the celebrations of Mitterrand's victory have died away the loudest noise in France will be that produced by a hundred thousand paper shredders working round the clock.)

I am afraid that, having lived through such scenes as these in the last week, I must report that the British media, whether through incompetence, ignorance or political favouritism, has missed the chance to present some wonderfully Balzacian scenes in our nearest foreign neighbour. It has been a strange, almost surreal experience, to have spent a week witnessing the results of the total conviction in all those in the know in Paris that Giscard had lost, and yet to read the cautious, pedestrian reports in the British press – some even predicting a Giscard victory. Perhaps the reason lies deeper than mere incompetence. After all, this was a week when the British media were mainly preoccupied with the drama of the Prince Charles tapes. Perhaps the British are simply too deeply monarchist to understand what a fundamental thing the assertion of the republican spirit can be. For that is what France has witnessed in the last few days – indeed many Gaullists I knew told me they were voting for Mitterrand not because they were on the Left or even because they were true Chiraciens, but 'parce que je suis républicain'. Even on election night the BBC cameras failed to notice the largest meeting in Paris – that in the Place de la Bastille. That meeting, in that place, and the general delirium of the Left have only one meaning: in France, once again, a monarchy has fallen.

11

The Pursuit of Sound Money*

In 1976 Gerald Ford campaigned for reelection as President under the slogan 'Don't let us follow Britain down the drain'. Not the least remarkable thing about this was that such a comparison could be made publicly. Not many years before the sheer belief in the uniqueness of American – what C. Wright Mills called 'American exceptionalism' – would have simply prohibited the use of such a rallying cry, particularly from anyone used to nursing the prejudices of the voters of Grand Rapids, Michigan. It was no mean index of the effect of recurrent devaluations, the onrush of foreign competition, and the pervasive evidence of imperial decline, that such a comparison could find an uneasy popular acceptance. Ford's message, of course, was that this fate could be averted only by a return to 'true conservatism'.

Six years have gone by and the parallels seems to have got closer, not further apart. Ironically, one reason for this is that both countries have returned to 'true conservatism'. In both cases this was heralded as a major new departure, produced by a great philosophical sea-change in public opinion. In neither case was this true.

What actually happened was that the gradual disintegration of an old leftish electoral bloc – the New Deal coalition in the US, the 1945 class alignment in Britain – simply removed the constraints under which post-war conservatism had had to labour. Faced with the power of that opposing block conservatives' only hope lay in conceding to it by recoming Butskellite or running liberal Republicans for President. With that opposing bloc in tatters and

---

* First published in *New Society*, 7 October 1982.

crucially weakened by centrist defections (the swelling Liberal–centre group here, the Anderson independents in the us), the right was presented with a walkover. Not only could the right win but it had no need for Butskellites or liberal Republicans any more.

The result, in both countries, has been the return of a primitive variety of knownothing conservatism whose cutting edge is sharpened rather than blunted by the fact that this is its first chance at power in half a century. There is nothing new about this: it is the revenge of Herbert Hoover and Montague Norman. The message is simple to the point of simplemindedness: arm against the Red Menace abroad, fight inflation to the death at home, and nothing much else matters.

The mania for rearmament (also called 'defence') is equally perverse in both the us and uk in that it means pouring money into non-productive assets which are actually *intended* never to be used, which will all be quickly obsolete, and for which there was never much demonstrable need. But in every other way Thatcher's gun-happiness is far less rational than Reagan's. At the end of the day the us will always have a truly independent deterrent, whereas Britain won't, quite regardless of how much is spent.

In addition, Reagan's programme means pouring money into the pockets of the huge private arms manufacturers of the sun-belt, thus rewarding his political friends and transferring resources directly from the public to the private sector. While, in the British case, some of the loot will go in the same direction, quite a lot will go to nationalised industries (British Aerospace, Rolls-Royce, and so on) and the lion's share will go abroad.

The Trident programme is essentially a matter of passing billions of dollars over to the us, after all, and even for the conventional defence of the Falklands we will be buying us jets. That is, while the arms race will at least stimulate economic activity in the us, it will be almost purely a dead loss for the uk. Given the strenuous curbs on all other forms of public spending which might stimulate the economy, to increase spending in the one area which provides the least stimulus and causes the greatest foreign exchange losses is an act of surpassing ideological silliness, even by normal Thatcher standards.

Arms spending is for both Administrations, though, quite explicitly an area unconnected to all others: none of the normal rules about public spending, enlargement of the state sector and increasing productivity apply to it. Among domestic policy areas, only law and order gets similarly favoured treatment. Otherwise the totality of public policy is subjected to a single overriding theme: the battle against inflation.

This in itself is fairly odd. While nobody favours hyper-inflation (though the Israelis, for example, have always lived happily with it), it is difficult to see what's supposed to be so injurious about the 10–20 per cent sort of inflation we've had. It makes life a bit more complicated for accountants but provided pensions and wages are indexed it's a perfectly tolerable state of affairs for most people. Indeed, while interest rates remained neutral or negative great swathes of lower – and middle-class people found that inflation was a wonderful thing, allowing them to acquire high-priced houses or other goods and then to watch their mortgages and debts erode painlessly away.

For most people the problem was not inflation, but the failure to index their wages and pensions to it, so that every group had to fight not to fall behind while the strongest groups took the opportunity to try to move ahead of inflation. Perhaps the clearest example was old-age pensions. Every year in Britain used to see a mighty struggle over the question of what the pension increase would be. Finally, pensions were indexed and the issue simply vanished from the political scene.

But there, of course, was the rub. Inflation might have been tolerable for 'most people' – but not for the really rich and not for the banks. All those debtors required lenders, after all. Inflation brought about the devalorisation of the assets of some of the very rich and it also made it difficult for them to invest for a positive real return. Moreover, while for the average middle-class family their house, and thus their mortgage debt, was by far their largest investment, the same was not true for the really rich.

If you own £10 million, after all, your house is still not likely to account for more than 5 per cent of your assets and you probably don't have a mortgage anyway. For this group of people inflation was the next thing to cancer. Bankers were able to cope better but they did not like negative interest rates and inflation offended against their whole sense of "sound money."

While it was the achievement of both Reagan and Thatcher to rally majorities of the middle and lower classes to their cause, the essential point about both of them was that what they really represent is this tiny minority of bankers and the very rich. (The standard Marxist formula of finance capital versus industrial capital only partly captures the nuance: a better formulation would be finance capital plus historic capital versus the rest.)

Hence the nature of the 'fight against inflation'. Instead of curbing inflation by indexation or incomes policies, both Reagan and Thatcher chose the Hoover–Norman route: less government, a balanced budget (or a shrunken budget deficit), 'sound money', carrots for the rich in the shape of lower taxes (called 'incentives') and sticks for the poor in the shape of lower benefits and wages (also, strangely, called 'incentives').

Foolishly, both Reagan and Thatcher began their Administrations with large tax give-aways, angled towards the rich. This produced a slump in government revenue and thus an increasing budget deficit, which had to be countered by exceptionally fierce public spending cuts and some tax increases in other areas. The theory was that, armed with these incentives, the rich were going to work harder and invest more. It didn't happen. Instead, unemployment soared and demand slumped. The chief sufferers were the poor, in all their varieties and industry which found its market diminishing.

Manufacturers countered with price-cuts, extra borrowing and more labour lay-offs. Finding they could now meet the decreased demand easily from existing production capacity, manufacturers saw no reason to invest in new capacity, so investment fell again. At the same time, both Administrations, hot on the pursuit of 'sound money', pushed up interest rates to ensure that whatever the rate of inflation, those with spare cash to deposit could get a positive real return. In the UK this produced an MLR at 17 per cent; in the US interest rates of 20 per cent plus.

This was delightful for those with large amounts of spare cash and for the banks. It was dreadful for just about everyone else. For the poor it was unrelieved misery. Even the solid middle classes found that their houses were losing real value rapidly, while their mortgage payments escalated along with interest rates. But the most surprised victims were the industrialists. They had all voted for Reagan or Thatcher and had confidently expected better times. To their dismay they found the opposite was true. They cut their costs to the bone but still found their profit margins under pressure. They remonstrated with 'their' governments in vain. Thousands went bankrupt – and not just the smaller fry: Laker and Braniff went down, as did De Lorean. Chrysler, Ford, International Harvester, Turner & Newall, Woolworths and a host of other household names were in deep trouble. Unemployment soared, the banks thrived, the rich took pleasure in their capital gains and the governments did nothing.

Under this draconian pressure, inflation fell as prices were cut and profit margins shaved. Interest rates followed down – but stayed real. According to the Thatcher–Reagan theory this was now the stage where an investment-led recovery would begin and both governments confidently prophesied its imminence. It hasn't happen. They have continued to prophesy it. It still hasn't happened.

Hence the present impasse in both countries. Both governments were hell-bent on the revitalisation of capitalism via higher profits and investment. Instead both have achieved huge falls in production and employment, slumping investment and profit margins which are still nosing down.

Most rational people, having followed a theory thus far and found that it produced effects quite opposite to those intended, would question their theory. Instead, there is every sign that both governments believe that salvation lies in repeating their earlier mistakes on an even bigger scale. Hence the rumblings in both Washington and London of even more massive public spending cuts in education, health and social transfer payments of every kind; this despite the fact that the original alleged objective of pulling down inflation has been already largely achieved.

There are only three things which can save us all from the terrible misery inflicted by this stone-age economics. The first would be a large recovery in world trade – but all the signs are that the opposite is happening. Second, there are the banks. Until now they have watched with equanimity as awesome damage was inflicted on the real economy. But they have begun to be aware that another wave of cuts will bankrupt many of their biggest industrial clients, leaving them with a mountainous chain of bad debts. This frightens them sufficiently for some of them to start throwing their weight against the idea of further deflation. The third hope lies with the ballot box. Here the Americans are luckier than us. All the indications are that Reagan will suffer sweeping mid-term losses in November, will lose control over Congress and, by the New Year, see Democratic challengers running ahead of him in the polls. This could well halt the Reagan experiment in its tracks.

The tragedy in Britain is that there is little present sign of the direct electoral pressures needed to bring Thatcher back to earth – though all rational industrialists should be praying for a Labour lead in the opinion polls. Failing that, both they and the rest of us have to place our faith in the power of the bankers to dissuade Mrs Thatcher from further carnage. It is no mean indicator of how badly our opposition parties have failed us to date that our best hopes may lie in wishing more power to the elbows of the lineal heirs of Montague Norman. . . .

12

The Great Debt Explosion*

Amidst the acres of newsprint about Mrs Thatcher's Falklands trip last week it was barely possible to find a snippet to the effect that the major British banks had informed their international counterparts that owing to the present political difficulties surrounding Anglo-Argentine relations they did not feel able to join in the banking consortium faced with the problem of Argentina $43 billion debt. It was a very curious piece of news selection. The debt crisis of the less-developed countries (LDCs) and Eastern bloc is not only a far bigger story than any amount of Iron Ladies at Goose Green – it is the biggest story of all. If this crisis is going to bring down the international financial system it will be because the great banks of the West fail to maintain a common front – so a split in their ranks is news indeed. One can't know when the chickens will come home to roost on this issue, but come home they eventually and certainly will.

The aforementioned fowls have been circling over the world financial system for ten years now, but to understand the situation one has to go back even further. At least since 1945 the terms of trade between the LDCs and the developed countries had been deteriorating in favour of the latter, so that each year it took more sisal, copper, sugar or whatever to buy the same tractor (for example). This process of deterioration was, though, a very gradual one and was punctuated by the (short-lived) Korean War boom of the early 1950s. It was also made slightly more tolerable to the LDCs through the fact that many of them were growing quite fast and that inflation was low. None the less by the late 1960s there was a growing realisation that the terms of trade were far more important than any amount of aid to LDCs and

---

* First published in *New Society*, 27 January 1983.

that further deterioration in these terms would make their escape from immiseration quite impossible.

Then came the synchronised boom of all the major capitalist economies in 1971–3. This quickly generated acute raw material shortages, an astonishing boom in commodity prices and thus – despite higher inflation – a major reversal in the terms of trade in favour of the LDCs. For the poor countries these were happy days indeed and many of them used their new gains to launch ambitious development programmes. The boom was just ending when the commodity price rise phenomenon reached the last and greatest commodity of them all, oil.

There followed the great world crash of 1974–5. Inflation soared simultaneously but commodity prices, with the exception of oil, fell like so many stones. Suddenly the LDCs found that not only had they been brutally stripped of their new gains overnight but that they were simultaneously having to face hugely higher oil bills while the price of those tractors was climbing at 15–20 per cent a year. If they were to pay their ordinary housekeeping bills, let alone continue their development programmes, they – and a number of Eastern bloc countries were in rather the same position – could do only one thing: borrow. If all went well their borrowing would enable them to maintain their investment programmes and thus their ultimate ability to repay in dollars whose real worth would anyway be eroded by inflation. And, who knew, the cycle might reverse itself in time.

The LDCs were, naturally, loath to accept a situation in which the optimal possible future on offer to them was one in which whatever development they could achieve would be mortgaged away under a mountainous debt. Moreover, the commodity price boom had allowed them not just to see but to experience how different things might be. Accordingly they made vehement demands for a New International Economic Order (NIEO) which, when stripped of all its rhetoric, amounted essentially to the freezing of real commodity prices at their 1971–3 levels, that is to say a permanent alteration of the terms of trade in their favour. There was never any serious possibility that the developed countries would agree to such a massive redistribution of wealth away from themselves. For a while the LDCs nourished the illusion that the OPEC bloc might altruistically use its 'oil weapon' to exact such concessions or that a NIEO might be achieved by the sheer political weight of their united numbers. As these hopes faded, the only alternative left was to borrow.

Happily, this was just what the big Western banks wanted. The OPEC nations were building up enormous cash balances with those banks who had no realistic possibility of lending it back out in the amounts required except to sovereign states with multi-billion dollar requirements. Thus they all but fell over themselves to lend to the LDCs and the Eastern bloc, usually at a rate of interest 4–5 per cent higher than they were paying OPEC on their deposits. It was a wonderful business – every $1 billion thus 'recycled' produced an extra cash-flow to the banks of around $50 million a year, much of it pure profit. Western governments were only too ready to applaud the 'success' of recycling, for they were conscious that without these loans the LDCs and the East would be unable to buy Western exports, producing a collapse in world trade. Moreover, if the private banks couldn't handle recycling then Western governments and central banks might have to. This would put everything on a state-to-state basis and thus politicise the whole process in just the way the advocates of an NIEO wanted and which, accordingly, the West did not want.

The only oddity in this Pollyanna world where everyone was happy – for a while – was the apparent fact that OPEC states were willing to let the Western banks take their enormous middle-man profits which they could, after all, have had for themselves by lending direct to the LDCs. Actually, OPEC was far cannier than the banks, for the OPEC deposits were entirely safe while the banks, in return for their 4–5 per cent margin, were carrying the whole of the risk that LDCs would be unable to repay their debts. At first the banks acted as though this risk was negligible. No country could default upon, let alone repudiate, its debts without being locked out of international credit markets ever after. Moreover, the international community as a whole would never accept a country defaulting for fear that the demonstration effect would produce a chain reaction of defaults with a consequent collapse of world credit and trade. It would be The End of the World As We Know It – and therefore unthinkable.

In this *bien pensant* mood the fact that LDC debt ratios were escalating to unprecedented and probably unrepayable levels was simply brushed under the carpet in 1974–5. When North Korea defaulted (and brusquely repudiated its debts) in 1974 nobody took much notice. After all, anyone who had read Kim II Sung's huge advertisements for himself in the press – ads for which the banks has really paid – knew that he was mad. In 1976 Zaïre defaulted but the debt wasn't all that big, and rescheduling (i.e. fresh loans to pay the interest on the old ones) was arranged. What could you do about Mobutu, sighed the bankers: another madman. Then came similar troubles with Peru and Turkey with similar solutions reached.

The only sign of public unease over this developing situation came during the 1976 West German election campaign when there was a brief flurry of panic that the real meaning of *Ostpolitik* seemed to be the expansion of German trade with the East financed on the back of huge German bank loans to Poland and others which could never be repaid. Such fears were quickly hushed as 'exaggerated'. Elsewhere in the West such fears did not surface at all during the 1976–7 recovery. The problems with Zaïre, etc., were dismissed as mainly the result of individual falls from grace rather than as part of a general phenom-
•enon. So while the miscreants had to be helped out, the international community (in the shape of the IMF) was pulled in, partly to help in a small way with the loans, but mainly to deliver stern lectures on the Friedmanite virtues and to impose tough conditions, usually involv-ing devaluations and cuts in imports and public expenditure.

Then came the second great downturn of 1979–82, with a further huge rise in the oil price, the advent of UK and US governments bent on competitive deflation, a stronger dollar and pound, and sky-high interest rates. These last two factors were crippling – well over half the loans were at variable interest rates so borrowers now faced repayments in currencies which were appreciating, not depreciating and at interest rates of up to 20 per cent and more. (Every 1 per cent rise added around $2 billion to the annual LDC debt bill.)

By late 1979 the writing was on the wall for all to see. But the big banks continued to shovel out loans as if there were no tomorrow. Well into 1980 I attended a bankers' lunch where one of my hosts told me with pride how he, acting for one of the biggest UK banks, had just taken part in a new loan to Poland. I could not desist from asking if he was betting on a Russian invasion or some solution whereby the Russians would assume responsibility for the Polish debt. I was reprimanded, no doubt rightly, for being 'too outspoken'. I got the clear impression that the loan was seen essentially as a Cold War move – bolstering Poland's ability (and Solidarity was then at its peak strength) to stand up to the USSR. Certainly the reasons for the loan could not, by that stage, have had much to do with banking. Except, of course, that, as in 1974–5, the oil price rise of 1979 produced huge new OPEC balances on deposit with the banks in

1980–1 which they were keen to lend out somewhere . . . anywhere.

The crunch finally came over Poland in 1981. The Poles owed some $26 billion, were in arrears, and couldn't pay. The complex minuet of debt negotiations began. Would the Russians or the (comparatively wealthy) East Germans help? Well, the Russians themselves owed $23 billion and the East Germans $14 billion and neither approved of the antics which had got the Poles into such a mess. The Russians would help, but only a bit. Some US banks toyed with the idea of just calling in their debts. Their exposure was relatively small – most of the debt was owed to European, especially German banks. This notion was not exactly discouraged by some of the wilder Reaganites in Washington. If debts were recalled then either a formal default would be declared – a crushing blow to the prestige and the pocket of the entire Communist bloc; or the Germans, desperate to prevent a default and preserve their Eastern bloc trade, would have to come up extra loans so that the US banks could be paid off. A simple recall, the Germans furiously pointed out, was a sort of Cruise missile with multiple targetting for Warsaw and Frankfurt. In the end a united front was – just – maintained and rescheduling (i.e. fresh loans) agreed.

It was, though, a major watershed. The great debt problem had surfaced at last and no amount of diplomatic silence would sweep it back under the carpet again. The problem could only get worse with time. Any number of ingenious 'solutions' were canvassed but there was no solution which wouldn't leave an enormous hole in someone's pocket. No one was willing to accept that now, so the problem was always pushed off till tomorrow. Thus it got ever bigger – and ever less soluble.

13

Oil, Credit and Crisis*

'Major US banks have arranged an emergency $1.5 billion rescue for Seaforth Corporation of Seattle, parent of the 26th largest US bank.'

Financial Times, 22 Jan 1983

'Business', as James Gillray said, 'is other people's money.' For no one is this truer than for bankers. In the 1970s many bankers seemed almost to forget this home truth as they made vast profits out of recycling (i.e. relending on) the OPEC money deposited with them to the Eastern bloc and the less-developed countries (LDCs). There was a collective aversion of eyes from the awkward truth that many of these borrowers were extremely bad risks who would be quite unable to pay back. After all, a country never defaulted, did it? Well, hardly ever. . . . The result was the construction of a great card house of international debt. The first sign that this whole house might fall came with the crisis over the Polish debt in 1981. In the end a Polish default was avoided, though only by the banks unhappily making new loans to Poland to enable it to pay the interest on the old ones.

With this, the lid was off the pot. What was sauce for Poland was bound to be sauce for a whole host of Third World geese and ganders as well. But the banks were already dangerously over-extended (they had plenty of bad debtors at home as well). If they continued extending loans to hopeless non-payers, they'd go bust – but if they didn't then they risked a chain reaction of international defaults in

---

* First published in *New Society*, 3 February 1983.

which case the banks would also go bust, with consequences for the entire international financial system which were almost too frightening to contemplate. The ensuing ripple of panic brought to the fore a whole series of conflicts and tensions.

Apart from the obvious clash between debtors and creditors there was the conflict between the banks' desperate desire to get their money back and the West's trading interests. The 40 per cent of Western trade directed to the LDCs and the East depended heavily on these loans. If new loans weren't made this trade would collapse and the world would sink into a far deeper depression than anything seen so far. There were tensions too between the private banks and their government central banks. When it had been a matter of making fat profits from recycling the OPEC surplus, the private banks had been only too keen to keep the central banks out. Now, when it was a matter of facing up to huge losses, the private banks pressed for the maximum involvement of the central banks, the World Bank and the IMF. There were tensions within the ranks of the private banks, with the smaller ones unwilling to 'take the long view' (whatever that was). They wanted to take their money and run – even at the risk of triggering defaults which would overwhelm the big banks too.

Finally, as the bitter quarrel between the German and US banks over Poland had revealed, there were growing political tensions between the various national banks, whose exposure to debt varied considerably. Thus the Japanese banks, though carrying $81 billion of international debt by 1981, were forbidden by Japanese law from lending more than 30 per cent of their capital abroad. Others were far more exposed: the top nine US banks, for example, had lent out 130 per cent of their shareholders' equity to Brazil, Argentina and Mexico alone. At the other end of the spectrum were the conservative Swiss banks who had held back from the grosser excesses of the lending spree and yet still seemed to have levers the others lacked. Thus even when Zaïre stopped repaying other banks it kept on paying the Swiss – a phenomenon apparently not unconnected with the fact that Mobutu's personal fortune of some $4 billion was under lock and key in Swiss vaults.

What made everything worse was a simple lack of information. Both banks and national treasuries were such secretive animals that it was impossible to be sure about even the crudest big numbers. It was only when a country was at its last gasp that its creditors were allowed to see the books. This frequently produced nasty surprises. Thus the

Polish rescue took place without the bankers ever discovering that a whole sixth of the Polish debt was held by Brazilian banks: this emerged only when Brazil came running for help.

Inevitably rumour was rife. Sometimes in such stories a country's debt or a bank's exposure varied by many billions of dollars. Brokers' circulars speculated as to whether Citibank or Chase was truly bust. There were recurrent rumours of a secret cabal of debtor nations planning a massive collective repudiation of their debts. But lack of information also allowed those who wished to pretend that things were not really so serious. This form of behaviour, known as 'maintaining confidence', was widely believed, especially in the UK, to be 'responsible'. Those who warned of the gravity of the crisis were indignantly shushed for mentioning such frightening things in front of the children. Hence the 'Crisis, what crisis?' remarks of the new Governor of the Bank of England in recent weeks.

But the Polish debacle of 1981 had already made such pretence absurd. Moreover, while fifteen countries had been in repayment arrears in 1975, by 1981 the number had grown to thirty-five. The banks began to draw back from further lending as hard and fast as they could, with half of the 1200 banks involved scrambling to get out of the business altogether. New loans to LDCs, which had grown by 40 per cent in 1981, fell by 32 per cent in 1982. The trouble was that many banks were in so deep that they couldn't stop lending now: even at the 1982 rate LDC debt was increasing at $100 billion a year.

Even this small contraction of credit only hastened the crisis and in August 1982 Mexico announced it couldn't pay the interest on its $80 billion debt. Almost immediately Brazil ($87 billion) and Argentina ($43 billion) followed. Thereafter it was a virtual cascade: Venezuela ($28 billion), Israel ($27 billion), Yugoslavia ($19 billion), Romania ($10 billion), Zambia ($4.5 billion) and Bolivia ($3.1 billion). A host of others were in trouble too. Frantic rescheduling has happened in every case so far but there is no sign that the queue is getting shorter. Indeed, Poland has just announced it can't even meet its already rescheduled 1983 payments. All told over $700 billion is owing and of that a full half looks hopeless – a sum equal to one and a half times the annual budget of Japan, the second greatest capitalist power on earth. And the total is still climbing fast.

Faced with the Mexican bail-out the private banks could no longer cope so, willy-nilly, the central banks were forced to come in. (Paul Volcker, the head of the US Federal Reserve, was summoned so abruptly that he had to transact some of the most crucial business in his pyjamas.) The heads of the private banks – the world's greatest capitalists – had taken their chance with the free market and lost. There are, though, few who believe in capitalism less than they and they look to their governments for rescue.

In response to their frantic urgings moves are now in progress to beef up the reserves of the World Bank, the General Arrangements to Borrow, and the IMF by a total of $47.5 billion, thereby enabling them to bail the private banks out. Great faith is currently placed in these moves but even if they all succeed $47.5 billion will, at the present rate, last only six months. It is no real solution. Similarly, the hopes now placed on the effects of a falling oil price are pretty empty. A 20 per cent cut in the oil price would improve Brazil's balance of payments by 6 per cent, but worsen Mexico's by over 14 per cent, Venezuela's by 18 per cent and Nigeria's by 19 per cent. Overall the effect of an oil price cut on the debt problem may be no better than neutral, but it will undoubtedly lengthen the debtors' queue (as OPEC states join it) and worsen the position of several countries quite catastrophically. Finally, one should note that two-thirds of the IMF quota increase will depend on a highly problematic vote in the US Congress. At present it is being blithely assumed that the vote will go through easily. This is typical of the wishful thinking which has dogged the debt problem all along.

So what are the real options? First, one could belatedly admit that the LDCs were right to demand a New International Economic order in 1974 – that is, a massive resource transfer from the developed countries to themselves. That the West's refusal of such a transfer was inimical even to its own trading interests is largely proved by the fact that such a transfer has been taking place anyway, though in an utterly crazy and wasteful fashion, with the money going to rich LDCs – the Brazils rather than the Tanzanias – and that merely for housekeeping rather than investment purposes. That is, we could now sit down and plan such a transfer on more equitable and sensible lines. This proposal is too rational to be even remotely likely.

The second possibility is a massive and concerted world reflation whose effect would be a large expansion of world trade, rising commodity prices and a depreciation of all currencies in which debts are held as inflation took off again. Under these conditions many, if not all, LDCs would find they were able to repay their debts after all.

This is an attractive option partly because it would mean debts don't have to be written off and partly because it would also trigger a world economic recovery. There are two problems with it. First, every previous attempt to get all the great capitalist locomotives to pull together has failed because all governments are frightened to be the first to reflate: their competitors may take advantage of them by pursuing more conservative policies and then pricing out of world markets the higher priced goods produced by the reflation leader. Second, the great crash of 1974–5 happened largely because of the synchronised boom of all capitalist countries in 1971–3 – there were no counter-cyclical countries taking off into boom when the others fell back, so everyone fell together: hence the depth of the slump. If we now deliberately plan another great synchronised boom we are also planning an even deeper synchronised slump a few years after that. But because this option is the least immediately painful to the West and would be nice for the banks it is bound to be tried to some extent.

The third possibility is that things will go on as now with the private banks being forced to extend more loans, with the central banks being pulled in more and more so that public money is shovelled towards the private banks to prevent them going bust. This is extremely likely, although it implies that the private banks will in effect be quietly nationalised, in effect if not always in name. It may well be that this option will be so distasteful to Reagan, Thatcher and Kohl that there will have to be some major bank collapse to make them change their minds. The private banks can put off this evil hour – which is what all governments would like – but only at the cost of the problem getting worse.

The final key feature is a growing hostility between the European and us banks. With the British banks refusing to touch Argentina and the French and Germans saying they will only help Brazil if their loans are used to buy their own countries' exports, there is a clear tendency towards a fresh demarcation of spheres of influence, with the Europeans accepting responsibility for Eastern Europe and Africa, the us for the (enormously greater) Latin American and Pacific basin debtors. Such a division would mark a major us retreat and would simultaneously deal the Americans a crippling economic blow. It seems unlikely that the Western alliance, already strained over defence and East–West issues, could easily survive such a show-down.

The most likely outcome is a combination of these last two scenarios – and all the dangers they imply. There is just no easy way out. At this point the new Governor of the Bank of England, Mr Robin Leigh-Pemberton, strides toward the centre stage with his 'Crisis? What crisis?' remarks. Like his patroness, Mrs Thatcher, Mr Leigh-Pemberton has been trained as a barrister, knows little of finance or economics, but shares her instincts of the Victorian governess. There was a time when the British Establishment really *could* dispose of minor crises by such displays of insouciance. That time has gone; this is not a minor crisis; and Mr Leigh-Pemberton's pretence is both pathetic and foolish. What crisis? *That* crisis.

14

The Holy Multinational*

As the Pope trips round the world – from Britain to Argentina, from El Salvador to Ireland, and back to Poland yet again – he enjoys a benign respect, even reverence, from the Western media which is as novel as it is curious.

It is novel in that the predominantly Protestant, if not downright secular prejudices which would not so long ago have greeted a Bishop of Rome are now almost wholly stilled. It is curious because even as the Pope preaches, for example, the indissolubility of marriage or inveighs against birth control, there are many whose lives would have been rendered unlivable without contraception and divorce who will join in the chorus that he is a wholly good and wise man.

If Reagan or Andropov or Mitterrand toured the world's trouble-spots, giving vacuous speeches in favour of peace and brotherhood while studiously avoiding all the truly burning issues, they would be greeted with derision. Not so the Pope and he does, like them, claim a world diplomatic role. What is curious, in a word, is the tendency to take the Pope, alone of all world figures, at the evaluation set by his own public relations machine. Anyone who, like myself, was born and brought up a Catholic can only blink in sheer disbelief.

'There is not, and there never was on this earth,' wrote Macaulay in 1840, 'a work of human policy so well deserving of examination as the Roman Catholic church. . . . No other institution is left standing which carries the mind back to the times when the smoke of sacrifice rose from the Pantheon, and when camelopards and tigers bounded in the Flavin ampitheatre. The proudest royal houses are but of yesterday when compared with the line of the Supreme Pontiffs. . . .

---

* First published in *New Society*, 16 June 1983.

'The papacy remains, not in decay, not a mere antique, but full of life and youthful vigour. The Catholic Church is still sending forth to the farthest ends of the earth missionaries as zealous as those who landed in Kent with Augustine, and still confronting hostile kings with the same spirit with which she confronted Attila. The number of her children is greater than in any former age. Her acquisitions in the New World have more than compensated for what she has lost in the Old. Nor do we see any sign that the term of her long dominion is approaching. She saw the commencement of all the governments and of all the ecclesiastical establishments that now exist in the world; and we feel no assurance that she is not destined to see the end of them all.'

Macaulay lacked our word for this 'work of human policy': the Catholic Church is the first and greatest of the multinationals, a structure which dwarfs Exxon or IBM in its global reach. Not even the Comintern at its zenith had a chain of command which branched so effortlessly into every corner of the globe. The church's adherents, nominally at least, are now nudging the one billion mark.

Which multinational could demand that all its staff work without salaries – indeed which other church could? Which other organis- ation could deny its cadres the right to marry? Even Stalin would never have dared ask so much. And which other organisation combines the ownership of churches and schools with that of banks and a large portion of the world's art treasures?

Beyond even that the church has an actual state, controlling a sovereign physical territory, its own radio station, its own worldwide ambassadorial corps. It issues its own passports, its own stamps. And which other organisation claims that its chief executive is literally infallible when he pronounces on key matters of company policy? It is the behemoth to end all behemoths.

The key to understanding the behaviour of this Pope, as also all his predecessors, is to realise that he is conducting not just state diplomacy but a global diplomacy of the sort only conducted and understood by the chief executives of other multinationals. He is like the chairman of Barclays with branches in both Nigeria and South Africa, or the president of Exxon with interest in both the Middle East and amongst the New York Jewish lobby.

Diplomacy at this level is quite inevitably amoral. All that matters is the maintenance of the balance most beneficial to one's widely spread interests.

There is no point getting upset about this. It is pointless to berate the chairman of Barclays for not taking a stronger moral stand against apartheid. He is not in business as a moral philosopher. His responsibility is to his balance-sheet and his shareholders. It is the same with the Papacy, which has far wider interests than Barclays and takes a uniquely long-term view of its shareholders' welfare.

The reasons why Pius XI supported Franco's insurrection against the legal government of Spain, or why Pius XII gave audiences to Ribbentrop (and provided him with Vatican police-car escorts flying swastika flags), had nothing to do with morality, everything to do with the church's far-flung European interests. The Pope's claim to be God's representative on earth had not, after all, prevented the Papacy employing war, torture, genocide, censorship and all other means to hand to gain its ends.

That this higher amorality of statecraft counted for far more than the Papacy's prodigious moral claims, used to be generally understood. It is the loss of the perception today which is so remarkable, which needs to be explained.

The answer has its roots in the utter trauma of the Papacy amidst the revolutionary turmoil at the end of the first world war. Before that war, Rome had railed furiously against any form of bourgeois republic, whose secular libertarian values it found deeply offensive. Catholics were instructed not even to vote in such states.

The bolshevik revolution and the wave of postwar revolutionary unrest changed all this. Within Italy itself, factory occupations, strikes and Red peasant league agitation seemed about to produce a socialist revolution. At the least, the church faced the loss of its working class following right across Europe; at worst the church might find itself wholly expropriated of all its property and privileges.

Anything – and that suddenly included the bourgeois republic – was better than this. The church threw itself frantically into the anti-bolshevik anti-socialist crusade, quickly set afoot the Catholic People's Party and enjoined Catholics to vote for it. It immediately emerged as the largest party in Italy, and held the Red tide at bay until Mussolini took over to do the job even more thoroughly in 1922.

The Papacy did not directly support the fascists – it did not like some of the wilder spirits around Mussolini or the fascist arrogation of state supremacy. But in the church's eyes Fascism (and later Nazism) was infinitely preferable to Communism. It had the great positive merit that it crushed the left, and the fascists were people one could do a deal with. The People's Party, which alone could have blocked Mussolini's quest for supreme power, was disbanded, and in 1929 the clerical–fascist alliance was sealed by the Lateran Treaty, which guaranteed papal sovereignty and made Catholicism the state religion of Italy.

This set the pattern for much of Europe in the years to come, so that by 1939 the church was maintaining relations of at least benevolent neutrality with fascist regimes in Italy, Hungary, Portugal and Spain. Relations with the Nazi regimes in Germany, Austria and Czechoslovakia were less warm – though this was more because Nazism was a form of Protestant nationalism than because of any principled dislike of concentration camps. The accession to power of Pius XII in 1939 owed no little, indeed, to his successful negotiation (as papal nuncio) of a concordat with Hitler in 1933.

Through its effective alliance with fascism, the church had surmounted the great bolshevik threat of the inter-war period. By 1943, however, the allied landings in North Africa and Sicily had put the writing on the wall for Mussolini, and the Vatican stealthily but decisively shifted its weight towards the growing anti-fascist coalition. Vatican diplomats opened up a close relationship with Allen Dulles (then head of the oss, and later of the cia) at his base in Switzerland, and provided invaluable political intelligence to prepare the groundwork for the Bodoglio coup.

By this adroit shift in *Realpolitik* the church was able, ex- traordinarily, to emerge into the post-war world as one of the leaders of the anti-fascist resistance. At the end of the war Piux XII even found some stern words to say about the German treatment of the Jews. At the same time, though, the church co-operated enthusiastically with us intelligence in protecting a number of major German war criminals – Klaus Barbie is only one example – and ultimately help- ing to smuggle them out to safe hiding-places in good Catholic countries like Argentina.

Peace brought a renewed threat from the left, however, and the church immediately took the lead in the fierce new cold war against Communism, setting afoot powerful Christian Democratic parties in much of Europe and in 1949 actually excommunicating those who joined the Communist Party. This medieval ultimate weapon – never used against the Nazis – entitles faithful Catholics to kill those excommunicated without incurring mortal sin. If taken seriously, it was an open invitation to murder. In Eastern Europe the church enthusiastically embraced the philosophy of the Dulles brothers

(Allen still at the CIA, John Foster at the States Department) about 'rolling back' Communism, even though it was tolerably clear that if such a policy were really pursued it could only lead to another world war. It was as part of this strategy that Rome supported the most intransigent anti-Communists within the Eastern European church – Mindzenty in Hungary and Wyszinsky in Poland.

At the same time, however, the church quietly reassessed its strategy towards Eastern Europe. It was clear that the Dulles brothers had led Rome into a blind alley there – the Communists were there to stay, if not for ever, then at least for a long time. Accordingly, although the church insisted that it should still be seen as the guardian of human rights there (a truly breath-taking piece of historical impudence, this), it also disembarrassed itself of the Mindzentys and Wyszinskys in order to seek a rapprochement with the state authorities.

This has been a notable success. The Communists, no doubt, realise exactly what the church is up to and the very definite limitations on its real friendship. But they too are masters of *Realpolitik*. It was a decided nuisance to have to govern against the sullen resentment of their often strongly Catholic populations and they jumped at the chance to improve the position. Their long-term aim is still to secularise their populations or at least to 'nationalise' their local Catholic Church in the way Henry VIII did in England; but for any present relief much thanks.

The result has been a delicate and indeed rather comic series of minuets, conducted with courteous distrust. Cardinal Lekai of Hungary has actually been decorated by Kadar for his contribution to church–state relations; Cardinal Tomasek of Czechoslovakia called personally on Husak to congratulate him on his seventieth birthday; General Jaruzelski was one of the first to congratulate Glemp on his elevation to cardinal; and the Pope has even been able to name cardinals in East Germany and Russia.

On the other hand the church has been careful to position itself to be able to seize the leadership (and control) of any dissident movement should cracks appear in the Communist monolith. This is precisely what has happened in Poland. The Solidarity movement was originally led by Lech Walesa and the Gdansk workers. As the dust now settles Solidarity has been smashed, Walesa is isolated and the church has wholly expropriated the movement's leadership, thereby increasing its significance, popularity and leverage upon the regime. Walesa is known to be bitter about this and says the church would like him to disappear through a trap-door now that he has served his purpose. To avoid such charges of collaborationism the church must continue to strike a high moral note of implicit defiance and independence. This is what brings the Pope to Poland again this week. Theoretically his visit is all about bringing Christ to the faithful; in fact he is performing a diplomatic tight-rope act for the benefit of multiple audiences in East and West. If he succeeds the church will further consolidate its hold over the dissident movement, allowing it to bargain for further concessions from Jaruzelski as the only institution able to provide peaceful social control over a restive population – while simultaneously gaining even greater renown in the West as the only institution capable of driving a wedge into the Communist control of Eastern Europe.

This is an ambitious strategy even for someone who regards himself as God's direct representative on earth. This is not to say it is beyond him. No one should underestimate an organisation which has produced the Inquisition and the Index but still manages to appear as the defender of Western values and freedoms; which has hunted with the fascist hounds, done deals with the Communist fox and even turned secularisation to its own account. It is a pity Macaulay is not alive to see the triumphant Papal procession through the streets of Warsaw. Even he might be surprised to see what this 'work of human policy' has now achieved.

15

How Russians See It*

It is a commonplace abroad, especially in Europe, that the British remain obsessed by the Second World War. There is no doubting the truth of this, nor is any end in sight. The Falklands war was revealed once again how rich are the rewards for British politicians able to harness the underground streams which flow ever onwards from 1940. Indeed, such is the British appetite for military heroics that even before that, the balcony antics of a handful of SAS men during the Iranian Embassy seige was celebrated over and over again as a major national achievement. In a climate where our newsagents' shelves bulge with military pap it is hardly surprising that successive governments have been able to get away with ludicrously high levels of defence expenditure and our nuclear debates are conducted, on both sides, as if we count for far more than we actually do.

What is less commonly recognised is that the conflict we 're-member' so well is not really the Second World War but a rather peculiar British version of it. This proceeds from Dunkirk via the Battle of Britain and the Battle of the Atlantic to Alamein, the Dam Busters and D-Day, with sidelong glances at the fall of Singapore and Wingate's war in Burma. Stalingrad, Iwo Jima and Hiroshima are familiar names, but how many Britons know much of (say) the battles at Leyte Gulf or Kursk? How many of us can even find these places on the map? Yet Leyte was the greatest naval battle of the war and saw the definitive reduction of Japanese naval power, while Kursk remains the greatest tank battle in all of world history.

If the British have their own version of the war, so do others, most notably the Russians. This matters a great deal more than is often

---

* First published in *New Society*, 21 July 1983.

realised, for if the British tend to view the world through glasses irreversibly tinted by the war, so do they. Given that Russian motives and perspectives are, in one way or another, the object of almost all Western foreign and defence policies, it is worth considering the major ways in which the Russian version of the war differs from our own.

The approach to war is viewed here largely as the story of appeasement, that is of Allied attempts to buy off the Axis powers by means which were misguided but on the whole well-intentioned. The Russian view of Western diplomacy is altogether more sinister – that it was a protracted attempt to divert German aggression eastwards with the ultimate objective of a German crusade against Bolshevism which the West would at least tacitly and perhaps actively support.

The Russians recall that their proposals first for total and then partial disarmament during the 1930s were almost contemptuously dismissed. As the German advance into central and eastern Europe began the Russians repeatedly pleaded for a collective security pact with Britain and France to contain the Nazi menace. They met with obfuscation and delay and when an Allied team did finally arrive in Moscow in August 1939 the Russians discovered that they had no authority from London or Paris to sign any military agreement. At this the Russians broke off the talks and signed the Nazi–Soviet pact as the only respite left to them.

War then broke out, but oddly the Allies carefully refrained from any aggressive move against Germany for seven months (the 'phoney war') as if they still desperately hoped to conclude a deal with Hitler which would redirect his energies back eastwards. This caused the Russians to eye with some nervousness the fact that the Finnish border passed within twenty miles of Leningrad and they sought a pact with Finland to pre-empt a possible German attack from that direction. The Finns refused. The Russians then offered to exchange for the Finnish salient territory near Leningrad twice as much territory in Soviet Karelia. The Finns again refused. At this point war with Finland erupted (the Russians say the Finns started it). The Allies furnished the Finns with large-scale aid and were preparing to send an expeditionary force of 150 000 men to Finland when in March 1940 the Finns sued for peace. The fact that the Russians had only security motives in mind was proven by their complete withdrawal from Finland after the war. The Russians bitterly contrasted the West's eagerness for involvement in a war against the

USSR, to which it was not a formal party, with its failure to initiate action against Germany with which they were, supposedly, at war. In the end the issue was settled not by the Allies but the Hitler's westward attack (on Denmark and Norway) in April 1940. Only then did the British appoint a leader (Churchill) willing to do war with Germany.

The Russians do not believe that the Western attempt to redirect the war into an anti-Bolshevik crusade ever quite ceased. They point bitterly to Harry Truman's remarks on the day after the German attack on Russia: 'If we see Germany winning, then we should help Russia, and if Russia is winning, we should help Germany; so that in that way as many as possible should be killed.' This, they feel, remained an ever-present, if usually subordinate, Allied motif throughout the war. Only this, they feel, can explain the repeated Allied delay in launching a Second Front in the West while Russia was fighting for its life in the East, and the bizarre decisions to give priority instead to the North African, Italian and even Balkan fronts. The Russians bitterly allege that their great victory at Stalingrad appears to have convinced the Allies that there was a 'danger' of Germany being overrun 'too soon' (i.e. by the Russians alone) and that Stalingrad was followed by an abrupt and unexplained cut-off for eight months of all Allied aid convoys to Russia and frequent unexplained interruptions thereafter.

Over and over again the Russians return to the fact that throughout the war they took the brunt of vastly superior German forces. In 1943, when Churchill proudly boasted that the Allies were holding down eighteen German divisions in Italy, Stalin pointed out that Tito's partisans were holding down the same number in Yugoslavia, while Russia was facing 180 German divisions. At the time of D-Day the Allies faced sixty German divisions in the West while the Russians faced 259 divisions in the East. Despite this the Allies actually had the gall to criticise the Russians for not advancing more speedily to liberate Warsaw during the uprising there, even while the Allies were finding German armies less than a quarter the size all and more than they could cope with in the Battle of the Bulge.

Finally, the Russians emphasise that their preponderant role in the fighting meant that they paid the lion's share of the war's cost. Almost all of western and central Russia was devastated in a way only Coventry and Dresden experienced in the West. At war's end the Russian economy had been pushed back to below its 1913 levels of production – a whole generation of terrible sacrifice had been wiped out. Twenty-eight million people were homeless. Most of all, the Russians suffered human loss on a scale it is still difficult to fathom. For every 2 American casualties in the war there were 3 Britons, 14 Japanese, 31 Germans – and 137 Russians.

One may dispute some elements of the Russian account, but it undoubtedly contains a very large share of the truth. Even on a question as controversial as the Russian failure to extend greater assistance to the Warsaw uprising it is interesting to note that it is the Russian, and not the Western, version which best tallies with German accounts. The Chief of the German General Staff, Guderian, talks proudly in his memoirs of the awesome losses suffered by the Russians in their repeated attempts to break through to Warsaw and concludes flatly that 'We Germans had the impression that it was our defence which halted the enemy rather than a Russian desire to sabotage the Warsaw uprising.'

Similarly, one notes that it has been standard West Point doctrine since 1945 that the war was essentially won and lost on the Russian steppes. The reasoning is inescapable: the Germans' major strength lay in their army, the finest of the war, which had almost effortlessly disposed of the the Poles, French and British. If Germany was ever to be defeated someone, somewhere had to confront that army head on in all its massed strength and destroy it. This the Russians did and from June 1941 to June 1944 they faced this juggernaut almost entirely on their own. The German casualty list at Kursk was five times as big as the entire German army that Montgomery faced at Alamein. . . .

The impact of the war on Russia will be felt for decades to come. As in Britain, the proud memory of the war has engendered a conservative patriotic nationalism which is a powerful force for social cohesion. Predictions of the imminent social collapse of the USSR should be treated about as seriously as similar predictions about Britain.

The war also left Russia with a defensive psychosis. While Western armies were soon fighting abroad again in Korea, Suez and Vietnam, it was not until 1980 that the Red Army again saw real action, in Afghanistan. But horror of war made Russia, like Britain, more not less military minded, especially given its legacy of a distrust of Western motives deep enough to survive any amount of détente. The lesson that one must never be caught unprepared again and that in the crunch one stood on one's own was, as in Britain, perhaps overlearnt. A vast standing Red Army was maintained despite the large domestic political risks that entailed and Russian defence expenditure was a world record. After the shock of 1941 the Russians tended to feel you couldn't have too much of a good thing and they are often genuinely surprised that their military might should be seen as threatening to others.

The grievances over the Second Front live on in the imperial Russian attitude to Eastern Europe. Had the Allies launched the Second Front earlier they might have met up with the Red Army at Brest Litovsk, not Berlin. In the end the Russians feel their hegemony in Eastern Europe exists because they earned it with their blood. If anything they stand amazed at their own generosity in having withdrawn from Finland, Austria, Yugoslavia, Romania and Albania.

Finally, the Russians are bitterly conscious that if they won war, the Americans scooped the fruits of victory. In 1945, with Russia, Japan and Europe in ruins, America bestrode the world. America alone was strengthened, not damaged by war and accounted for half of all the world's production. This dominance has now been eroded by forty years of peace, to the great discomfort of the US. The Russians mortally fear American nuclear superiority for they believe that the US could have a clear national interest in starting a nuclear war in order to re-create the world of 1945. A war which destroyed Russia and Europe would restore American hegemony, albeit this time in a condominium shared with the Japanese.

Ironically, the best guarantee against such an apocalypse might be a strong, militarily independent Europe without the Americans. The original idea for such a European Defence Force died because neither the British nor the Russians could bear the thought of a Germany armed with nuclear weapons. But in the end whether we can avert the next world war could well come down to a question of whether the British and Russians both can finally emancipate themselves from the fears and prejudices engendered by the last one.

16
Nuclear Doublethink

This autumn's great debate over Cruise and Pershing-II has had a surreal air – though not, one hastens to add, for any lack of reality in the fateful issues involved.

The pro-missile camp have argued that the emplacement of these new missiles is a measured retaliation for the siting of the Russian ss20s, something which Andropov can avoid if he wants to be reasonable. Their *bête noire* is the ss20 which, symbolically, stands for the whole phenomenon of Soviet imperialism. The unilateralists, on the other hand, have tended to argue that since all nuclear weapons are bad, and since Cruise and Pershing are refinements on previous nuclear weapons, the new missiles are very bad indeed. Their *bête noire* is Ronald Reagan in particular, and each and every nuclear weapon in general.

Both sides have missed the entire strategic point behind the emplacement of the new weapons: the pro-missile camp deliberately; the unilateralists, I suspect, thoughtlessly.

For there are only two important things to know in this debate. The first is that the emplacement of the new American missiles has nothing to do with retaliation, and not that much to with Ronald Reagan. The decisions to develop Cruise and Pershing were taken long before Reagan came to power, and largely as a result of the insistent Congressional pressure of the US military and defence industry lobbies. The assumption was already absolute that they would be placed in Europe (for neither weapon can reach the Soviet Union from America), and there were no ss20s to worry about at the time. The ss20s are being used as a currently convenient excuse. But if they didn't exist, no doubt some other 'reason' would have been found.

The second point is that Cruise and Pershing are in no way an equivalent to the ss20s. These latter are medium-range missiles. They can threaten Europe but cannot remotely threaten the USSR's main opponent, the US. The Pershings and Cruise, on the other hand, constitute the most direct threat possible to the USSR, especially as they dramatically reduce the warning time available to Moscow in case of nuclear attack. Missile flight times are, of course, a hotly disputed subject. But while it takes 20–30 minutes for an ICBM to travel from the USSR to the US, it will take only 6–12 minutes for the Pershing to travel from West Germany to the USSR. Cruise takes far longer but it is radar-invisible. It too thus cuts warning time: if launched at night perhaps even to nil. Beyond even these there is the (radar-invisible) Stealth bomber now in development by the US which, when based in Europe – the presumption is absolute that it will be, though Europeans haven't been asked – will similarly reduce warning time for the USSR.

Viewed from Moscow – and in this context this is the only view that counts – the emphasis of all these weapons seems quite clear: the US is equipping itself with the capability to launch a surprise attack from bases which do not even put the US in danger, an attack which would rob the Russians of the time needed to mount a coherent response. If this happens the balance of deterrence has been disastrously undermined and there would be a real temptation for the US to launch such a first strike – which it has, unlike the Russians, always refused to rule out.

The Russians sought desperately to preserve the old nuclear balance in the Geneva talks. But their only real answer is to find a way to reduce the nuclear attack warning-time for the US in similar fashion, or at least to ensure that they have a completely secure counter-strike capability.

The only way to achieve the first objective is to position large numbers of Soviet submarines close up to the American coastline with their missiles set for depressed firing trajectories.

Now the natural habitat of the missile-firing submarine is the deep ocean. The Americans have invested enormous resources in installing a network of ocean-bed microphones, developing new depth sonar, and even implanting listening devices into wandering dolphins in order to track Soviet subs. The fact remains that the oceans are vast and deep, and have shifting currents, temperatures and sandbanks – so detection remains difficult.

But this will no longer be good enough for the Russians. Their subs will have to prowl in the shallow waters off the New England and Californian coasts, where detection will be far easier. There is another problem too. All subs leaving the northern USSR either have to leave from Murmansk, which is frozen up for much of the year, or, if they come through the Baltic, have to pass through the Kattegat, where it is easy for NATO to track their passage. All subs bound for the New England or Florida coasts have to come this way.

There is considerable evidence over the last few years that the Russians have been tackling this problem by testing new anti-detection techniques, deliberately pushing their subs right up against the Scandinavian coasts in what can only be dry-runs for the real thing. Time and again the Scandinavians have detected such subs. The full fury of NATO detection attempts have followed – always in vain. The Russians seem to have made their subs virtually un-detectable, even in tight, shallow waters.

None the less, the approach problems to the eastern coast of the US remain and there is evidence of a shift in Soviet attention towards the Pacific west coast. The Russian subs which approach such waters are based at the giant Soviet naval base at Sakhalin. They can, if they wish, hide themselves in the massive expanses of the Pacific, or tread a path towards the western United States along some of the greatest 'deeps' in the world – the Japan, Kuril, Kamchatka and Aleutian Trenches.

Not surprisingly, the United States has become deeply interested in what is happening at Sakhalin – and the Russians equally determined to prevent any surveillance of this base. It is, to put it mildly, highly suggestive that only a few weeks before the final emplacement of the Pershings and Cruise – from which date Sakhalin becomes the nerve-centre of the Soviet counter-move – that we have had a major international tragedy which centred on Russian fears of US surveil-lance of Sakhalin. The real secret of the shot-down Korean airliner may well lie, indirectly, in what is now happening at Greenham Common and elsewhere in Western Europe.

If the Russians find that the problems of detection off the American coast are insuperable, they have a fall-back. Their subs could lurk in the Pacific deeps and, if they hear Pershings and Cruise have been launched against the Soviet Union, strike at the US with long-range missiles. Until now, however, the Russians have lacked missiles with sufficient range to do this, or submarines large enough to carry enough missiles to pose a realistic counter-threat.

The Russians will now fill this gap with their new Typhoon-class submarine – at 25,000 tons the largest such craft in the world, carrying 20 new long-range missiles, MIRV-ed to deliver 80 nuclear warheads. The Russians had offered to halt the deployment of the Typhoon if Cruise and Pershing did not go ahead but once they did, the first Typhoon went into operational service in late 1983. Ultimately there will be a fleet of 12 Typhoons operating from a secret new base in the Kurile Islands; that is to say, again within the area overflown by the fated Korean airliner on September 1. . . . There are, indeed, many questions concerning the airliner's flight which remain unresolved. The possibility that it *was* involved in a surveillance operation can hardly be ruled out and it is even possible that the tragedy was deliberately provoked by the US to produce a climate in which the Cruise–Pershing deployments were bound to go ahead.[1]

It is very difficult to raise uncomfortable questions such as this in the fevered climate of renewed Cold War: to do so is to risk the immediate charge of 'anti-Americanism'. Something of the same applied to the debate over Cruise and Pershing, and it was this which so largely accounted for the surrealism of the debate. The pro-missile camp defended hotly on the grounds of deterrence theory. The peace movement, dominated by unilateralists, does not, of course, accept the whole notion of nuclear deterrence and tended, indeed, to attack it. The more damning fact was that the old balance of terror had its charms and that Cruise and Pershing were actually undermining that balance to the advantage of the US. Anyone who made this point was equally likely to find himself branded as 'anti-American'. In Britain, at least, this is regarded as an epithet of great stopping force.

It is worth lingering on that epithet, though. Orwell believed that the original corruption takes place at the level of language, then of thought, and then everything was possible. Something like this is now happening. When nuclear missiles arrived at some of the 102 US bases in Britain those who protested in the name of national survival were attacked as anti-American, even unpatriotic. Not long afterwards the US invaded Grenada, an independent Commonwealth country. Some English politicians protested – and so a number of Tory and SDP politicians bought space in the American press to condemn this

---

[1] The circumstantial evidence for such a conclusion I presented in '007: Licence to Kill?', *The Guardian*, 17 December 1983.

criticism and protest their loyalty to . . . America. In the same week an opinion poll showed that 94 per cent of Britons were sufficiently anxious about US intentions to want dual-key control over the new missiles. What to think of British politicians who show such solicitude for the anxieties of the US electorate, while dismissing the anxieties of their electors as anti-American – except that they wish or even believe themselves to be members of the US Congress rather than the British Parliament? There is a problem here of national identity.

The way this works is as follows. Traditional British patriots – and super-patriots – have, for two generations now, inbibed a form of 'NATO consciousness' which supersedes the older patriotism. The polarity of the Cold War is seen as a sort of supra-historical fundamental. The fact that we once fought shoulder to shoulder with the Russians, lauded them for their heroism and sacrifice – even for a period had them as allies while the US remained neutral – is not something to be dwelt upon. Opposition to Soviet Communism must be seen as a *permanent* fact of life: *We Have Always been At War with Eastasia.* The highest form of patriotism is thus anti-Communism. The most secure form of anti-Communism is found in NATO. America is the heart of NATO. So the purest form of British patriotism is loyalty to America. What of those who claim to be old-fashioned patriots who simply don't want their country exposed to mortal danger for the sake of another country? This is nonsense. Such patriotism is unpatriotic. Those who would wish to be free of this relationship with the US are warned that the price of such freedom is subjugation by the USSR: *Freedom is Slavery.* But doesn't alliance with the US involve us in the risks of war which they, not we, may start? Nonsense: the more nuclear missiles we have the safer we are: *War is Peace.* But what if the US gets up to reprehensible things, takes aggressive actions, invades other countries? It would be better not to discuss such things. Who can it help? Better even not to know them at all, the Alliance is more secure that way: *Ignorance is Strength.* None the less, surely one can't help having doubts and anxieties about this relationship to the US? They are so much more powerful than us. We cannot control them. We are clearly the subordinates in this relationship. And it doesn't stop at politics: the image of America bursts from our screens and into our homes at every hour of every day. However much we are pushed and cajoled along surely it's only human to resent a presence which is so overwhelming? No. As O'Brien explains to Winston Smith: *Intellectually there is very little wrong with you. It is only emotionally that you have failed to make progress. . . . You must love Big Brother. It is not enough to obey him: you must love him.* The fact that the same analogies could be made with at least equal force within the Soviet bloc is hardly any comfort. For that too was true in *1984 . . .*

17

Towards an Independent Europe?

On 19 November 1983, in a vote which is still reverberating through Europe, the West German SDP brought four decades of bipartisan foreign policy in the Federal Republic to an end, pronouncing against the emplacement of Cruise and Pershing II missiles there by a 96 per cent majority. Willi Brandt announced that in 1984 he would 'move on to the offensive', issuing the call to all European socialist parties to campaign in the Euro-elections on a platform of European independence from *both* super-powers. Already the German opinion polls show large majorities, stretching far beyond the ranks of the SPD, sympathetic to such aims. There is no need to remind anyone that it was in precisely similar fashion that Brandt launched the policy of *Ostpolitik*, and that that policy is now a fact of life.

Interestingly, at almost the same moment, Sir Geoffrey Howe, the British Conservative Foreign Secretary, speaking in the aftermath of the US invasion of Grenada, made his own call for a movement towards an independent European foreign policy. Similar noises were heard all over Europe, from Denmark (which has long refused to have nuclear missiles of any sort of its territory) to Greece, which has reaffirmed its wish to close all US bases there. But what might such an independent European foreign policy look like and how might it be brought into being?

In the past the chief impulse towards an independent European stance has come from the growing economic divergence between the US and Europe. To some extent this was a matter of straightforward rivalry in world markets: the US share in those markets was contracting rapidly and the European share was growing. Oddly, perhaps, the industrial competition between the two blocs, though it has thrown up occasional sharp differences – over steel quotas, for example – has proved manageable enough. The really bitter competition has only arisen in the last decade and it is over food. Again, oddly – when one considers the industrial strength of the US – food products constitute by far the largest single component of all US exports. As EEC agricultural self-sufficiency steadily increased, US exporters found they were losing their best market and protested bitterly. Worse, with its growing agricultural surpluses the EEC began to appear as a major threat in third-country food markets. At this US ire knew no bounds. Every indication is that this peculiarly bitter competition will intensify in the years ahead. Although the argument always takes the form of bitter wrangles over the worth of subsidies doled out to the absurdly mollycoddled farmers of both blocs, underlying it is a deep European resentment that the US should mind at all about European self-sufficiency – and a suspicion that the US would like to maintain Europe in a state of food-dependency. In 1982 the value of US food exports actually fell and in 1983 there has been a further 11 per cent decline – a loss of $4 billion in a single year. Clearly, this sort of thing cannot go on much longer before a dramatic crunch comes.

The second field of major economic tension has been energy. The crisis of 1973 opened up a split which has never been healed. Kissinger sought then to rally Europe behind schemes to bring OPEC to heal. It was, he argued, an intolerable situation for the US to be dependent for its vital oil on imports from sources willing and able to exercise 'blackmail'. Nothing less than the strategic security of the West was at stake. Neither the use of military force nor 'the food weapon' should be ruled out. The Europeans were appalled and pointed out with some asperity that dependence on oil imports might be something new for the US, but it was a fact of life Europe had always lived with. The US had better learn to live with it too. Meanwhile Europe would have nothing to do with actions likely to produce a major Middle East and perhaps world conflagration. Kissinger retired, defeated, in a furious cloud of invective.

This divergence has remained, sporadically resurfacing whenever the US military presence in the Middle East and the one-sided US view of the Arab–Israeli question threaten to disturb Europe's oil supplies. The uncomfortable fact is that the US military presence in the Middle East was both far larger and far more adventurist than the European presence, even though the Middle East is in Europe's backyard. The bottom line here is that the US has a large degree of control over Europe's oil supply – and the fear is never quite absent that this could be used as a form of leverage. In 1981–3 this fact underlay the furious dispute over the Russian gas pipe line to Europe. Although the argument was conducted in terms of the pros and cons of the Cold War, this was merely a form of code. What was really at stake was Europe's attempts to diversify its energy dependence away from the US and the US attempt to block the pipeline by forbidding US companies to supply components for it. To Europeans, who were well aware that US coal industry interests were pushing hard to make Europe take its supplies instead, the US intervention was intolerable. It was not just that the US was going ahead with grain sales to Russia – so that a European refusal of Soviet gas would mean that they were paying the costs of US foreign policy. It was more the sheer presumption of the US attempt to dictate where Europe should get its energy supplies from – Europe had no ambition to tell the US where it should buy *its* gas from, after all.

Incidents of this sort have proliferated in the period since 1973, each time leaving Europe angrier at its dependence on the US and the way that dependence is, as Europeans see it, exploited to US ends at the cost of European interests. Awareness has grown, too, that Europe has fared far worse in the post-73 recession than the US – there was by 1983 hardly a single European country where unemployment was not far higher than in the US and sometimes it was, as in Holland and Belgium, double the US level. The feeling has grown that this is no accident, that Europe is being made to carry an unfair share of the costs of recession. The virtual interest rate war of 1981–3 was largely about this issue.

One reason for US indifference to all these noises of complaint is simply that Europe matters less to America than it did. For years British politicians wilfully deluded themselves into believing that the UK had a 'special relationship' with the US. The awkward truth is that not even Europe as a whole can feel secure in such a 'special relationship' now. The real US 'special relationship' is with Japan, the second greatest capitalist power on earth. It is bound to be so. As the shift in the centre of political and economic gravity within the US has gravitated remorselessly towards the south-western sun belt, the notion has grown that the US must move towards 'the Pacific Century'. On the fringes of the Pacific stand not merely the US and Japan but several other of the world's most dynamically growing states and one-half of the world's population. Europe has no lure to compete with this.

The US has, of course, a very simple rejoinder, which is that the maintenance of US forces in Europe is extremely costly and by no means uniformly popular with the American electorate. Europe has a bigger population and a larger combined GNP than the US; indeed, a growing number of European states (West Germany, Norway, Denmark, Sweden, and Switzerland with Holland, Austria, Belgium and France close behind) actually have a higher GNP per capita than the US. Let them pay (at least the NATO members among them) for their own defence. To date this argument had led to Europe paying an increased share in the offset costs of maintaining US forces in Europe. But this process is clearly not indefinitely extensible: the point could theoretically be reached when Europe was paying the whole of such costs and the US army in Europe had effectively become a mercenary one, hired out to European states. It is doubtful whether such a situation would be tolerable to the US. For Europe would doubtless be unwilling to pay for the whole of the piper without also being allowed to call the tune. Some way before the point when US forces in Europe began taking their orders from politicians in Bonn, London and Rome it is safe to predict that Washington would simply order them home.

Europeans have always balked at this spectre. In part this is because of the fact that the US has twice in this century arrived as a virtual saviour to end European wars; this has engendered deep feelings of gratitude and psychological dependence. Moreover, those conflicts have left many Europeans unhappy at heart at any idea of seeing a militarily strong Germany again – and it clear that Germany would have to play a leading role – perhaps *the* leading role – in any European self-defence force. Then again, to mount a European defence effort which was a full replacement for that currently mounted by the US in Europe would be enormously expensive. And it would not be a matter of just paying for this or that weapon. The present arrangement gives Europeans indirect access to the fruits of the whole military technology base on which the US has lavished such enormous investment over a period of decades. To replace the US fully would mean nothing less than the replication in Europe of that entire technological base, which involves many fields in which Europe has little historic expertise. This in turn would require the annual diversion of quite enormous resources from European budgets over a steady period of years. Given the annual fracas over the EEC's budget for the Common Agricultural Policy – despite the huge political power of its beneficiaries, Europe's farmers – one may legitimately doubt whether Europeans would ever agree to fund such an effort, or that they could do so without periodic budget crises which would be very destructive to the long-term investment build-up required.

Anyone who doubts the cogency of such factors has only to glance at the history of Britain's 'independent' nuclear deterrent. As the V-bomber nuclear strike force neared the end of its useful life in the late 1950s Britain fell back into partial and then total reliance on the US. The process began with the stationing of the first nuclear missile in Britain – Thor in 1958. Then when the British Blue Streak rocket was cancelled in 1960, Britain agreed to take the US Skybolt instead and, in return, to allow US Polaris subMarines to use the Holy Loch base in Scotland. When Skybolt was cancelled in 1962 Britain agreed not merely to leave the Holy Loch bargain untouched but to buy Polaris subs itself. As the Polaris system aged there was never any doubt that Britain would look to the US for its replacement – Trident. This collapse into complete reliance on US technology took place, more-over, in a state which was outspending all other European states on defence as a proportion of GNP.

Despite repeated debate over the wisdom of such reliance, or even over Britain possessing nuclear weapons at all, each successive British government since 1962 has happily embraced that reliance once in office – for only a few back-of-the-envelope sums were needed to see that the Polaris deal was hugely more cost-effective than any conceivable alternative. If this could happen in the case of Britain – where no international agreement was required – what hope could there be for an independent European nuclear force? Every decision would require ten (and soon twelve)-nation agreement and at every stage the purchase of US weaponry would always be by far the cheapest alternative. If the funding of a European defence effort meant, for example, cutting back hard and regularly on the CAP subsidies to Europe's farmers, what realistic hope would it have?

Accordingly, although Europe's growing economic conflicts with the US produced a steady impulse towards the notion of a more independent Europe, this wave has broken every time on the rock of Europe's military dependence on the US. Now, however, an increasing number of Europeans are becoming discomfited precisely by that military dependence. The US military posture is viewed by many as both belligerent and unreliable, a source of insecurity rather than security. For the moment the old view of the Western Alliance holds – the emplacement of Cruise and Pershing II has gone ahead. But it is clear that this view no longer commands the consensus it once did and that that consensus is unlikely to return. It now seems certain that each further move in the arms race, even if only a 'modernis- ation' of existing weapons, will face a rising wave of opposition across Europe. Moreover, for the first time unease over Europe's military relationship with the US has broken out of its traditional ghetto of the old pacifist Left. Distrust of US intentions, including a concern that the US would not come to Europe's aid in a crunch or that the US might choose to fight a limited war in Europe while remaining *hors de combat* itself, has now seeped into a far wider and more 'respectable' constituency. It seems unlikely that this genie can be got back into its bottle again. If so, the momentum towards an independent European foreign/defence policy is likely only to grow from now on, probably quite rapidly. The question any British government – whether under Thatcher, Kinnock or anyone else – must face is how it is going to fit into such a movement and what such a policy might look like in the end.

One's first reference-point has to be de Gaulle, who foresaw the problem long before others. In the event of a successful Soviet invasion of Western Europe, he argued, no responsible US President would expose his country to probable nuclear suicide for the sake of holding Paris or Amsterdam. In any case, he felt that the presence on French territory of foreign armies and weapons, over which France had no control, was a violation of national independence. France had been through that experience twice before and it was called an Occupation. In 1966 he summoned the NATO Commander, General Norstadt, and asked to know the targets of all US missiles emplaced on French soil. Norstadt declined, saying it was a military secret.

De Gaulle swore that no French President would ever have to accept such an answer again and withdrew France from the NATO Integrated Command (though not from NATO itself). The US bases went. De Gaulle then developed an independent nuclear deterrent, his famous *force de frappe*. He accepted that you couldn't be a Great Power, or face up to other Great Powers, without nuclear weapons. He also accepted that France would never have a nuclear force equal to that of the USSR. But that didn't matter. He didn't want to win a war with Russia, he only wanted a 'force for dissuasion'. Anyone who thought of attacking France would know the French could inflict quite unacceptable damage on them – 'tearing off an arm', as he put it. Anyone – the US or USSR – who thought even of leaning on France would think and think again. He then proceeded to conduct an independent foreign policy of surpassing insouciance. It worked.

The French example is particularly crucial to Britain. All the other European countries decided they would not develop nuclear weapons themselves but would shelter under the US nuclear umbrella instead, accepting US bases on their soil. The French showed that if you had your own nuclear weapons you could do without the US bases and missiles – and, what was more, you could still remain a NATO member. The British, all alone, and quite illogically, did both things. They had their own nuclear weapons but they also had the US bases and missiles. Without much doubt Mrs Thatcher is still as ignorant today about the targets of the US missiles in Britain as de Gaulle was in 1966.

In the Britain of the 1950s the Campaign for Nuclear Disarmament (CND) used to argue that Britain could give a 'moral lead' to the world by unilateral nuclear disarament. Nowadays CND does not repeat that silliness but tends, instead, to hope for a similar act of renunciation on a European scale. This too is silly. The first thing that has to be recognised is that all European countries currently shelter under a nuclear umbrella, whether their own or the Americans'. They cannot be expected to give up that protection in return for nothing. The Germans know that what is only a limited war for the rest of Europe will be a war of survival for them and the French won't dream of giving up their *force de frappe*. On the other hand the French find the maintenance of their nuclear strike force a great financial strain and have repeatedly approached Britain – the last time in 1979 – to collaborate with them. They have always been refused.

Britain's first move towards a European orientation is thus clear enough: instead of buying Trident from the US to pursue nuclear co-operation with the French instead and, like them, to aim only for a limited, dissuasive nuclear force. And, again following the French, Britain would then ask for the removal of all US bases and missiles from its territory – while remaining a NATO member.

Without doubt this would trigger very strong echoes elsewhere in Europe – the agitation to get rid of US missiles would become stronger everywhere. Britain would then take the initiative of proposing a full-scale European Defence Community. This would exactly reverse the post-war position where Britain refused to join an EDC, which then collapsed through French fear of having to see a rearmed Germany with no British counterweight. This time the EDC would be based around the Anglo-French nuclear force, but the rest of Europe – especially the Germans – would be asked to help pay for it. In return Britain and France would provide tactical nuclear weapons to those European states who wanted them – in practice only the Germans – while maintaining control over the production process.

The formidable financial and technical objections to an independent European nuclear deterrent would have to be met head on by accepting from the outset that no full-scale replacement of the US nuclear force in Europe was possible and that Europe would, instead, adopt the French *force de dissuasion* concept as its own. Immediately this would mean the pooling of the nine French and British nuclear submarines; a plan to expand that fleet with European financial assistance (and perhaps mixed European crews); and co-operative development both of an alternative to Trident and of the tanks, aircraft and short-range missiles the EDC would need.

At this point – with US bases still dotted across much of Europe and with perfectly credible plans for the expansion of the European nuclear force on the drawing-board – it would be possible to open separate European negotiations with the USSR on nuclear disarmament. In essence the objectives would be two: the removal of all Soviet land-based missiles (the ss20s, etc.) facing Europe plus a relocation of the Soviet air/space-based deterrent away from Europe – and a binding commitment that the Red Army would stay within its western border. This would imply not merely the dismantling of all Soviet bases in Eastern Europe but a public repudiation of the Brezhnev doctrine allowing Soviet intervention in Eastern Europe: no more Hungarys or Czechoslovakias. Full on-site inspection of military facilities would, of course, be required to ensure full enforcement.

In return Europe would offer to get rid of all the remaining US bases in Europe, make a similar commitment not to intervene in Eastern Europe, propose that both Germanies should be de-militarised, and suggest that the European nuclear effort could be scaled back in return for reciprocal Russian concessions. It seems most unlikely that the Russians could look such a gift-horse in the mouth, for it would then be free to concentrate its attentions solely on the US and China.

At the end of such a process both Europe and the USSR would retain nuclear-armed submarines and probably also tactical nuclear weapons on the nearest militarised borders. The nuclear submarine strike force would stay because no on-site inspection would be effective with them and the French would never give them up anyway. They would go only as part of a truly world-wide process of nuclear disarmament which, for the present, seems Utopian.

The gains to Europe would be very considerable. It would be truly independent of both super-powers and the *force de dissuasion* stance would leave no doubt that war would never occur by Europe's choice. The nuclear threat to Europe would be very greatly diminished and the actual defence burden would hardly be intolerable. The ensuing relaxation of tension could well open the way to further benefits. Most obviously, the Eastern European states would be far less inclined to cling to Russia's skirts and with the certainty that the Red Army couldn't intervene whatever they did, a wave of liberalisation right across Eastern Europe would be pretty well inevitable. Both sides would have an enormous interest in sticking by the spirit as well as the letter of such an agreement – there would have to be no covert attempts to subvert or destabilise states in either part of Europe – for failure to do so would imply a ratcheting back upwards of the other side's military strength and posture.

There are several problems with such a scenario. Getting agreement among the bevy of European states will never be easy. The Chinese would protest bitterly at the freer hand the USSR would have to deal with them. The Americans may well try the same argument – though the rejoinder that they will now be rid of an onerous defence commitment of which they have often complained, seems unanswerable. The European peace movement will doubtless denounce the new status quo and try to push on towards unilateral disarmament. None of these problems seems intrinsically insuperable, however – and the first of them is probably the most difficult.

The real problem lies in the evolution of US–European relations. The key fact to grasp is that the US is a declining imperial power. Having accounted for a full 50 per cent of total world production in 1945, the US had declined to a 30 per cent share by the late 1970s and will decline to an 18 per cent–20 per cent share by the year 2000. Americans are in no way reconciled to this contraction and have sought the typical way out of all such declining powers – an ever greater build-up of military strength to compensate for shrinking economic leverage. While the continuation of this trend of decline will leave the US decreasingly able to afford its European commitment, it is also quite likely to make it keener than ever to maintain it all the same. Indeed, the more the US is relying on its military leverage to squeeze economic concessions out of its clients, the more it has to lose by relaxing that leverage. In addition, of course, the US would have every reason to fear that other regional blocs would take their cue from Europe and that the present world-wide US military deployments would soon be in headlong retreat. The threat to US interests from what would in effect be a massive process of decolonisation could be very considerable – certainly enough for the US to regard its eviction from Europe as an unfriendly act of ingratitude. No amount of flannelling about Europe's undying regard for America and its people would get round or over that.

The reverse side of this is the enormous investment – political, psychological and emotional – which European elites have made in the American alliance over the past forty years. This has been so great that among many European conservatives loyalty to this alliance seems a higher good even that patriotism. In effect the Cold War has, in these milieux, created a complete identification between patriotism and anti-communism – and loyalty to the Atlantic alliance is seen as the benchmark of anti-communism. Moreover, this message has been endlessly sold and oversold to European electorates for more than a generation – at the same time that the world of popular culture has been selling an equally positive picture of America to even the most apolitical members of every European society. The cumulative effect of this multi-level and historically unique volume of propaganda has not merely been to socialise whole generations into pro-American attitudes but even to make many feel that American culture and values are part of *their* identity. The European politicians who lead the way towards independence from the US may well find their greatest problem of all in this psychological and emotional dependence on the US which they have helped to foster, particularly if (as must be expected) American politicians attempt to appeal over their heads to European electorates in favour of a continued US presence in Europe.

What makes it all the harder is that many of the conflicts and divergences of recent time between the US and Europe have been carefully kept within the confines of a small European elite: it has never seemed sensible to give wide publicity to European economic grievances for their expression might have fuelled a popular anti-Americanism which could, in turn, have undermined the Atlantic Alliance. This hyper-protective attitude has frequently had bizarre results: American Democratic Presidents have quite ordinarily been more popular in Europe than at home and conservative European newspapers like *The Times* continued to support the US war in Vietnam long after their American analogues had ceased to do so. There is an enormous task of political re-education to be carried out here – which will have to begin by Europe's elites being a great deal more forthright about their divergences from the US.

The point may never come when European electorates are fully prepared for such a break, any more then the French electorate were for de Gaulle's break from NATO in 1966. Opinion only lined up solidly behind de Gaulle some time after the Gordian knot was cut. Without doubt the fact that de Gaulle was both a conservative and enjoyed a unique national legitimacy eased the process: had the knot been cut by a politician of the Left, the Right would have contested it for years. Within a few years it became clear that, in France at least, there could be no going back: any politician who attempted to lead France back into the NATO Integrated Military Command would be taken to be a traitor to national independence. There are clear lessons for the European political elite here.

In fact the two great problems – the angry American response and the psychological unpreparedness of European electorates – may well be the opposite sides of the same coin. Probably Europe will only find its true self-definition and identity in opposition to the US, just as English national identity was first forged in opposition to the Spanish Armada. It would be pleasant to imagine that a US – European divorce could be negotiated with good will but the experience both of diplomacy and the divorce courts suggests this may be less than realistic. At the least such a separation would probably occur in great clouds of vehement rhetoric and bitter self-justification. As Europe used its new-found freedom to assert its own economic interests the probability of US reprisals would be considerable and it is possible that the US would seek to destabilise some of the weaker European states. More likely, perhaps, the US would regard the very proposal that US bases should leave Europe as *de facto* evidence that Communist subversion had already *taken* place. This would lead to a heightening of East–West tensions just as the divorce was about to take place, with the possible result of some of the more timorous European states losing heart and clutching desperately for the old US alliance against the Russian bear. Almost everything depends on the Europeans starting the process with a united front and maintaining it through such trials. If they succeed in this they would not only succeed over all, but would come through at the end with a greatly enhanced sense of European unity and identity.

If the precise dynamics of a US–European separation are imponderable, the likely outline of a European foreign policy thereafter is hardly less so. Almost certainly this separation would give an enormous push to a world-wide grouping of regional blocs. Europe's *de facto* dominance in Africa would probably increase and in the Middle East Europe would find itself – in some ways it already does – in a three-cornered struggle for dominance. One descries, dimly, Orwell's three great power blocs in *1984*, Eurasia, Eastasia and Oceania.[1] In *1984*, of course, Britain is part of the Oceania bloc with the US, Europe has thrown in its lot with Russia to form Eurasia and the three blocs are perpetually at war. Like not a few other of Orwell's forewarnings in *1984*, this seems unduly pessimistic. Indeed, it seems safe to predict that Europe would retain an overriding interest in world peace, not merely because it would be militarily the weakest of the big blocs but because a US–USSR war would actually see long-range nuclear missiles tearing over Europe in both directions.

The scenario sketched above whereby Britain leads the way to a fully independent Europe is, of course, only one of several possible scenarios. It does not take much thought, though, to see that neither France (already half out of NATO) nor any of the smaller, non-nuclear European states can lead such a movement. Only Britain or Germany can lead the way. Already there are stirrings of this sort in Germany (and not just in the SPD). They centre, inevitably, around the never-to-be-abandoned dream of a reunited Germany. Equally, it takes little imagination to see that this is the maximally destabilising way in which such changes could take place. Any attempt to reunify Germany on Western terms would lead directly to nuclear war; reunification on Soviet terms, with a united but neutralised Germany outside NATO would create a new super-power of 80 million people with an industrial base of Japanese proportions. The very existence of such a state would terrify Western Europe (particularly the French)

---

[1] It is interesting to note that this terminology has begun to creep into the strategic vocabulary. Thus the US Defense Department's *Soviet Military Power* (1983 edn) speaks of 'a general East–West conflict across the face of Eurasia' and 'the land war in Eurasia' (e.g. p. 13).

and would probably rule out any further possibility of concerted European action.

Thus it would be far better if Britain led the way – indeed, in a sense only she *can* do so, for a German-led initiative could well produce something far less satisfactory than a united Europe. There is even a certain urgency to such a British initiative. It is not just that the continuing contraction of US power will make an independent Europe inevitable in the end and that Britain may as well lead the tide rather than follow it. It is more that if Britain doesn't act, Germany, sooner or later, will. The SPD will come to power again at some point – and even before that it may push a Christian Democrat government in the same direction anyway. The bait of a nationalist reunification of Germany is so alluring to the German electorate that no government will be able to stand out against it for ever. Once that bait has been trailed before the German electorate, German politicians of all stripes will find themselves impaled irreversibly upon the hook. Once that has happened a British initiative might well be too late. If control over the momentum and terms of a European divorce from the US slips into the hands of German nationalist opinion there will be no getting it back.

Britain is, in any case, ideally suited to such a role: she is already an independent nuclear power; she is a full member of NATO; and she is still probably America's most trusted European ally. Britain could, moreover, stop being embarrassed by her relative weakness and take advantage of it instead. For the brutal fact is that Britain is both economically and demographically too weak for other European states to fear that a British-led initiative could ever lead to a Europe dominated by Britain. There would, none the less, be considerable advantage to Britain from such a policy. She would recapture, at least in part, the political leadership in Europe for which she has yearned. In return for her supremely European act she might well be able to get a reformulation of the Common Agricultural Policy, perhaps even a Common Industrial Policy as well. Her national security would not be impaired and might well be strengthened – certainly the immediate risk of nuclear annihilation would recede.

The problem for the British elite is that such a policy amounts to nothing less than the repudiation of the Churchill tradition in favour of de Gaulle's. The meaning of this tradition was clear from the moment in 1940 when Churchill withdrew the RAF from the defence of France and decided to pull British troops out at Dunkirk and leave the French to face the Wehrmacht's fury on their own. True, it was Churchill who first launched the call for a European Defence Community after the war – only to reject it in horror when Britain was asked to join ('I meant it would be a good thing for *them* – not for *us*'). It was Churchill who enshrined the notion of a 'special relationship' between Britain and the US. It seemed natural for Orwell, writing in 1948 to place Britain in *1984* as the eastern edge of the (US-led) Oceania bloc, fighting against Eurasia, which began at Calais. And, when the EEC was in its crucial stages of formation in the early 1950s, it was Churchill who so decisively spurned the notion that Britain might join such an association, even though he could have dictated almost any terms he liked for such an act. All of this was perceived by de Gaulle when, in 1963, he rejected British membership of the EEC on the grounds that Britain would be only a 'Trojan horse' for the US.

Successive British governments have endorsed the Churchill tradition almost as a matter of second nature and they were humiliated as well as enraged by de Gaulle's words in 1963. It will not be easy for the British to conduct what will, in effect, amount to their own de-Stalinisation ritual over Churchill. But, quite clearly, de Gaulle was right in 1963 and Churchill was wrong at every stage. He was – like Stalin – a great war leader, but had a parochial and limited vision of the world. The logic of Churchill's world could only be maintained if the British could hang on to their empire – which was why he fought so hard to keep it. He was, despite the superlatives lavished on his historical writings, a poor historian with no real sense of historical change and certainly no understanding of the great historical process of decolonisation. He had no vision as compelling as de Gaulle's independence from the US or his 'Europe from the Atlantic to the Urals'. It was no accident that while de Gaulle's post-war career saw him triumphantly reshape his country into a successful modern state, Churchill's post-war career was a thing of shreds and patches – irresponsibility in Opposition, drift in government, a lot of windy rhetoric and too much drink. It is time, indeed it is high time, that the British took a less sentimental look not only at Churchill and de Gaulle but at their allies and their own real situation. And· they could do worse than remember de Gaulle's maxim that 'A man may have friends, but a nation never.'

Part Two
Britain: The Eye of
the Storm

1

Enoch and Edward

' . . . it must have been in 1927, when I opened my first German book. Here was the language I had dreamed of but never knew existed: sharp, hard, strict, but with words that were romance in themselves.' Thus Enoch Powell of his first great love. One of the difficulties in writing about Powell, such a passage reminds one, is that he is a man of great literary precision whose occasional shafts of self-disclosure reveal the man more accurately than any biographer can do. For there are Powell's characteristic tastes set out for one, even in the right order. Romance is important – but it comes last. He liked German not despite but *because* it was 'sharp, hard, strict'.

It is necessary to cling hard to that insight for, as so often happens, the essential character of the man is more obscured than revealed by the brilliance of his later career. And it was brilliant. A Fellow of Trinity, Cambridge, at 21 and the youngest professor in the British Commonwealth at the age of 25, Powell has always towered above his political peers in intellect. He is, moreover, the last great orator in an unrhetorical age. Over and over again one has seen him lead a poorly educated audience through complex and arcane subjects, making careful distinctions, using long words and making no concessions; and hold them utterly rapt as he does so. This has been an exceptional gift in any age. (I have met cockney taxi-drivers who, while averring their disagreement with Powell's policies, have rhapsodised over his 'beautiful use of language'.) For years on end he was by far the most-admired as well as the most-hated politician in the land. And even now that his hour is long past, his utterances command a respect and attention not accorded to many of his generation who rose to far higher office than he.

But the secret of it all is back there with that already rather isolated and lonely boy of 15 with his German book. It is not difficult to sketch the elements behind this brown study. The parents of humble origin, Welsh schoolteachers both; the dominating mother, the determination to get on, that their son must grasp the chances they never had. The equally determined embrace of the dominant English world and the Latinate high culture within it. Classics the only real subject; hard, rigorous but the only true sign of the educated gentleman, the real scholar. The son accepting the gospel of ferocious work, knowing the love behind the strictness, becoming known as 'the professor' by the age of 3. Birmingham in the 1920s. The shadow of Chamberlain, but even more the shadow of the Great War, the knowledge that those who went before had made the greatest sacrifice of all. No way to show your patriotism in the same heroism of self-immolation but the utter yearning to do so. The maps on the schoolroom walls with the vast Empire still painted in blazing red. A world ruled by Kipling, Buchan, Saki and Rider Haggard, but most of all a world ruled by ghosts.

The boy could only be a Tory and, given how clever he was and how hard he worked, he could only succeed. But the thwarted patriotism which burnt within was far stronger than mere cleverness. A feeling that one's private likes and interests would not only have to be subordinated to the higher Cause if necessary, but that they were almost ignoble in themselves. The higher Cause? To submit oneself utterly, glorying in the privation of it, for England (quite consciously England, not Britain). The greater the sacrifice, the higher the glory, with no shrinking from the supreme sacrifice itself.

Thus when war broke out in September 1939 Powell instantly resigned his chair in Sydney, sailed round the world to Britain, and enlisted in the Army *as a private*. Immediately he became the best turned-out and most conscientious private in the company; spent his off-duty hours reading Clausewitz and Field Service Regulations; and set himself the target of early death or promotion through the ranks to Major-General. Others might have waited the call to colours; and most professors would have taken a commission or a safe desk job in intelligence (and Powell would have been a fearsome code-breaker – an Enigma machine all by himself). But for him that would have been cheating. To be strict and hard with oneself, to humble oneself as a private before the majesty of the Army, to court the glory of an early death – and *then* to excel. Only in such self-prostration lay the true romance.

He was, naturally, a brilliant soldier and there are many stories of how he risked his life quite heedlessly, even needlessly. Yet one moral of the story was that he ended as a Brigadier. A remarkable achievement – but one rank short. It was to be the same in politics. Every cause he took up – the Empire, defence, the free market, immigration, the EEC, Ulster – was part of a passionate crusade in the cause of England. He was a better political strategist than is generally appreciated, but the Cause was the thing. What matter if it meant damage to one's own career? And so, again, he ended one rank short.

But there was more to it than that. In a way Powell was an anti-politician. Two examples may illustrate the point. At one stage he brought the fury and contempt of Fleet Street upon himself by announcing that within Whitehall were real enemies of the people and the state conspiring to make the immigration situation worse by deliberately falsifying the figures. This sudden outburst – which was no more explained than that – caused even many erstwhile supporters to conclude that this time he was *really* mad. A few months later Roy Jenkins's Home Office admitted sheepishly that it had been miscounting immigrant entrants; that the error had been discovered some time before; but that it had been hushed over for a while so as not to alarm people unduly. It seems tolerably clear that Powell had had an advance leak and that the truth was forced out of the Home Office when it became evident that they could no longer maintain their secrets. The really odd thing was, though, that Powell made no 'I told you so' speech, so that many failed even to connect the two events. Perhaps he felt that that sort of self-justification was simply beneath him, but it is difficult to imagine another politician deliberately allowing such an opportunity to pass and so unfortunate an impression of himself to remain. He had spoken for England and that was enough; further references to it could be only self-serving. Similarly, he allowed the Toxteth and Brixton riots to pass with hardly a reference to his famous 1968 immigration speech in which he had predicted violence of just this sort.

Or again, take the occasion when Powell addressed a student audience in Oxford on devolution. The audience was perhaps 10 per cent black and included many who were bitterly hostile to him. Speaking for an hour without notes, he wove his extraordinary spell. With some amazement I realised that it was quite likely he would emerge with a standing ovation. Then, at the very last moment, in answer to a concluding question, he threw in several bitter, wounding references to immigration. The audience's heads went back as one, stunned and shocked. They trooped out in silence. I asked him why on earth he had done it. He had had them in the palm of his hand; immigration was quite irrelevant to the topic under discussion; and there was simply no need for it. He laughed, acknowledged that he had appreciated the situation perfectly, but averred that he didn't want partial support. If people were to accept him, they must accept all of him, 'cloven hoof and all'.

Now in a way this is admirable. But it is also peculiar. Time and again Powell did this sort of thing on a grand scale, disregarding the conventional deference to party, to received opinion, to his leaders. And yet he *was* a politician and was always quite frank in his ambition for power. We are used to politicians who are good tacticians but have no strategic sense, but the combination of powerful strategy with no tactics at all is far rarer. And who better able than he to understand how destructive of his ambitions his behaviour was bound to be? Instead, as he threw over the traces he affected, time and again, a certain determined *naïveté*, a sort of contumacious innocence. How could anyone blame him for expressing his deep opinions? Could they not see that he could not act otherwise? Why should the generals and sergeant-majors of the political battleground take against him when everything he did could be supported by the letter – the rigorously argued letter – of Field Service Regulations?

A general faced by this sort of private, or a party leader faced by this sort of backbencher, is bound to feel exasperation. Anyone who knows the Regulations backwards and is as clever as Powell also knows, dammit, that a time comes to ignore the book's letter and follow its spirit. The one thing the fellow can't pretend to is stupidity. And, if he persists, the one thing he won't get is promotion.

The man who actually had to face such decisions was Edward Heath. There was a strange symmetry in this, for alone among the Tory leadership Heath came from a background even more modest than Powell's – his father a carpenter, his mother a housemaid. Both had climbed the greasy pole of Tory Party politics in a way that few indeed achieve. But, despite another ambitious mother in the background, Heath's boyhood in Broadstairs, Kent, had been very different from Powell's. Broadstairs is an utterly isolated part of England; softer, rural, a world almost to itself, untouched by the harder – and bleaker – urban culture of industrial England. It was a world where the Anglican Church, cricket and being a good, solid chap were what counted most.

Heath's mother was ambitious for her son but she did not dominate him so much as spoil him. From an early age he was able to organise the family around his needs – his mother doted on him and his father simply retreated, unable to understand or even communicate much with his son. For already Teddy, though not brilliant, was a determined, tireless worker but aloof and even curt, the whole of his energies organised around getting on in the external world of school. Even there, though he did well, he was not much interested in anything which might distract him from getting on, such as sporting activities or friends. He was a prim, disciplinarian prefect – his first experience of formal authority, and one he relished. He was decidedly unpopular and a self-contained loner. He had none of Powell's imagination and a mere fraction of his intellect. His scholarship to Balliol and his career at Oxford had more to do with organisation drive and a firm conviction that if you did the Right Thing you got on. And get on he did, although his peers had already begun to liken his progress to that of a tank.

Entering the Tory Party via the *Church Times* Heath was made Chief whip in a period (the late 1950s) when there was much grumbling on the backbenches (along which it was his job to move) that the Tory party had drifted a sight too far away from free enterprise towards Butskellism. As a young meritocrat Heath was naturally sympathetic with these stirrings and was not a little warmed that they came from knights of the shires, for he could not be unaware that he was something of a social freak in such company. Accordingly, when he got his chance to go out and bat for liberal capitalism – over EEC entry and the abolition of RPM – he did so with a will. He was formidably efficient – as Whip he could always forecast a majority exactly and kept an unrivalled card-index of every MP. More remarkable was his remorseless self-confidence. He clearly lived in a world where all the shots were self-righteous straight drives and where anyone spinning the ball was told that he'd jolly well better bowl straight or else. This self-confidence, on the part of a social inferior moving among social superiors, was peculiar. True, young Edward now mimicked the accents of his betters, but that fooled no one. The secret was that he knew if you did the right thing, firmly and straightforwardly, you got on. He was still a school prefect.

Then, lo! It was felt that the Tories must efface their Etonian image

by electing a leader who, preferably, should be a meritocrat like
Wilson. And so young Edward rose to fresh heights, propelled by the
backbenchers he had cultivated. He was not surprised. If you did
right things, then right things happened to you. Only five years later
Edward became Prime Minister. Again, he was not surprised, and for
the same reason. He chose a Cabinet with as many meritocrats as he
could find. This was not many, the Tory Party being what it was, and
the most notable among them, a grocer's daughter who made much
of the fact, had in fact built her political career only after she had
married a great deal of money.

In power Edward continued to be efficient, forceful and managerial – and wholly without friends. Even his political secretary and
closest confidante, Douglas Hurd, called him 'Mr Heath' or, as a sign
of intimacy, 'EH'. But the strains of office were such as to dent the
self-confidence of even such a man. Had he been less buttoned-up,
less wholly self-contained, this might not have been so. Time and
again those who tried ever to make small talk with him found the
conversation immediately closed down – not as a hostile act, but
because that was the only way he could behave. The strain told most
clearly in his voice which could not always maintain the even
upperclass tone he had affected. Hurd became increasingly concerned
at the prospect of His Master's Voice going off like some ghastly
wooden hooter, wrecking the effect of speeches Hurd had helped to
write: 'The voice', wrote Hurd,[1] 'might change its quality. The
vocabulary might become stilted, the tone defensive. The thread of
the argument might become lost. . . . Instead of speaking to people,
Mr. Heath would too often speak at them.' Unable to hold out
longer, he would still never give way. Then we get 'EH exploded' or
'EH retires in a cloud of stubborn and unconvincing negatives'.

Then came the mighty blow of the 1972 miners' strike. Edward had
to give in and a wrathful rumbling began on the backbenches.
Edward performed U-turns. The rumbling got louder. For the first
time, perhaps, in his entire life, Edward began to lose confidence. He
had done the right thing but the right things weren't happening to
him. He knew the backbenchers had put him where he was and, given

---

[1] D. Hurd, *An End to Promises: Sketch of a Government, 1970–74* (1979)
p. 73.

his origins, he could hardly ignore them the way Macmillan had. Anyway, they wouldn't take it from *him*. So when the wretched miners started trouble again, he was jolly firm with them. Or tried to be. But it wasn't any good. The school prefect dithered. To give in to the miners was unthinkable – his backbenchers would never stand for it. But not to give in to them was pretty unthinkable too, for it seemed unlikely they could be beaten. There was no right thing to do – a situation which he had hardly believed existed. After a lengthy and public period of indecision, during which his cabinet all but disintegrated under him, he decided, inevitably, that he had better be jolly firm. With everybody. He would shut his backbenchers up by calling an election. He would be jolly firm with the miners by making the election a referendum on their strike. And he'd be jolly firm with the electorate by decreeing a three-day week, claiming that this was the cost of the strike. That would show them all.

During all this time Powell had dogged Heath at every turn. He had run against him in the leadership contest in 1965 and, when beaten had not taken his defeat easily. Instead, on one issue after the other Powell had, though a member of the Shadow Cabinet, staked out wildly independent positions, each time professing surprise at Heath's evident annoyance. The climax came with Powell's 1968 immigration speech. As Hurd would put it, EH exploded – and sacked Powell. Powell maintained his challenge and more or less single-handed (as the polls revealed) propelled Heath into office in 1970 with a series of inflammatory speeches on immigration, pushing a huge swathe of racialist votes towards the Tories. Powell may have expected the reward of office (on his own terms) for this achievement. If so he was disappointed: Heath was more determined than ever to be jolly firm against him.

Thereafter the gulf of hatred between the two men never ceased to widen, fuelled more by their similarities than their differences. Undoubtedly both realised it was a contest between men of like steel and ambition, men who had risen both against the odds towards the Tory summit, men who, unlike so many Tories, had only their political careers. There was no country estate for them to retire to – it was all or nothing. What could the effete and hereditarily wealthy rows of Tory MPs know of the struggles they had waged, the effort they had given?

Each easily convinced himself that the other spoke against the national interest. Each time Heath moved towards Powell on immigration Powell denounced him for not going further. And no sooner had Heath achieved his great ambition of EEC entry than Powell, reversing his earlier views, concluded that this was a treason against the nation. When Heath's hour of trial with the miners came in early 1974 Powell was ready. There was only one way to destroy Heath and that was by electing Labour and so, astonishingly, Powell threw his immense electoral weight on that side, overthrowing the Tory convictions of a lifetime. It was enough. In a desperately close election the polls revealed that Powell had shifted several hundred thousand votes towards Labour. To achieve this final revenge Powell had even to surrender his own Commons seat, but no matter: Heath was beaten.

Immediately it was back to Edward the school prefect. He stubbornly refused to go, desperately attempting a coalition with the Liberals. The Tories wanted him to stand down as leader. Again, he stubbornly refused and lost – to none other than the grocer's daughter. Both men had been too preoccupied with their titanic struggle – Powell had now led a desperate attempt to reverse even Heath's EEC triumph in the 1975 referendum – to pay sufficient attention to this freakish outsider. Both were furious. Powell made bitter noises about the flukish and circumstantial nature of all Tory leadership choices. Edward couldn't accept it at all. After all, he had done the right things and the grocer's daughter hadn't, but the right things were happening to her, not him. He sulked, repeatedly refusing her peace overtures. He is still sulking. When the head prefect is demoted back to the third form there isn't much else he can do: to stop sulking would imply that he accepted that there was some justice in his demotion. This was – and is – unthinkable.

Both men had in the end destroyed the other, and in their struggle had changed their country's political landscape for ever. Heath wandered the world being important, awaiting the summons back to the head-prefectship, a summons which would never come. Powell was exiled in Northern Ireland but his case was more curious. Mrs Thatcher was, as even she knew deep down, the poor man's Enoch Powell: her views on every subject from race to the free market were merely bowdlerised versions of his own. She regarded him with something akin to veneration, wanted him in even her most intimate discussion groups, to which her own cabinet colleagues were not invited. But back into the cabinet – never. After Powell's expulsion from those ranks in 1968 any Tory leader who summoned him back into the fold would face intolerable pressures from their party, the media and even from abroad for 'giving way to racism'. Heath's stroke against Powell had been decisive too.

It may seem peculiar to have laid such stress on the class backgrounds of Powell and Heath, but in England this sort of thing is still necessary. In a society so deeply divided by class, culturally as well as socially, those who remain at the bottom of the heap suffer not only a multiple deprivation of life-chances, but, frequently, an abiding sense of helplessness and inferiority. Any child growing up in a lower-class family learns very young the human damage done by class. The child feels the oppression of his social position and wants to escape. In general the brighter the child the more determined the wish to escape. Some actually manage it. What is often not appreciated, however, is the heavy price that even they pay, for they have to make of themselves people which their environment could never 'naturally' make. This sort of herculean effort exacts large and unavoidable costs, and this is the story of both Powell and Heath.

Like so many able children of the lower classes Powell and Heath – Enoch and Edward – were blinded early by the lure of success, achievement, getting on. It was a dream they learnt, literally, at their mothers' knees, and the means to it was work, work and always more work. Both men learnt this lesson prodigiously and pushed themselves to their limits and beyond. The price of this was that both became loners, indeed, complete isolates. They also learnt a degree of inflexibility which long served them well until it served them fatally.

But the price was higher than that. In Heath's case the effort was such that it led to a sort of evacuation of the areas in which a private, inner life should have been lived. This left him entirely devoid of the talent of friendship and, indeed, something of a wooden prig. To be sure, he always remained rather like a spoilt child, stubborn, a bad loser, and in that sense self-centred. But it was a peculiar form of self-centredness, for he lived only in and for the external world. Throughout his life even those who worked long and closely with him were to confess that they had never got to know that self. Great mystery was made of this but, almost certainly, this was not a self that Heath knew either.

Powell was very different – self-aware, imaginative and more complex. He could escape into flights of romanticism, expressed through the medium of Greek, Latin and German literature and history; he didn't just see black people, he saw 'the Tiber foaming with blood'. He could dream of glorious self-immolation, of prostrating himself utterly before the flag, and this added to his other talents a rare courage. And he knew his own worth. Bowing to the flag was one thing, but bowing to the men of the Establishment whom he knew to be his real inferiors was something he found it all but impossible to do. And in politics, particularly Tory politics, this is a very necessary art. Behind even this lay a spark of lower-class rebellion, 'a bit of the devil' as the English often say. In part this expressed itself simply in ambition, but it came out too in a continual propensity to be awkward, to tweak ears and singe beards, to play the barrack-room lawyer. He knew how formidable he was and could not really bear to be anything other than top-dog. Resigning he could do with furious panache and did so in 1958 and again in 1963. But to be beaten by a lesser man for his party's leadership and then to be publicly humiliated by having that man dismiss him – that was too much, an intolerable affront. He had topped every class, beaten every rival, won every prize. The one thing he could never be was dismissed. And so the deadly battle was joined until the two men had destroyed their careers and one another. No doubt neither man would see his career in sociological terms. None the less, what Powell and Heath built in the end was a monument to the hidden injuries of class.

2

Tom Nairn and the Break-up of Britain[1]

For a long time now anyone who wanted to know what was 'wrong' with British politics had only to glance at much that was written on the subject to realise that this literature was part of the problem, not part of the solution. Not only were many of the best general works written by foreigners (McKenzie, Rose, Hechter, Beer) but so were not a few of the more detailed works (Stokes, Eckstein, Wilson, Roth). The best of the natives were generally interested in Abroad (especially France), Sociology or the latest euphemism for poor countries. What there was of a *literature indigène* hovered uncomfortably in a stodgy nether-world peopled by the ghosts of Burke, Bagehot and Jennings. The best empirical work was generally done in biography or contemporary history; beyond that topics often appeared to be chosen on the grounds of their truly heart-breaking triviality and boredom – the organisation of the civil service, local government, ombudsmen, the Commons' committee system or the world of the lobby correspondent. The world passed such writing by and most students, thank heavens, passed it up.

It is in part this dismal context which makes Tom Nairn's book so refreshing. This is true despite the fact that the book is in fact a collection of essays, none of which are brand new. For Nairn argues with power and sophistication, situates all he says in historical context and broaches the large question of the decline of the British state. He writes with the polemical thrust and analytical sophistication one has come to expect of editors of *New Left Review* but with something more as well. Mr Nairn lives in Scotland these days and has clearly received a large intellectual and emotional jolt from the

---

[1] Tom Nairn, *The Break up of Britain, Crisis and Neo-nationalism* (1977).

rise of Celtic nationalism. The result is a mood of chastened and rather angry realism, with Marxist theory more frequently than not found wanting. This is not a book which ends by charting the true path to revolution. Indeed, Nairn clearly neither hopes for nor expects the fulfilment of his (past?) socialist hopes but he is altogether more interesting than the usual socialist renegade. What Nairn has clearly broken from (and with some force) is not socialism so much as from a metropolitan intelligentsia which is in part socialist. The basic position of such an intelligentsia, he writes, 'is one of frustration at home, they have found it difficult not to make a mythology of anti-imperialism . . . history has forced most of them to be content with home-movies of the world revolution'.[1] In particular such intellectuals have found themselves acting simultaneously as cheerleaders of 'progressive' Third World nationalisms while deprecating any dim echo of domestic nationalism. Vietnamese patriotism (for example) is splendid, heroic; British (or Welsh or Scots or English) patriotism is ludicrous, even monstrous.

Nairn is keen, above all, to re-establish the relevance of the 'national question'. For all that Marxism may have provided the nearest means to understanding the phenomenon of nationalism, it has not been near enough. The phenomenon took its definitive modern form in the nineteenth century states of central and eastern Europe and moved outward, throwing its awakening touch onto the scores of new nations of the Third World. But how now to explain the turning of the wheel full circle, the recrudescence of nationalist movements in the imperial heartlands of the Old World? Part of the answer, of course, is that nationalism is a very various and variable phenomenon even if, in some conceptual sense, it does remain a single phenomenon. It is now such a generally available form of expressive and instrumental social protest that it may be appropriated in almost any set of circumstances. Thus the gradual economic unification of the world by the universalising forces of capitalism had the paradoxical result of creating both a degree of economic and social homogeneity and also a widening circle of political resistances to the ingress of these new forces on established communities and social structures. So that the economic internationalisation of capitalist

---

[1] First published in *Planet*, no. 40 (1977), and *Political Studies*, vol. XXVI (1978) 1.

market forces and institutions produced not political internationalism but an ever more fragmented map of local political nationalisms. As these in turn ran their course and imperial units disintegrated in favour of local particularism, so the unity of the old imperial states themselves came to be called in question. In this case, however, the motive power of nationalist resurgence is not the brutal thrust of new economic forces but rather the opposite, the dismal awakening to the fact of (relative) economic decline. Such, crudely expressed, would appear to be Nairn's main hypothesis. But his argument is too subtle and multi-faceted for Grand Theory to do it justice. And his various essays on Welsh, Scottish and Ulster/Irish nationalism show a keen regard for the local peculiarities of social and historical evolution – they are not being fitted into an already established theoretical grid. The main thing is, quite simply, that nationalism will not lie down. No theory which dismisses it can succeed; there is no doubting its continuing power; and yet the sources of that power remain ultimately mysterious.

It will be clear that the central theme of Nairn's perspective has, perforce, to lie in the decline of the British (imperial) state, to which the first quarter of the book is devoted. It is this chapter, above all, which delivers such a welcome blast to the stodgy world of British political studies. The British state, Nairn argues, is a true *ancien regime*. It is a unique form because the happy combination of isolation and possession of the greatest empire the world has ever seen enabled its ruling classes to carry through modernisation and industrialisation without ever suffering either a revolution from below or having to effect (*à la* Germany or Japan) a revolution from above. The cumulative, encrusted result is a monstrosity of neo-feudal survival which prolongs itself endlessly by virtue of its own mystique, myopic expedient, and the incorporation not only of a Labourist proletariat but of a uniquely continuous intellectual class who have become past masters in the strategy and practice of social containment. Thus Britain, the world's first industrialised state, has never properly experienced a bourgeois-democratic revolution. We are not citizens, but subjects. The people are not sovereign, parliament is – or, more accurately and tellingly, the Queen in Parliament. An antique social order – replete with monarch, dukes, barons, and knights – has withstood successive waves of change and reform and now stands poised to preside over the continuing and rapid decline of the imperial state. Ahead Nairn sees 'rapidly accelerating backwardness, economic stagnation, social decay and cultural despair'. Unsurprisingly, the national minorities of the periphery are determined to leave this sinking, demoralised ship.

The implicit model is, of course, Spain. In the sixteenth century Spain acquired an empire from which it extracted a steady flow of tribute whose domestic effect was to freeze and ossify an antique monarchical and social system, providing it with both an 'artificial' invulnerability to challenges from below, the means by which to avoid painful programmes of modernisation *and* a ruling class with the lunatic self-confidence to believe that it could all be sustained thus for ever. Gradually the Spanish imperial state declined; Spain was overtaken by the Low Countries, by France, by Britain – and finally she lost her empire too. The result of this long drawn-out process was stagnation, growing instability, and ferocious political reaction, culminating finally in the Civil War. Britain's path has been similar but the contraction of imperial power, though it has occurred far more quickly, is still incomplete. But, Nairn suggests, the end of the road is only too likely to be the same: 'There exists in modern history no example of a national state afflicted with this kind of decline and traumatic loss of power and prestige which did not, sooner or later, undergo a strong reaction against it.'

Nairn warns against any simple extrapolation, however. British decline lurches downward from one ephemeral plateau to another and the search for panaceas and escape-routes is never-ending. Perhaps something will 'turn up' via North Sea oil, a 'technological revolution', or the EEC? The (hopeless) search will go on. Meanwhile British politics is essentially the political management of imperial and relative economic decline. The job of all politicians has been and is to manage the descent to the next plateau, to sell this to an increasingly embittered electorate and to do so in part by holding out these promises of pie-in-the-sky. Thus far they have made an astonishingly good job of it. The fall since 1945 has been so far and fast that the continued survival both of democratic forms and the old state in all its neo-feudal trappings is a fairly major feat. The giant still sleeps.

But what or who is this giant? Nairn sides strongly with all forms of peripheral nationalism – not because he believes in them but because he sees them as helping towards the necessary explosion of the grotesque incubus of the imperial state. (It is a slight oddity of the book, deriving from the fact that much of it was written in 1975, that Nairn displays a total confidence in the eventual triumph of these nationalisms which fewer now would share.) But whatever a few million Scots, Welsh, and Irish may decide to do or succeed in doing, *they* are hardly the giant. The answer must, necessarily, lie in England. It is here that Nairn is disappointing. His chapter on the English nationalism of Powell is a simple reprint of a seven-year-old essay which, in the light of Schoen's work, now looks sadly incomplete. And the chapter on 'The English Enigma' is, revealingly, the shortest in the book when, arguably, it ought to have been the longest. In surveying the English political culture of the 1960s and 1970s Nairn espies the rise of racism, Powellism and (extraordinarily) 'a gathering movement of historical revision and socialist culture', exemplified in CND, *New Left Review*, and the History Workshop movement! Putting in a plug for one's friends and their publications is one thing: historical wish-fantasy on the grand scale quite another.

No, the true sleeping giant is an English populist nationalism which Nairn instinctively dislikes and fears. Thus far it has shown only glimpses of itself in anti-immigrant agitation and the Little Englandism of the anti-EEC campaign. If this giant ever truly awakes it will be little to do with the History Workshops. The central failure of nerve of the English left has, surely, been its inability to embrace the fact that the truly popular mass movement it seeks will be anti-aristocratic *and* racist, will use referenda not just to reject Europe but *also* to bring back the death penalty, will, in a word, not draw any fine distinctions in its anti-elitism. Faced with this the Left (including Nairn) turns tail, finds itself fighting for the nonsense of unrestricted immigration, supporting the EEC and taking silent comfort in the elitist structure of power which bars the way to such a monster. The intellectual Left is, after all, part of that (metropolitan) elite itself in the last analysis.

Nairn, for all his protestation, is very much part of it too. He is steeped in his examination and loathing of 'English bourgeois culture' to the point where he is not unlikely to commence his analysis (as in his *The Left Against Europe?*) with a long discussion of a *The Times* editorial. Wherever the New Jerusalem is to be built, one doesn't, surely, get to it from there? One is reminded of some American Marxists (Magdoff, Baran) whose staple reading is the *Wall Street Journal* and *Fortune*. Opposition to capitalism ultimately implies fascination with it and such men become more expert decoders of the Dow-Jones index than all but the most sophisticated stockbrokers. Similarly, Nairn's somewhat literary cast of mind and the deep repugnance in which he holds the world of *The Times* and Weston Park (which features over and again in *Break-Up*'s pages) makes him one of Rees-Mogg's most devoted readers. One result is a tendency to overstress Gramscian, cultural factors in his general schema of explanation. There is, for example, no analysis at all of the central role of London as the key political, social and financial focus of the British state, nor of what the decline of the state implies for that city and vice versa. (Why have no Scottish Nationalists apparently even noticed that London is just as over-represented at Westminster as is Scotland, perhaps more so?) There is also no adequate account of the changing international and market position of the British state. It is surely pertinent, after all, that Germany overtook Britain economically around 1900; was forcibly immiserated and pushed back to second place in 1918; had overtaken again by 1939; was forcibly reduced in strength and size (again) by 1945; has overtaken again – and that, finally, Britain has acknowledged defeat by joining the German condominium that is the EEC?

These are not just quibbles, but nor should they be taken as dismissals. Nairn has written a powerful, sophisticated and provocative book. Those who wish to make the study of British politics the study of ombudsmen and select committees will doubtless ignore it. But nobody with any sense will. Equally, though, anyone who wants to understand the weaknesses and limitations of our radical intelligentsia should also read this book. And wonder.

3
Prophets of Doom*

In the past few years we have gradually become used to a new *genre* in staple television fare, the series based in our imagined totalitarian future. There is a clear futurological consensus among our television writers, for the scenario is roughly the same: riding on a law 'n order backlash against strikes, protesters and permissiveness, an authoritarian government of reaction has come to power.

To keep the populace in order, it utilises a strange (and photogenic) mixture of futuristic electronic gadgetry, appeals to Conservative half-truths and, above all, a terrifying order of military police rejoicing under menacing Newspeak titles such as the Guardians, the Protecters or some such. Against these dark forces is ranged a tiny band of heroic resistants with whom, of course, our sympathies lie. Typically, our heroes anguish in their own moral dilemmas about the use of counter-violence, torture and blackmail, revealing that human nature's dark side is truly ubiquitous.

Quite invariably, such series – as also their eco-sisters. *Doomwatch* and its more recent successors – are politically naïve. They are based on very simplistic and sixties-ish notion about the nature and dangers of Conservative backlash, and they are sometimes quite unbearably patronising in their preaching about the Beast Within or, in the eco-series, the Danger Without. They are all clear lineal descendants from Orwell – somewhat ironically, for it was Orwell's acquaintance with the BBC which furnished him with the idea of Newspeak in *1984*. Imitation is the sincerest form of plagiarism, of course, but what, one wonders, would Orwell make of the reduction of *1984* to formula

---

* First published in *New Society*, 18 May 1978.

television, a first cousin to Newspeak? The main point, though, is just that such series continue – they are clearly popular.

Now if television writers, producers and advertisers can make a good living out of prophesying doom, why can't politicians and economists? These latter are, as they say in the City, professionals in the futures business; but in their case the foresight of trouble simply brings it on their own heads Three examples stand out: Powell's 1968 prophecy of 'the Tiber foaming with much blood' over race and immigration; Benn's 1975 prediction of the likely sequel to EEC entry; and, most recently, the forecasts of the Cambridge Economic Policy Group warning that only import controls can prevent a tidal wave of unemployment. All three predictions were greeted by roars of outrage from the massed ranks of opinion-makers and, on the evidence thus far available, they were all right.

Take Powell. What he declared himself to be saying (at least) was that a continued flow of coloured immigrants would, in time, bring racial tensions in urban areas sufficient to produce large-scale civil violence. Ten years on, this prediction looks pretty good, even if there still some way to go. Racial tensions rose, especially in the great cities; it proved possible even to launch a new party (the National Front) on the single issue of race; from about 1970 on, a clear pattern of private violence ('Pakibashing'), became discernible and, since 1976, we have settled down to a steady round of open street-fighting between organised groups. The young Left militants who confront the NF in such clashes may not enjoy the thought that they are helping, prove Powell correct; but that is, of course, what they are doing.

Second, there is Benn. During the referendum campaign he insisted that EEC entry would be followed by higher food prices, higher unemployment, the accelerating erosion of our manufacturing industries and thus all-round falls in real incomes. It is difficult to deny that all this has either happened or begun to happen. Those who argued on the other side, then, have not merely fallen silent now, but in many cases have fallen from sight. Lord Stokes of Leyland, for example. From public platforms he extolled the glittering economic opportunities afforded us by the EEC; he got his way: his own company was engulfed in the predictable, indeed, predicted, flood of car imports; went bankrupt, and was nationalised. [Lord Stokes, following this staggering act of economic hari-kiri, has become entirely invisible.]

Third, there is Wynne Godley and his Cambridge associates who, for several years now, have been predicting that, on present policies, we face a prospect of rapid deindustrialisation, up to 4.5 million unemployed, and a vertical fall in the value of sterling – unless swingeing import controls are applied. It is early days yet to say that this is completely right. But already industrial production has stagnated or fallen for five years, the pound is down and under pressure, unemployment is high and there is a clear drift towards protectionism. [All the more impressive as evidence since the government is going Godley's way reluctantly and under protest.] If I were a betting man – and I am – my money would have to be on the Cambridge group.

Now all of these prophecies, both explicitly and in their implications, are at least as frightening as anything cooked up by the latter-day Orwells of Broadcasting House. And, to put it mildly, they seem a great deal more plausible. But Powell's career was ruined by his 'Tiber' speech (usually, and revealingly, referred to as his 'rivers of blood' speech – a phrase he never used). Benn's referendum speeches helped establish him as a vote-loser of major, nay unique, proportions. And each fresh report from the Cambridge group provides the occasion for universal salvoes of vituperation – even, recently, from the soft *Guardian* centre. Whatever the other merits of these predictions, they are, clearly, not show business. Why?

First, all these predictions pointed quite explicitly – in a way the TV series are careful not to do – to some major fault or mistake that had *already* taken place. Powell was asserting that too many coloured immigrants had already been admitted for trouble to be averted, and accused the Home Office under Roy Jenkins of compounding the fault by publishing figures which falsely underestimated the numbers entering. (Later, this, too, turned out to be true.)

Benn and the Cambridge group were effectively saying much the same thing. For if we stand in need of stringent import controls now, it was clearly quite crazy to have entered the EEC free market. The past and present leaders of all the parties and virtually the whole of the press supported EEC entry. It now emerges that at precisely the point when our industries were in need of increased tariff protection, our leaders all joined hands in dismantling what protection we had. The flood of foreign cars which brought such bathos on Lord Stokes were Renaults, Fiats and Volkswagens: the Datsuns and Toyotas only came later and still amount to only 11 per cent of cars sold here. The present fuss about Japanese and Third World imports is, in fact, an elaborate (and deliberate) diversion of attention from the far more fundamental onslaught of the EEC.

It is all very embarrassing. To admit the predictions of Powell, Benn or Godley means that a large number of men of great sagacity and principle in politics and the media must now admit that they were silly and wrong. This is asking a lot – and television doomsters are careful to pose no such questions. If doom there is to be, it must be doom without fault, without guilt.

Second, the predictions of Powell, Benn and Godley all looked to solutions within an autarchic national framework. Powell's nationalism was most explicit: he insisted, quite simply, on the right of any sovereign state to decide who should or should not be allowed to cross its frontiers. In the last analysis this was an absolute, primary right, whose assertion immediately relegated all questions about past commitments to East African Asians and passport holders to the level of trivial technicality.

Messrs Benn and Godley have been a lot more hesitant, even timorous, in spelling out their assumptions which are, in fact, much the same as Powell's – namely, the right of any sovereign state to determine which goods should or should not be allowed to cross its frontiers and enter its markets. In Powell's case this right was invoked in the name of the national need to maintain social homogeneity and social peace. In the case of Benn and Godley it was invoked in the name of the national need to maintain employment and social peace.

Such ideas can be made attractive and undoubtedly can still be phrased in such a way as to evoke a deep popular response. But the demands they contain for strongly restrictionist policies, whether against imported goods or imported people, and their evocation of the primal rights of national communities – are profoundly, desperately unfashionable – are, indeed, often dismissed with the single phrase '19th century'. We bask in a climate of *laissez-faire*. In the end, to be sure, this *laissez-faire* is limited, even hypocritical. We are against Powellite imigration restrictions – but not in favour of unrestricted free entry for all-comers. We are in favour of free trade – within a protectionist EEC bloc. We are in favour of liberty, not licence. And so on. But these contradictions are too remote to trouble the intellectual climate where every species of *laissez-faire* – free speech, free trade, permissiveness, dislike of 'narrow nationalism'. and several varieties of radical individualism – are utterly dominant, at the level of theory, anyway. In the end this current is so powerful that, [whatever happens at the fringes] it paralyses nationalism at the centre. And in the end, [whatever the resistances] it corrodes socialism and undermines conservative backlash quite equally.

The Conservative backlash state of the television series is, in, this sense, a paper tiger. The writers of such series, for all their 'bold' moral earnestness, their 'controversial' social comment, are asking us to swim *with* the tide. We are on the side of the heroic libertarians in the resistance, for freedom, against the strong state. The futuristic trappings and gadgetry should not fool us: we are being asked to refight the old battles of Wilberforce, Hampden, even Robin Hood.

But Powell, Benn and Godley, somewhat to their own embarrassment and reticence, are not fighting such battles. They *are* evoking nationalism, they *are* championing the rights of the sovereign state, they *do* want restrictions. Whatever the merits of their respective cases, however valid their statistics and arithmetic, however valid their predictions, they are, in the present climate, sitting ducks. If the forces of which they foretell really were allowed to let rip, the intellectual climate might indeed then change. It is much more likely, however, that their political clothes will be stolen (as has already happened to Powell) and that they and the principles they evoke will continue to be reviled.

Finally, there is the crucial fact that the prophecies of doom enunciated by Powell, Benn and Godley are given – and *received* – in deadly seriousness. For all the transparent preachiness of the television doomsters, their bleak prophecies are seriously given but received, correctly, as fantasies. They are popular, in the end, because we don't believe in them. There is, of course, nothing to stop the BBC or ITV sponsoring a series in which the Britain of the 1990s has become an under-developed region, awash with mountainous unemployment and racked by continuous race riots. Even to describe the project thus far makes one realise how unlikely it is. There is deep unease about allowing the NF air-time, even on *Open Door*. But what about '1990, scene 2: a pogrom in Brixton. Take 3'?

Perhaps, indeed, we should be cheered by the popularity of the present doomster series. Their commercial success is the clearest indication we can have that their intention to convince has failed, and failed because it deserves to. *1984* itself could hardly have been such a huge success if Orwell had not been so wide of the mark. We like our fantasies neat – and woe betide those politicians or economists who forget it.

4

A Prodigal Period*

This summer is beginning to feel oddly like 1959. In that year, in a warm daze of economic wellbeing and delightful weather, the country returned a government to power for a record third time. The shattering crisis of Suez, Eden's departure into disgrace, the problems of sterling and empire – all apparently dissolved into a distant bad dream.

In 1978 something very similar seems to be under way. The great crisis of 1974–6 seems far behind. The departure into obloquy of both Heath and Wilson stirs as few spirits as Eden's once did and, with every passing poll and sunny week, the voters' hearts are melting visibly in the government's favour. Callaghan can hardly claim that we've 'never had it so good', but there are signs of economic cheer and another three-in-a-row electoral sequence appears distinctly possible. Literally and politically, the country dozes in its deckchairs, much to the advantage of Sunny Jim.

This mood, while it lasts, depends on an enormous act of collective suppression, a recapture of equanimity by pretending that problems aren't there, that they almost never happened. It is, of course, the 'spirit of '59' which is unreal. Suez happened all right. The agonies of decolonisation and imperial decline returned soon enough, as did sterling crises galore. Moreover, Suez had holed the ship of state below the waterline, leaving water seeping quietly in, with results by no means wholly clear as early as 1959. Will it be the same again with the crisis of 1974–6?

It was, after all, a prodigal period. The year 1974 began with the country plunged in cold, darkness and a three-day week – a combi-

* First published in *New Society*, 22 June 1978.

nation even the Luftwaffe never succeeded in inflicting on us. The Heath government fell in its own trap, the greatest blow to authority the Establishment has suffered in recent time – though not long after the Protestant workers of Ulster achieved an even greater denouement with one of the most successful political general strikes in history. Amid continuing terrorist activity in Ulster (and a bombing wave in London), the economy was hit by the spreading wave of world recession and the oil crisis, producing soaring unemployment, record inflation, steeply falling investment and production, and a major property and secondary banking collapse. The government confessed its weakness by throwing to the country the EEC issue, acknowledging the need for supra-parliamentary legitimation for the first time.

Meanwhile, there was a growing backlash from the extreme right, with the formation of several private armies and a mounting wave of fierce racialist animosity directed against the coloured population. This wave produced an ugly multiplication of violent, even murderous, attacks on individuals, race rioting and an escalating series of street battles, as well as increased support for the National Front. In May 1976 the Front won 18 per cent of the vote in local elections in Leicester. If one allowed for the fact that none of these votes came from Leicester's coloured population, the sensational fact emerged that a quarter of the white electorate of a major English city had voted for an openly fascist party.

Later that summer the currency collapsed, the pound falling to $1.50 before the IMF loan was secured. As the recent *Sunday Times* series on the loan negotiations reveals, Callaghan was reduced to pleading with the US Treasury that nothing less than the survival of British democracy was at stake.

Over and around all of these events swirled the Great Fear. Fear of the unions, of inflation, of bankruptcy and of unemployment; fear of being 'swamped by the blacks', of the 'takeover by the left', and of the 'fascist threat'; fear of parcel-bombs, of street violence and (if one was black) fear of being killed; and, finally, a generalised fear of social or national disintegration.

Arch-Conservatives ceased, suddenly, to argue for the status quo and began, with equal force, to decry it. In vogue books like Moss's *The Collapse of Democracy* or Haseler's *The Death of British Democracy*, the whole system was claimed to be at, or beyond, the point of collapse due to the work of left subversives, with a need for stern, even authoritarian measures to stop the rot. Formerly staid academics joined in: books like S. E. Finer's *Adversary Politics and Electoral Reform* and Nevil Johnson's *In Search of the Constitution* demanded sweeping changes to the political system in a desperate search for prophylactics against this same imagined threat from the left.

The new villain of the piece was 'adversary politics' – the process whereby oppositions oppose a government and, if elected, change its policies. This overtly anti-democratic note was echoed by others who hinted that we would do best to wind up parliament completely in favour of 'Great Britain Limited' – a sort of Securicor state.

Different people had different fears and there was, at least, no doubting the reality of inflation, unemployment and racial tension. But a great deal of the panic was wild and inchoate, overheated and nonsensical – and this was not a little alarming in itself. *The Economist*, reviewing *In Search of the Constitution*, referred to its author as behaving like a 'headless chicken' and, indeed, there were many intellectual farmyard noises to be heard. It hardly inspired confidence. A future social historian may well experience some difficulty in comprehending the cacophony of the Great Fear – particularly since many who were loudest then are, in the new 'spirit of '59', often quick to deny they were frightened at all.

Quite clearly the crisis frightened Conservatives, causing them to turn right. By the same token it frightened many on the left who glimpsed an open threat from an extreme, even fascist right, leaving them much preoccupied with the question of how best to pre-empt its rise or resurgence. They would do well to read Mike Newman's article, 'Democracy versus dictatorship' in the current issue of *History Workshop*.

Newman's article examines the tactics and analyses of the British left in the 1930s, the last occasion when it was faced with the rise of a significant fascist movement in the midst of economic depression, and comes to some paradoxical conclusions. The Labour Party, he suggests, attempted no serious analysis of the nature of fascism or of the conditions which had led to its conquest of power in much of Europe. Rather, it was viewed as merely a variant of extremist dictatorship – which could be avoided if the left adopted a policy of conscious moderation, tolerance and constitutionalism. The extreme Left (the Communist Party) offered a more sophisticated analysis of the fascist phenomenon as capitalism-in-crisis, but argued quite erroneously from this that the British middle classes would turn to fascism unless the way was barred by mass action.

The results – then, as today – were that the Labour leadership sought to deny popular support to the fascists by impotent appeals to the electorate's democratic instincts, while the extreme Left fought the fascists on the streets. This latter tactic was effective not in itself but because *mêlées* such as that in Cable Street produced an indiscriminate public revulsion against violent extremism of *any* kind. This was largely a reaction in favour of Labour's moral perspective and helped ensure the passage of the Public Order Act. Socialist Workers' Party militants please note.

However – and this is the crucial point – the real reason why the fascist danger was averted in Britain was that the upper and lower middle classes – the groups crucial to fascism's success – could look with confidence to a strong Conservative government. The best guarantee against fascism was, in the end, neither preachy tolerance nor mass mobilisation but . . . Stanley Baldwin.

The parallels for today are obvious enough – up to a point. The street fighting between SWP and NF has produced much the same revulsion against right *and* left extremism. And we have a conservative government which enjoys the confidence of the City and is led by a man whom even Conservatives compare with Stanley Baldwin. Callaghan is the SWP's best guarantee against fascism, not because he fights it, not because he's Left-wing, but because he's there.

However, the great difference is that the NF is only part of the problem. More serious, perhaps, is that in 1974–6 important sections of the middle classes did lose confidence. For the first time parts of the Establishment began seriously to consider alternatives to our present form of parliamentary democracy. This was the real significance of the Great Fear, of the sentiments so frequently expressed in *The Times* at that time that democracy on these terms no longer commanded allegiance, of the oft-repeated claim that the middle classes were in decline. One of my colleagues who commutes frequently to Whitehall told me during this period that many of the senior civil servants with whom he dealt talked quite seriously of one day seeing tanks coming up the Mall. 'Not that that frightens them,' he added, 'in fact, most of them give the impression that they'd be rather glad.' He wasn't joking though I suspect the civil servants concerned would now claim they were, such is the change of mood.

The Great Fear of the 1970s had no real parallel in the 1930s. Were it to return, were it to take concrete form, it would pose problems of an entirely different order than those at present considered by the Left. For the moment, though, the beast sleeps. It may be dying. The NF has lost support and may lose more. Private armies have become a joke. We hear less of Great Britain Limited and fewer feverish voices from academe. The Great Fear is, temporarily, at least, dissipated. Which is not to say that the establishment has become reattached and reconciled to the present order. As with Suez the real damage may have been done below the waterline, and may not yet be wholly visible.

A third consecutive electoral win for Labour would undoubtedly cause many of these fears to resurface. Labour has already won four of the last five elections and yet another Labour win might well make many Conservatives despair. Such an outcome – especially if accompanied by the onset of deeper economic woes – would undoubtedly see the present embarrassed grumbling take on a more strident tone, with the same desperate 'solutions' that were canvassed during the Great Fear returning to the fore. Even the mildest of these – proportional representation – implies the risk of a National Front block of MPs playing coalition games at Westminster. We shall see. Meanwhile, such discontents are stilled, even numbed, by the 'spirit of '59'. This mood has little to recommend it. It's empty; it's boring; it solves to problems and, indeed, dishonestly pushes them under the carpet. But it's nice while it lasts.

5

Generation Game*

If one is in the education business, summer is the season of goodbyes as one's pupils or students depart in great annual waves. Watching over the timeless ritual of Oxford Finals is always a bitter-sweet occasion for me. One invigilates several hundred sub-fusced young men and women writing and pausing and writing in purposeful unison. They are so rapt in the immediacy of their present while I am so conscious of the fact of their leaving. I am always put in mind of Philip Larkin's *Whitsun Weddings*:

> and none
> Thought of the others they would never meet
> Or how their lives would all contain this hour.

The poignancy of Larkin's bridal couples on a train or the massed ranks of examinees derives from essentially the same source: it is a picture of a whole age-cohort gathered together for perhaps the only and certainly the last time, providing an appearance of unity which cannot long survive. For they are gathered thus to be shot into the wider society where their common possession of a marriage certificate or a BA will hardly ensure a common destiny. They will go their different ways as managers and housewives, journalists and dropouts, civil servants and junkies – or as couples, divorcees or single parents.

> there swelled
> A sense of falling, like an arrow-shower
> Sent out of sight, somewhere becoming rain.

---

* First published in *New Society*, 20 July 1978.

But all this lies ahead. The magic of the moment is that it does lie ahead, that the whole cohort, with only its glittering prize to hand, stands

> Ready to be loosed with all the power
> That being changed can give.

The world which awaits this year's students seems a quite unfairly greyer place than that into which their '60s predecessors embarked, and not surprisingly they depart for it with less confidence. In retrospect nothing is more striking than the gathering *élan* with which the student generations of that period attacked the Establishment; first in rather self-righteous moral tones (CND); then with gleeful ridicule (the satire wave); then as Kennedyish social democrats, urging Labour on to victory in 1964; then as radicals, recoiling to the left of Labour over Vietnam; and finally as Marxists and re-volutionaries (from 1968 to 1973), taking on just about everyone in sight. Behind the growing pessimism of these radical critiques lay an increasing optimism and self-confidence about what the student age-group could afford to take on and attack. It was a long upward swing: last year's high-tide was next year's low-water mark. In Oxford, at least, 1973 was the end. After that successive cohorts became first Liberal, then Conservative, then apolitical. The only strong political sentiment shared among today's (1978) students seems to be an abhorrence of the National Front.

How much can be learnt from all this? During the 1960s it became common form to use the changing political mood of the student generation as a barometer of wider social significance, a habit greatly reinforced by the discovery of the importance of 'political gener-ations'. This theory had several legs to it. First, it was found that voters tended to plump very early in their adult life for one party or another and then to repeat their preference over and over again at subsequent elections. Second, it was found that 80 per cent of voters who remembered both their parents sharing a single political preference inherited that preference themselves. And third, to the extent that political change took place from one generation to the next, the decisive variable seemed to be the state of the political climate which young voters encountered as they entered adult life.

The influence of parental preference was overwhelming – but it was also something nobody could do much about. Changes in the political climate were possible enough, however, and so everyone watched the young – not just because they were liable to keep their early preferences but because they were clearly an excellent weathervane. It seemed only a small further step to pay particular attention to the political attitudes of university students. They were, helpfully, more visible, more articulate than the rest of their age-group and were more likely to become influential. Just as the middle-class young were fairly reliable pace-setters in changing social and sexual mores, so they might be in political terms too.

When Butler and Stokes[1] first introduced the theory of political generations in 1969 their findings were universally read as a favourable portent for Labour. For, as they pointed out, the generation leaving the electorate (through death) consisted mainly of those born at the turn of the century who had come to age politically in the (Tory) 1920s and thus tended to divide 3 : 1 or 4 : 1 against Labour. Thèy were being replaced by young voters born after 1945 of parents who were at least 50 –50 Labour, and who, accordingly, could be expected to favour the Left. The student leftward wave of the '60s was at its height when these findings were published, making the prediction seem almost a truism. Conservative Central Office naturally took a dim view of this. Iain Macleod published a marvellously wrong-headed attack on Butler and Stokes in *The Times* – but then, a year later, was apparently vindicated by the Tories' shattering election victory.

What had gone wrong with the theory? First, Butler and Stokes had not sufficiently stressed that only 40 per cent of voters could remember their parents sharing the same political views, so that no more than a third of either major party's support was a simple inheritance effect. There is, moreover, every reason to believe that inherited views are far weaker and less stable than those which one has come to via one's own experience. And finally, young voters often don't vote at their first opportunity to do so – the replacement effect takes some time to take place. What Butler and Stokes had anticipated for 1970 may have only been taking effect (to Labour's advantage) in 1974. With such modifications the theory survives.

The idea that student political attitudes are a reliable guide to anything does not stand up to much examination, though, and not

---

[1] D. Butler and D. Stokes, *Political Change in Britain* (1969).

just because students are more middle class than the rest of their cohort. Student political organisations are certainly no guide. They are notoriously oligarchic and unrepresentative: the overall rightward shift of the last ten years in student opinion as a whole has merely seen the old Right-wing Labour clique that used to run the NUS give way to a Broad Left (i.e. CP) one. Just as trade union leadership gives no hint of the number of Tory workers below, so student political leadership is often quite absurdly biassed towards the Left.

More important, though, is the fact that those who celebrated the emergence of an autonomous 'youth culture' in the '60s failed to notice that it was almost entirely a phenomenon of a newly enlarged stratum of the educated young, with no necessary connection with the rest of the age-group. The year 1968, for example, is remembered as the high point of youthful radicalism throughout the West – and so it was. But in that same year larger numbers of young people than ever before also defected to the Tories here, to George Wallace in the US and to the Gaullists – *against* the student radicals – in France. 1968 belonged not to Cohn-Bendit but to Powell, Pompidou and Nixon.

The isolation of the student group is not new, even if the group thus isolated is larger now. There is, for example, a certain line in 'period' writing which suggests that during the 1930s the young were mainly involved in anguish over Spain, the Left Book Club and Oxford Union debates about not fighting for King and Country. Did not the flower of the generation – Auden, Spender and Co. – go around being 'committed'? As for the working-class young, they were all marching in procession from Jarrow or somewhere, weren't they? Brave images, but hardly the whole truth, as the Tory landslide of 1935 showed.

I can do no better at this point than to appeal to the case of my own father. He wasn't at any Oxford Union debates and he didn't go on any hunger marches (though he was often unemployed). He simply survived the Depression as best he could. He never voted. During the War he was an engineer on oil tankers which ran the gauntlet of the U-boat packs. I well remember him telling me how often he sat and sweated in the Liverpool Port Office waiting to know if his convoy was routed to Murmansk (shipping losses averaged 50 per cent on this run) or for the Atlantic (where losses were only one in three). Aghast at the notion of a young married man (as he then was) having to play this sort of Russian roulette for years on end, I asked him why he did it: fighting in any of the Services would have been a soft touch by comparison. He agreed that patriotism had had nothing to do with it – the men in the Port Office were all the sort who walked out of cinemas while the national anthem was being played. And he agreed that he too now thought such behaviour crazy. The important thing, he told me, was that every man in the Port Office had known the reality or at least the fear of long-term unemployment. If you learnt one thing, it was never to refuse a job. 'You could never have fought the war', he claims, 'if my generation hadn't been completely cowed first.'

This story has two further points. First, the immediate social experience of a young adult may shape his political views, but that experience is itself capable of quite radical reinterpretation later. (In my father's case post-war full unemployment made him realise how he'd been 'taken advantage of' before. His parents were both solid Tories, but after 1945 he voted Labour.) Second, the decisive factor in shaping the experience of young adults is likely to be the state of the labour market as they enter it. This factor in turn is also affected by generational factors – in general a large age-cohort entering the labour market all at once will find life far more trying than a smaller one.

I am, though, uneasily conscious that this has not been true for my own – extremely large – cohort of those born in the 1942–8 baby boom. We have been uniquely lucky – enjoying the first fruits of the NHS and then of the 1944 Education Act, finding conscription abolished just as we became liable for it, emerging into higher education just as Robbins was taking effect and then entering the labour market during a period of headlong economic expansion. Most of my generation had little real competition from the (far smaller) pre-1942 and post-1948 cohorts and, as a result, are now safely esconced in good jobs which they came by easily and in which they have risen fast. It is a cohort of vaguely leftish hue – its parents were swinging to Labour just as it was born, and it entered political life in the great Labour swing of 1963–6. While its radicalism has been considerably eroded by its dramatic upward mobility, there seems little to stop this cohort from dominating British life for the rest of this century, just as the Resistance generation dominated France for decades after the war. The irony of this supremely lucky generation is that it – we – owe our good fortune entirely to the fact that our parents were imprudent enough to have babies in the middle of a world war. . . .

The reverse is true of the present young adults. Those born in the baby boom of 1955–64 – the children of confidence and expansion – are emerging into the shocking labour market of the '70s and '80s. To be sure, the students I have been saying goodbye to will not know the worst of it – they are hardly typical of their age-group. Not the least indicator of their change of mood, though, is that whereas the *enragés* of '68 made large claims to representative – or at least vanguard – status, this year's young seem happy enough to believe that they represent only themselves. It's quite enough.

6
Political Posturing*

Richard Nixon, who certainly knows imitation to be the sincerest form of flattery, can hardly have failed to realise during his recent visit that, judging by that criterion, this is the country where he is most admired. Not only are we enjoying an entire season of scandals quite sufficient to justify Equity's most extreme demands for a closed shop, but the term 'cover-up', with its distinctive bouquet of Watergate '74, is bandied wide across the land. The dramatic entertainment is only heightened by the fact that private cover-up jobs are as nothing compared to the comprehensive smothering process effected by our legal system and the fear it generates.

First, we had the Rhodesian sanctions brouhaha. Up and down the country you could hear animated conversations in which – dare one say it – participants were often so wanton as to impugn Harold Wilson's integrity. But journalists, dancing with rage and conviction though they were, were sharply restrained in their comment by the knowledge that Our Fallen Leader is a handy man with a writ.

There followed the case of the grave allegations made against Lord Chalfont that he had received all manner of largesse from the Shah's corrupt and oppressive regime in return for writing that it was actually a jolly good regime despite all the awful and torturous things it did. Lord Chalfont has naturally issued writs to prevent this slander from going any further. This has, equally naturally, stilled all comment. Indeed, if a case comes to trial, large sections of the Iranian populace are in some danger of being cited for contempt of court for suggesting by their present behaviour that anyone who defends the Shah is culpable of something pretty bad. (Their defence, presumably,

---

* First published in *New Society*, 21–28 December 1978.

will be that they object more, not less, violently to those who perform such a propaganda function on a free, unpaid basis.)

Finally, the nation has been shocked by the Thorpe Trial, or the Minehead Disaster, as, day by day, more bodies were brought to the surface. The grim toll is the talk of every pub and club, and the air is thick with fascinating stories which only the media are forbidden to discuss. We have even witnessed the remarkable spectacle of two such notoriously discreet men as the Secretary of State for Health and Social Security and the Master of University College, Oxford, bursting to tell us things for once, and not being able to do so.

Happily, a partial exception has been made for the latter. While, naturally, it would be grossly improper for anyone to cast doubt upon the veracity of any of the Minehead cast, the legal eminence of Lord Goodman is so great, and the occasions on which he wishes to enlighten the public as to what he gets up to so few, that he has been allowed to refer in print to the 'demented allegations' of those who have dared mention him.

Now while nobody could wish to deprive the great British public of its enjoyment in these *affaires* – to do so would constitute a significant diminution of our Christmas cheer – these entertainments do have a negative side. For these cases (whatever their final results) have already thrown into a new, sharp and possibly distorted relief, three of the main political actors of the last decade. In the consequent reinterpretation which may result, matters of real importance to our own history could well be overlooked, even submerged.

Take Wilson. The real point about the sanctions fiasco was not that British oil got through to Rhodesia. Anyone aware of (a) the South African refusal to apply such sanctions, (b) the position of the British oil companies in South Africa, and (c) the continuing arrival of oil in Salisbury, would have had considerable difficulty in putting two and two together and not getting four out of this.

Nor was it particularly the point that the pretence of oil sanctions was assiduously maintained, even to the point of bogus naval blockades. Any self-respecting journalist could, and should, have blown that pretence sky-high by early 1966 at the latest. The real and more interesting point was that the government quite deliberately – with, as it were, lunacy aforethought – committed itself to a policy which it knew in advance to be unworkable.

The policy resulted in practice from the progressive elimination of workable alternatives.

Ian Smith was given an assurance that whatever he did, there would be no British military action against him (Wilson as Man of Peace). Smith, thus encouraged, proclaimed UDI, and slapped Britain in the face. In order to show we were not lightly brooked, sanctions (minus oil) were ordered (Wilson as British Bulldog). This produced a furious onslaught against the inadequacy of British policy by a large majority of UN members, leaving Britain more isolated in the Security Council than she had been even over Suez. So oil sanctions were then conceded (Wilson as Conciliator), although by then Lyndon Johnson and not a few others had explained to Wilson that these would be unworkable.

And so the charade began, essentially because Wilson had boxed himself into a position where no consistent long-term policy *could* be applied. This he did by proceding from posture to posture, each echoing some imagined aspect of our national 'greatness'. This preoccupation with 'greatness' led Wilson ineluctably (like Nixon) towards the squalid and the trivial. It did, however – and this was what mattered – help Wilson's short-term run-up to the March 1966 election. (At this election, incidentally, the Liberals fared disastrously, not having been helped by the fact that Jeremy Thorpe had been rash enough to argue for the quite workable policy of bombing Rhodesia's supply routes from South Africa.)

What, the recent uproar over this fiasco obscures is that, under Wilson, policy was quite ordinarily worked out in this way. The very next year, he launched a frenetic bid for EEC membership, knowing full well that with de Gaulle still at the Elysée and more powerful than ever, the approach had almost no chance of success. But the disastrous June 1966 deflationary measures had just been brought in, killing George Brown's expansionist Department of Economic Affairs. It had taken Wilson only 22 months in office to return to the stop–go policies he had promised to banish for ever.

He needed a diversion smacking of action and purpose with which to distract the electorate, and he also needed to keep Brown from resigning. Brown was, luckily, a star-crossed Europhiliac, and the offer of the Foreign Secretaryship was irresistible to him, when combined with the prospect of a wild-goose chase around the capitals of Europe. While the chase continued – as it did until de Gaulle said his inevitable No – a breathless press followed the hare (Brown), relieving Wilson on the stricken home front.

This Laurel and Hardy turn was followed by the even more filmic pantomime, *In Place of Strife*. Knowing that the wage freeze must end in 1969 with a wage explosion amid a plethora of strikes, Wilson looked around for some means to convince the middle classes that he was 'tough with the unions'. Barbara Castle obliged with her notorious bill, although her labour relations experts unanimously warned that its proposed measures could have no effect on the incidence of strikes or on wage levels.

Wilson campaigned strongly for the measure, citing its economic advantages which, again, were known to be illusory. With his eye now firmly on the 1970 election he thus charged into the brick wall of union resistance.

While he was normally willing to drop major national objectives (like an end to stop–go) fairly lightly he was always willing to fight quite tigrishly for this sort of short-term political advantage.

It would be a pity if this richer and fuller picture of Wilson's premiership were now to be obscured by such trivia as his grotesque final Honours List or his recent 'explanations' about oil sanctions.

The occlusive effects of Minehead are potentially even more serious for the contemporary historian. Jeremy Thorpe has, after all, played a significant role in British politics during only one brief period, the Liberal revival of 1972–4. It was, one remembers, the era of the great property boom which brought the public to near panic with an unprecedented explosion in house prices. It was also the era of 'community politics', on which the Liberals capitalised so heavily and successfully. For many the two concerns came together in the reviled spectre of the office-block speculators who ripped communities apart to build monstrous and unlettable Centre Points. Such developments enormously enriched those who financed them, but they blighted city centres by driving land prices to a zenith at which young families could hardly compete in the housing market.

At the peak of the Liberal revival the property boom folded. Amid the wreckage was Jeremy Thorpe, director of London and County Securities, a fringe bank which had been fuelling the speculation for all (and more than) it was worth. Astonishingly, Thorpe escaped electoral retribution by admitting to a certain lack of business judgement.

This was not quite the point. The Liberals, Thorpe at their head, were riding hard with the hounds of popular discontent. At the same time, it now emerged, Thorpe had been running comfortably with the hares all along. The admission that his lapine career had been poorly managed hardly answered all the outstanding questions. But it was enough to satisfy the press which, in those far-off, pre-Minehead days, positively bulged with commentators who were enjoying the Liberal revival and were indeed part of it.

One such was Lord Chalfont, then in passage from being a Labour minister towards his present position on the far right. Again, there is some danger that Lord Chalfont's present troubles may cloud a proper appreciation of his interesting career.

His sympathetic reporting from Tehran, as also from Pretoria, has been motivated by an entirely laudable concern to support these Western bulwarks against the Russian menace. In particular – and this is what links Iran and South Africa – he has become almost obsessed by strategic threats to our safety lurking in the Indian and South Atlantic Oceans. So grave is the threat of strangulation posed to the Cape sea route by Soviet submarines (he has repeatedly warned) that we must not merely increase our own naval strength, but also face up to the need to support Iran and South Africa in their defence against communism.

Now, the importance of the Cape sea route is by no means a strategically uncontroversial question. Strong arguments have been mounted by defence experts that Chalfont's present position is based on a ludicrous anachronism. Among these experts, indeed, Lord Chalfont himself occupies a leading position. Back on 14 July 1970 he asked the House of Lords:

> Does anyone . . . seriously believe there is any kind of situation in which these [Soviet] submarines would be able to interfere with our shipping in the South Atlantic except in circumstances of such a grave crisis, if not a war, that the whole of the western alliance would be involved? . . . The only threat to our sea routes in the South Atlantic is the threat of war, and the next war is not going to be a war of naval engagements in the South Atlantic. The nuclear weapon has changed all that, and those who talk of 'showing the flag in the traditional way of a great naval power' are . . . indulging in the . . . worst excesses of prenuclear fantasy.

There is, of course, also the small matter that Lord Chalfont's position in the Wilson government was that of Minister for Disarmament, while in the 1970s he has become best known as a leading campaigner for the greatest possible rearmament. What is perhaps most impressive is the fact that he has shown the same strident confidence in both sides of these arguments – just as he has strongly supported Wilson, then Thorpe, then Thatcher, without the slightest trace of embarrassment to enfeeble his case. Indeed, he has been so unwilling to suffer gladly those foolish enough not to share his views at any particular moment that he has been willing to brand as 'fellow-travellers' or 'agents of influence' those who still hold his own (1970) views.

Thus the danger in the present troubles of Wilson, Thorpe and Chalfont. Our legal system is splendid, and does its best. Our lawyers, too, are wonderful. These bulwarks may not be enough. It would be tragic indeed if reputations so securely grounded in the history of our times should be affected by the present scandals. None the less, the Oxford Union, in bringing Richard Nixon out of his burglarious post-Watergate retirement and treating him as a world statesman once again, has shed a little hope for all politicians, even if all else fails. For when Samuel Johnson said that patriotism was the last resort of the scoundrel he was ignoring the even greater possibilities of the Oxford Union.

7

London Rules OK?*

The great revolt against London appears to be over. In the wake of the 1974 elections, with the Welsh and Scottish nationalists in full cry, it really seemed as if the movement against 'London rule' might get somewhere. For a while, at least, it even seemed possible that the vocal Celtic rejection of the capital's over-mighty sway might awake a true sleeping giant – the ever-present anti-London feeling of the English 'province' (London's word, not theirs). Consciousness of this deep, growling, regional resentment against Whitehall and 'London folk' – and what it might do if ever stirred to full life – almost certainly accounts for the speed with which the Labour Party discovered its great attachment to the cause of devolution.

But it never quite came off. In May 1979 the rebels were put to flight in all directions. The SNP collapsed. The Plaid Cymru leader lost his seat. Eddie Milne (who had toyed with the project of a North-East regional party) lost heavily in Blyth. Even amidst the carnage in Thorpe's North Devon seat, with the Liberal vote disintegrating to the benefit of all others, the Wessex Regionalist candidate could manage only 50 votes – 29 less than Auberon Waugh's Dog Lovers' Party. Whatever else Waugh may have achieved, he helped prove the point that even (?) dog-loving is more popular than regional autonomy in the Britain of 1979. . . .

All of which is a pity, for the rebels had – have – a good case. The dominance of London *is* oppressive and illogical. After all, no one who attempted to design our institutions *a priori* would place the seat of government in the far bottom corner of the country, closer to Holland, France or Belgium than to Yorkshire or Northumberland,

---

* First published in *New Society*, 24 May 1979.

let alone Scotland, Wales or Ireland. Nor, if such a blunder were somehow committed, would they then centralise all our other social, economic and cultural institutions there as well.

For it's not just that Parliament and Whitehall are in London. So are the national press, radio and television, the High Court and Inns of Court, the national museums, libraries and archives, the national theatre, opera and ballet (heavily subsidised by the 85 per cent of the population who do not live in London), the City, the company headquarters, the biggest university, the publishing companies, the national sporting stadia – the list is virtually endless. It is, indeed, easier to work backwards by asking which institutions do *not* centre their existence in London.

What annoyed the anti-London rebels was not merely this ludicrous and unequal centralisation of institutions, but the so-called 'London attitudes' which were its inevitable concomitant. By this was meant not merely a *de facto* parochialism (rubbish piling in the streets of London was a national crisis; the same thing in Manchester was just a pity), but a bland, self-indulgent presumption of the natural-ness of London's dominance. For several decades now the real centre of our major national sport, soccer, has lain in Lancashire but it's 'natural' that the cup-final and international games should be at Wembley. When regional TV companies were set up their head-quarters were 'naturally' sited in London. When the v & a was forced to make economies it 'naturally' cut its service to the regions first. When the motor show was moved to Birmingham from Earl's Court there was a huge chorus of complaint: such transplantation was 'bound' to be a disaster. (In fact it was a howling success, easily breaking all the old attendance records in London.) London staged the Olympics in 1948 – and if we are hosts in the future they'll be in London again. Naturally.

More serious are the social and economic inequalities which cement metropolitan privilege. For decades recessions in Britain have seen cruel-to-be-kind men in Whitehall deciding they must deflate the economy and pulling the levers whereby mass unemployment is inflicted on Scotland, Wales and the North. Only in the 1970s did a few London boroughs experience the 10 per cent unemployment rates which had long been commonplace in Northern Ireland and all too frequent in the North. A great hue and cry followed. London must be saved. The Location of Offices Bureau had to redirect itself. Massive discriminatory shifts in the rates burden were ordained to help the capital. The necessity for inner-city relief was suddenly discovered and the lion's share of the funds pumped towards London. Throughout all this unemployment in London remained by far the lowest of any major British city and the capital simultaneously experienced a massive tourist boom which left the regions untouched.

Nobody outside London needs to be told things like this. They may not know the details of their disadvantage, but they know the fact of it in their bones. A man who lives in, say, the North-East may not be able to tell you exactly how much greater than a Londoner's are his chances of being unemployed; of his wife dying in childbirth; of his children failing to reach the age of five; of his being working class; of (which is different) his being paid less; or of his dying sooner. But, if he is at all typical, he will know some of these things vaguely, will often feel inferior in his 'provincial' backwardness, and, in a rather defeated way, will feel that his inequality is almost 'natural' too. It was this sense of 'naturalness' that the anti-London rebels wished most of all to challenge, this feeling of defeat they wished to change. Whatever their demerits, it is difficult entirely to rejoice in their defeat. London's over-privilege has, moreover, grown with its own demographic decline. This decline was slow but apparent through the 1940s and 1950s, but has recently accelerated greatly. In the 1960s the process was largely concealed by a high birth-rate and the inflow of half a million Commonwealth immigrants into London. (In 1971 over 40 per cent of all our Commonwealth immigrants were living there.) The fallen birth-rate and the cutting of the immigrant flow have, in the 1970s, dramatically revealed the underlying erosion of London's population, now dropping at a smooth annual rate of around 75 000. (Nor is it true that London is simply relocating – the South-East is losing population at an almost equal rate.) Not, of course, that these facts have sunk in. In 1977, during one of the periodic crises of the *Evening Standard* one printers' union leader was heard to declare that a city of eight million *had* to have two evening papers. But in that year London had dropped below seven million. . . . Today it barely tops six and three-quarter million. London privilege may have been more defensible in the 1930s when nearly one Englishman in four lived there. It is more difficult now that less than one in seven does.

The Celtic nationalists, like the hedgehog, knew one big thing: that it would take nothing less than the direct assertion of political power to change such enduring inequalities. But the nationalists have been beaten almost out of sight. The new prime minister sits for Finchley and, London chauvinism aside, she owes her position quite particularly to the huge swing to her in the capital. The 20-seat swing between the parties here made all the difference between a slim and a comfortable majority. London, in a word, has won again – heavily.

There are, though, two possible reasons why this victory may not endure. One is the simple fact that third parties always prosper most under Tory governments. For the Liberals this amounts to almost an iron law, but it was also under the Tory government of 1970–4 that the Welsh and Scottish nationalists witnessed their most dramatic growth. Given a Tory government which tramples on all hopes of devolution and reinforces every stereotype of London rule, they could rise again. It seems a slim hope, though. It's difficult to see Plaid Cymru ever quite overcoming its referendum thrashing and there will be no second North Sea oil excitement to boost the SNP.

The second possibility is that Labour may become the *de facto* regional party of the North and the Celts. Undoubtedly 1979 has given it a big push in that direction. Labour has been virtually wiped out in southern England (outside London), where it took only 7 out of 154 seats. Even the 41 seats out of 92 it gained in London will, it is safe to predict, never be repeated. For London may have fallen far from its 124 seats of 1945 but it is still (surprise, surprise) massively over-represented – far more than Scotland or Wales ever were. In anything remotely resembling a fair redistribution London will lose 15–20 seats. Given that most of the rotten boroughs are Labour-held, the result will be a good dozen Labour losses. Labour could find itself pushed into ever greater reliance upon its Celtic and northern bastions, gradually taking up the cudgels of 1979's defeated rebels to become a more powerful anti-London party than the nationalists could ever be.

This is possible – but a glance at the Labour elite suggests it's deeply unlikely. Like their Tory counterparts Labour candidates compete fiercely for the luxurious convenience of a London seat. Finding these harder and harder to come by, the Labour sections of the metropolitan intelligentsia and professional classes simply go searching for a seat in the provinces, regarded, for the most part, as a sort of necessary inconvenience. The result is a great bevy of unshakeably metropolitan barristers, lecturers and media men sitting, anomalously, for Durham or Sheffield or Swansea.

Beyond this, of course, Labour does still recruit some of its provincial representatives from the local grass-roots. But these tend to divide into two parts. First, there is the dull, older, lobby-fodder of trade union MPS. Such men are moderately likely to remain quite attached to their regional grass-roots – but they seldom, if ever, make it to the front benches. Second, there are the young provincial bright boys who make it to parliament. But that is the whole point – 'make it': 'making it' means moving to London. For many of these recruits the aspiration to become sophisticated metropolitans themselves is quite as important a part of their general upward mobility as becoming an MP at a young age ever was – the two things go hand in hand. By the time they make it to the front benches it is most unlikely that there will be much real sense of provincial rootedness to them. The thing that most people now remember about Tony Crosland's death was that he asked for his ashes to be scattered in the waves off Grimsby. A mark of such real attachment to a provincial con-stituency was such an honourable exception to the general rule that it was accounted striking, even eccentric.

On the whole, though, the most striking thing about the attach-ment of the Labour elite to the regions they represent is their disinclination actually to live there. Wilson sits for Huyton but when he's not a London resident he's most likely to be found in the Scilly Isles. Foot sits for Ebbw Vale but lives in Hampstead. Hattersley romances about his Yorkshire roots and sits for Sparkbrook – but his celebrated jogging is actually done in Highgate. Benn represents Bristol, but his children graced Holland Park comprehensive school. Perhaps most striking of all was Callaghan. When, in recent months, things were going ill for him he was wont to threaten retirement to his Sussex farm. No one bothered to ask why Cardiff wasn't 'home' when he'd represented it for thirty-four years. . . .

A mere glance at this elite is enough to tell one where its heart lies. In the last analysis – and usually long before – it is not with the anti-metropolitan rebels. On this, surely, the nationalists were right: only a regional or national party without ambitions beyond its 'province' can be relied upon to fight for regional or national interests. First the Liberals, then Labour, and, for a while, the Tories under Heath took up the cause of home rule. None of them really meant it and devolution only got put on to the agenda when the nationalists put it there. A regional or national party fights for its particular interest because it has no alternative if it is to survive. The other parties will always find an alternative in the end. What odds now that the Tories will forget Heath's original pledge of devolution? Or that Labour will have forgotten Callaghan's by 1984? Some things *don't* change. London rules OK.

8

Let the Bland Lead the Bland*

Ralf Dahrendorf, addressing a seminar in Oxford last year, threw out the question as to whether any Western government would ever again be brought down over the issue of unemployment. The last few years, he pointed out, had seen governments happily returned to power in Italy, France and Germany despite record levels of unemployment in every case. (Labour's subsequent defeat in Britain hardly dents his case. Victory went to those who promised an even tougher, cruel-to-be-kind attitude to unemployment.) The students at the seminar stared blankly at Dahrendorf's question and quickly pushed on to more theoretical ground. Unemployment was a fact of life, an act of God. And, actually, rather boring.

This scene recurred to me a week ago as I went round the Hayward Gallery's recent exhibition of *engagé* contemporary photography. The exhibition was dominated by the work of the Hackney Flashers, a feminist photography group. There was much stirring stuff on the need for nursery schools, about women's oppression and their relentless trivialisation by the world of cosmetic and detergent ads. It was all very effective, if sometimes a little self-indulgent – the worst offence being a portentous little placard asking, in *New Left Review* language, what it might be to define a practice of feminist socialist photography. Or, perhaps, a feminist photographic socialism – I forget.

It was only after this and a brief but intriguing section on blacks in Britain that one came, at the back of the hall, to a section on mass unemployment today. It simply halted one in one's tracks – the gaunt images of boarded-up factories, the silhouettes of rusting pit-heads

---

* First published in *New Society*, 2 August 1979.

and, above all, the telling, timeless faces in the dole-queues and streets. A careful calculation on a mounted board showed that even if one discounted 200 000 of the unemployed as unemployable, the number of workdays lost due to unemployment last year (over 307 million) was thirty-four times greater than those lost due to strikes (9 million).

Suddenly the feminist images one had just seen faded to insignificance. That section had included pictures of women at work, secretaries with their heads bowed symbolically over their typewriter as powerful male figures held centre stage. Here, though, were labour-exchange scenes where pert young women dealt, seated and impassive, with steel-workers who stood, hoping for work after five years on the dole. Men (one could see the thought in both minds) 'old enough to be her father'. The point now seemed just that these young women, heads bowed or not, had jobs; that their sisters bent, drudge-like over washing-machines had modern appliances; that nothing Daz, Revlon and Jimmy Young could do to you mattered very much compared to the simpler devastation of worklessness. There was no need for placards asking how a socialist photographic practice might be defined. Such clever-clever pretension would, indeed, have been an insult. Anyway, the faces of the workless – men and women, black and white, young and old – told it all.

Now, clearly something rather remarkable has happened if the issue of mass unemployment can be elbowed aside by the trendier politics of personal experience and consciousness (feminine, black or gay). That this order of priorities should exist even on the left goes a long way to explain the currently rather blasé attitude of Messrs Thatcher, Joseph and Hoseltine as they prepare to wield a joyful knife against public-sector jobs. Unemployment, it seems, simply doesn't matter so much any more.

This comes as a considerable jolt to those of us brought up amidst a post-war consensus which saw the dole queue as, short of war, the greatest evil our society could inflict upon its members. We imbibed, if not with our mother's milk, at least with our National Health orange juice, the strong belief that governments – of whatever complexion – would 'never again' tolerate the miseries of the 1930s. If we all agreed on one thing after 1945 it was that we had put Jarrow for ever behind us.

Yet here we are with unemployment at $1\frac{1}{2}$ million – that is, allowing for our system's chronic under-counting, already 2 million in real terms; a figure which, on benign estimates, is expected to double over the next ten years or, on more pessimistic estimates (those of Clive Jenkins, for example), to go far higher still; and, currently, a government which seems not disinclined to add its own little push to help matters along. For – one hears the argument on all sides – governments can now get away with this. A new political wisdom, a new social *Realpolitik*, stalks abroad: provided a majority remains in work and its real income goes on rising, it may now be electorally acceptable to allow the devil to take the hindmost. Because we don't really care as much about unemployment as once we did. But why should things have changed so much?

The stock answer – that a more generous unemployment benefit has taken most of the sting out of unemployment – won't really do. One doesn't need to starve to death on the dole now, it's true (even in the 1930s that seldom happened). But it's pretty miserable trying to raise a family on supplementary benefit and the loss of confidence and self-respect suffered by the workless in a work-ethic society have not diminished. The view that unemployment is no longer a hateful condition is not one I have heard articulated by anyone actually unemployed. It is a view one hears most from those in secure jobs which, should the need arise, they would fight like cornered tigers to retain. (Much the same applies to those who argue, well-meaningly, that 'We must teach people to realise that the work ethic is a curse, that there need be no stigma attached to not working'. Invariably, one finds, they identify with the 'we' rather than the 'people'. *They* will be actively employed changing the hearts and minds of the workless while they teach them basket-weaving or communal mushroom farming.)

Perhaps the beginning of wisdom is to acknowledge that not that much has changed. In 1935, after four years of unemployment averaging 2½ million, a Right-wing government was overwhelmingly re-elected. Jarrow may have haunted the conscience of later decades but it didn't make much impact on the huge majority voting for Baldwin then. There was no reason to believe that peacetime Britain would see anything other than a succession of hard-faced Conservative governments winning one comfortable election victory after another.

The post-war consensus was just that – post-*war*. It was only after six years of wartime full employment that a majority came to regard the 1930s as a retrospective nightmare – which they were determined not to have to dream again. The precondition of the post-war consensus was not the Depression but the *War*.

Moreover, the consensus was always something of a fraud. After 1945 the permanent arms economy and the beneficent effects for world trade of the new American imperium together produced a full-employment economy without government having to do much besides. Politicians (of all stripes), being politicians, naturally ascribed the labour market's happy new era to the successful operation of their own policies. The belief that they had held at bay the returning tide of Depression by their own sagacity and de-termined humanitarianism did wonders for the self-regard of the political elite but it should not, perhaps, have fooled an electorate familiar with the tale of King Canute. Now that the conditions of the international economy have so decisively changed we should not be so surprised to see the Great Panjandrum of the post-war consensus evaporate like the mist – for it was always largely myth.

Some things have changed, though. Today's fatalism is, surely, powerfully affected by there being little real sense of an acceptable alternative. In its own way this is rather surprising. In the 1930s large numbers of intellectuals, repulsed by the evident failures of capita-lism, confidently viewed the USSR as providing a workable and superior alternative; this despite the horrors of collectivisation, starvation in the Soviet countryside and the Moscow Trials. Today none of these horrors exist, the Soviet standard of living is enormously higher (the East German one is actually higher than ours), and all the Soviet-bloc countries are desperately worried not by unemployment but by severe labour shortages. The regard in which this alternative model is held by Western intellectuals has, however, declined *pari passu* with its relative success.

In effect this has meant that critics of capitalism's current crisis have very little to offer at all seriously in its place – the attempts by the new radical movements of the last decade to define their own alternatives have never got beyond a formless Utopianism. Accordingly, neither revolutionary socialism nor the Alternative Society (communal mushroom farming again) have much following among the unemployed. There is, indeed, no sign of any movement threatening the system by expressing the collective grievances of the unemployed – no Jarrow marchers this time. Altogether more pre-sent are movements (the National Front, the Rastas) expressing conflicts *between* the groups under greatest threat of worklessness.

Such movements confuse and weaken the general political impact of unemployment and are, accordingly, attributed by some to the Machiavellian cleverness of the capitalist system. The opposite is the truth: they are a manifestation of the fact that capitalism is making a very poor job of the brutal house-cleaning its system periodically requires. The 'point' of a depression, after all, is to restore profit levels by lowering wage costs. This is best done by kicking large numbers of older, more expensive, less energetic (and probably more trouble-some), workers out of their jobs and replacing them by younger, cheaper labour which is wet behind the ears when it comes to union rights and which energetically undermines the general level of wages. If this prescription were followed employers would be eagerly enrolling large numbers of women, blacks and school-leavers at low rates of pay. In fact the very opposite is happening and it is precisely these groups on to whom the maximal incidence of unemployment has been unloaded. The reason why this is happening remains obscure. (At first sight it would seem to be a tribute to the unionised power of those still in work – but comparable trends are visible in countries like Italy and France where the unions are notoriously weak.) Whatever the reason the political results are different from that of the 1930s crisis. The unemployed male young are allowed to dissipate their energies in ethnic strife on the streets while the women unemployed become, happily, invisible by staying at home. Either way they are, in the end, quite easily ignored.

Paradoxically, the implication of all this is that anyone who believes the current public tolerance of high unemployment can continue indefinitely may be making a very large mistake indeed. If capitalism makes a hash even of its own purgative processes then the outlook for the system as a whole is hardly very bright – and, indeed, most long-range unemployment forecasts already reflect this fact. If these prove right then a crisis incomparably greater than that of the 1930s is in store for us. It is worth remembering that in that crisis those states with large colonial empires (Britain, Belgium, Holland, Portugal and France) were able to fall back within their imperial trading blocs and avoid the worst. The 'worst' was what the non-imperial states suffered: in the US unemployment hit 25 per cent and in Germany, at Hitler's accession, there were six million unemployed. Compared to that we hardly had a Depression. It goes without very much saying that our vulnerability now to the cold winds of the international economy is far greater than it was then.

Thus, if we take seriously the estimates of three, four and five million unemployed in the Britain of the 1990s (and there is no reason not to take them seriously, save for an illusory present comfort), two things become apparent. First, we have no national experience of what so great a crisis might be like and what its political results might be. Present unconcern may evaporate as easily as the old post-war consensus did. And second, long before such trends peaked, unemployment would be heavily visited upon the politically important labour market core (white adult male married men and children) which is currently still relatively well-protected. What experience we have suggests that things begin to change quite sharply if this core group is at all badly hurt. All of which may seem a somewhat harsh exericse in thinking about the unthinkable. The problem is, though, that the unemployment we already *have* is unthinkable and the current response is, accordingly, not to think about it. Blandness in the face of present suffering is blindness in the face of the future.

9

The Selling of the EEC*

The year 1979 – when Britain first elected its Euro-MPs – may yet prove more significant as the year in which British opinion turned, finally and decisively, against the whole European connection. Not only have seven years of membership failed quite remarkably to consolidate a conservative public opinion behind the new status quo, but the trend is clearly the other way. The polls show a 5:2 majority believing that membership has been harmful to Britain; and an increasingly large group who are unwilling to accept the argument that since we are in we simply have to stay in.

Thus, on the eve of the abortive Dublin EEC summit, ITV pollsters asked voters what we should do if we failed to gain a satisfactory reduction in Britain's budget contribution. They found 15 per cent who wanted us to obstruct the workings of the EEC, and 9 per cent wanting to block them completely. The largest group (40 per cent) were for simply getting out entirely. Only 29 per cent said we should do what we are in fact doing – stay in on present terms. This only four years after a referendum in which 67 per cent voted for membership on those self-same terms. Seldom, if ever, can there have been so swift and great a falling-off.

That ITV poll made front-page headlines in *Le Monde*. But it was impossible to find in the pages of the British press. The only respectable explanation for this curious fact is that public hostility to the EEC is hardly news in Britain. Edward Heath, after all, negotiated our entry in June 1971, with the polls showing a 59:23 per cent majority against such a move. There was still a 47:36 per cent plurality against entry when the Commons ratified it in October 1971.

---

* First published in *New Society*, 10 January 1980.

Thereafter, feeling against entry remained remarkably constant. Even in June 1975, when the electorate was casting a huge 2:1 Yes vote, polls showed that voters still thought (by 51 to 40 per cent – including a third of all Yes voters) that we had been wrong to enter in the first place. Indeed, apart from the short bursts of (well-orchestrated) euphoria, which have greeted the recurrent announcements of 'successful negotiations' or 'renegotiations', the normal posture of British public opinion towards the EEC has, for more than a decade now, been one of routine dislike.

On the other hand, if our EEC membership has never really enjoyed the electorate's full-hearted consent nor has it – at least until now – excited their full-hearted discontent. If the EEC was seldom popular, it was also an issue of low political salience. Voters were always conscious of their own large ignorance of a subject which was, in any case, debated in abstract terms ('Sovereignty', 'being a good European') which lacked any sense of political immediacy. Anti-EEC feeling was, accordingly, general and diffuse – but not deep. It was this very 'soft-centredness' which made the anti-Market cause so vulnerable to the repeated media blitzes mounted on the occasion of each fresh diplomatic initiative, 'breakthrough' or 'triumph'.

The strength of the pro-EEC lobby resided in a quite opposite configuration. Although its popular appeal was always limited, its cause was progressively adopted and then unwaveringly supported by the strategic elites which stand at the centre of British political society: the major party leaderships, the whole of the press, key sections of the bureaucracy (especially the Foreign Office) and, most important of all, the City.

In the end the City's historic dominance over British industrial capital ensured that the business community as a whole rallied behind the cause, even though for many of its members EEC entry was an act of virtual hara-kiri. Few businessmen were more vocal in support of the pro-EEC cause than Lord Stokes of British Leyland, whose career and company alike were swiftly overtaken by a ruinous inrush of Fiats, Renaults and Volkswagons.

With all the central blocs of the Establishment thus rallied to the pro-EEC cause, the issue quickly took on familiar class tones. Indeed, the class alignment soon became sharper on this issue than on any other, with middle-class Labour supporters rallying to the Jenkins–

Williams banner on the pro side, while working-class Tories found their natural leaders (Powell, Paisley, the National Front) within the anti-EEC camp.

Leadership of the resistance to EEC membership naturally devolved upon those fringe figures and organisations which speak for the 'out' groups in British society. The result was an unholy alliance of antis: the National Front and the Communist Party; the Labour left, the TUC and Powell; Paisley and the SDLP; the SNP and Plaid Cymru. The only consistent principle forming this alliance was that all parties to it had (or wanted to have) large working-class followings and were thus anti-Establishment.

Hence the near-hysteria with which pro-Marketeers originally resisted the notion of a referendum. Defeat in that would have been a far more thorough and alarming blow to the Establishment than any mere Labour-over-Conservative victory could ever be. The antis could only win by galvanising a great united tide of working-class populism directly against all the key elites in British society. Even the possibility was very frightening; by implication a great deal more than the EEC cause was threatened.

It didn't happen. Perhaps oddly, the best understanding of what did happen may be gained from reflection on an American parallel, the strange electoral career of Richard Nixon. Under 'normal' conditions Nixon's cause — like that of EEC entry here — was not a winner. He lost to John Kennedy in 1960, lost again in California in 1962, and scraped into office in 1968 by a hair's breadth and on a minority vote only after abdication, assassination and sheer fixing had removed the three leading Democrat contenders from the race. Then, in 1972, this routine loser manufactured the largest landslide in US history.

The result was obtained by an awesome array of electoral advantages: the exploitation of office, the support of a united business community (and Right-wing labour leaders); a huge superiority in campaign funds, enabling the Nixon forces to stage a crushing media blitz; a popular vice-president (Agnew); a well-staged diplomatic 'triumph' over Vietnam; and, of course, dirty tricks. Nixon's hapless opponent, McGovern, had all the best arguments — he cried foul over the Watergate bugging and pointed out the hollow nature of the Vietnam triumph — but it was no good. He was successfully depicted by Nixon as a dangerous extremist from whom the country had to be saved – a judgement in which the (overwhelmingly friendly) press concurred.

We know the rest. Agnew, among others, was soon on trial and discredited. McGovern was proved right about Watergate. The 'triumph' of Vietnamisation simply unravelled in no time at all. Nixon, the lost leader, was left only with the legitimacy bestowed by the landslide of 1972. It did him no good at all, indeed probably made things worse. To recall 1972 was to goad voters to even greater fury by reminding them of how successfully they had been taken for a ride – by someone they'd never *really* liked anyway.

The 1975 referendum here proceeded in somewhat similar fashion. The pro-EEC forces had much the same advantages: office; more popular leaders; the support of a united business community and Right-wing labour leaders; and a huge (125-fold) superiority in funds, enabling them to stage a crushing media blitz (they outspent the antis by a factor of three in press advertising, a factor of nine in polling, a factor of 42 in television publicity). And they too had their diplomatic 'triumph' – the Wilson–Callaghan renegotiation to secure the 'right terms'. Benn was cast as McGovern – a Yes vote was the only way to 'save' the country from him.

A united and vociferous pro-EEC press concurred. When Benn claimed that EEC imports were costing British jobs, the *Mirror* reported the speech in two front-page leaders headed LIES, MORE LIES and THOSE DAMNED STATISTICS and THE MINISTER OF FEAR. It was also the *Mirror* which provided a double-page spread of Marje Proops with her two grandchildren headed THESE ARE THE TWO MAIN REASONS WHY I SHALL VOTE YES. The *Sun* led with SACK BENN while the *Daily Mail* threatened NO COFFEE, WINE, BEANS OR BANANAS, TILL FURTHER NOTICE if we voted No. The *Telegraph, Times* and *Express* were barely more restrained. No single major paper supported the antis.

Dirty tricks? Well, perhaps not quite – though a great deal was done which would never have been tolerated in a general election. The ballot paper was headed with a reminder of the government's success in renegotiations and a 'positive' form of question chosen. The government spent taxpayers' money to circularise every household in the country with its pamphlet, *Britain's New Deal in Europe*. Many large companies (Marks & Spencer, GKN, Wimpeys, Rank-Hovis-McDougal) called on their employees to vote Yes – GKN telling them that 'our futures and our families' wellbeing' was at risk if they didn't. Only the TV authorities stood against the general tide, resisting the bitter arguments of Sir Con O'Neill (the chairman of Britain Into Europe) that his side should have the bulk of broadcasting time on the ground that the government and most MPs were pro-EEC.

Again, we know the rest. In the heroes of the Yes campaign – Thorpe, Wilson and Heath – we now have not one but three lost leaders (though only one has been on trial). The diplomatic triumph of renegotiation has unravelled as quickly and comprehensively as anything Kissinger achieved in Vietnam. Benn was quite right about the lost jobs. All that's left is the sheer fact of the referendum landslide of 1975 – and soon it may not be very clever to remind voters too much of that.

For things have changed. The days when a media blitz could manufacture even a temporary pro-EEC majority are probably over. The tissue has become more salient and less abstract. Few readers of even the popular press are ignorant of the fact that we are paying over £1 billion a year to our generally richer partners. This time there is no diplomatic 'triumph' in sight. Moreover, attention is currently riveted on the famous £1 billion. It is not yet generally realised that the scale of our budget contribution is still building up, and will soon be far higher. Nor is it yet realised that the budget is a minor issue, compared to the fact that EEC membership has transformed our trade surplus with the EEC into a £3 billion annual deficit.

What we are buying with our pricey membership fee is our own industrial ruin, as British companies and jobs sink beneath a tidal wave of imports. The problem is, though, that even in the decade since we entered there has been a quite irreversible shift in our trade flows. Moreover, our special trading relationships with the old Commonwealth have gone for ever. However unsatisfactory our EEC membership now is, it really is true now, even if it wasn't in 1975, that simply removing ourselves from the EEC is not a very happy solution either.

This is what makes the political implications of our present situation so hard to assess. Almost certainly the EEC will remain deeply unpopular with a majority of the British electorate even if, as seems likely, they will not vote to leave it in the crunch. A good part of the problem is that it is now widely realised that the pro-marketeers, including virtually all the 'moderate' and 'decent' elements in British public life, sold the electorate a false bill of goods. This helps create the mood of deep, grumbling resentment and virtually guarantees that the Labour Party will stay wedded to an (increasingly unrealistic) policy of immediate exit from the EEC. The same mood means that the Tory Party will probably treat the issue like law and order; something you bash on about to popular acclaim, but never actually 'solve'. As for Benn, right though he was, it seems unlikely that his reputation will ever recover from the media-bashing he received in '75 any more than McGovern's did from '72.

With all these reputations on the line – and with the press itself having played a cardinal role in the great con of 1975 – it is perhaps too much to hope that we will manage to discuss the EEC issue soberly and seriously now. But it would be nice if any discussion could manage without pictures of Marje Proops's grandchildren. And however embarrassed the British press may be by its past behaviour, it would be nice not to have to read *Le Monde* to find out what is happening here.

10

Some British Might-Have-Beens*

One of the more notable trends of 1980 has been the sudden emergence of a new genre, history-by-hindsight. The Hollywood version of this is to be found in films such as *The Final Countdown* (where the Americans refight Pearl Harbor with the help of a nuclear aircraft-carrier). The literary version is represented by books such as John Grigg's *1943* (how we won the war by launching D-Day a year early) or Hugh Thomas's colossus of wishful thinking, *An Unfinished History of the World*. Professor Thomas has probably secured a lasting place for this work by his remarkable refusal of the £7000 Arts Council prize awarded to him, on the grounds that he did not hold with state patronage of the arts.

I hasten to add that personally I can only revere a man of such awesome consistency. Since, however, the Arts Council now have seven grand burning a hole in their pocket and since my own views on state patronage are, happily, a formless mess, I hereby submit my own rather more parochial *Unfinished History of Britain*.

*   *   *

Looking back to 1945, it is not easy now to realise how bold Attlee's government was. Its critical perception was that while the electorate believed we had won the war, the truth was that we had only just survived it. The latter insight implied the need for sweeping retrenchment, the former provided the popular will and confidence necessary to make bold measures acceptable. Attlee set the tone with his firm pronouncement in August 1945 that his government had neither the inclination nor the means to fund a nuclear weapons programme.

---

* First published in *New Society*, 3 July 1980.

Churchill was aghast but, as he later admitted in his memoirs, found himself impotent. 'The hunger for peace, the joy of victory, and the popular revulsion over Nagasaki and Hiroshima the week before all conspired against us. Had the matter been dealt with responsibly as a high security affair, the first public discussion occurring only after we had procured the bomb, then Britain might have become a nuclear military power. But Attlee knew as well as I that if the case against a nuclear bomb was made public before we had one, the cause was lost.' Even Churchill quickly gave up the thankless task of trying to sell the bomb to a public more interested in rapid demobilisation than a fresh mobilisation of military effort.

It is clear, in hindsight, that Attlee laid a further trap for Churchill over decolonisation. Prior to 1947 the premier contended himself with homilies about 'a war fought for freedom' and the general need for Britain to look at a non-imperial future. In the debate on the India (Independence) Bill Churchill, as Attlee had anticipated, rose to the bait. 'India has always been the heart of the matter', thundered Churchill. 'If we are now to discard this very jewel of empire, what rationale can there be for the preservation of our wider possessions?' Attlee's famous deadpan reply was, however, the real thunderbolt. 'My honourable friend is, as so often, quite right. We shall, in answer to his query, shortly lay before this House bills providing for the independence of Malaya and a number of our African and Caribbean dependencies.' Again, once the word was out there was no going back.

The granting of Malayan independence in 1948 was accompanied by a peculiarly hypothetical public debate over Attlee's assertion that Britain was thereby pre-empting the possibility of some form of military 'emergency' in the peninsula. Since no such 'emergency' took place it is difficult for the historian to place much weight on this assertion. Rather, in retrospect, the capital importance of this move would seem to have lain in the abandonment of the Singapore base and the complete retreat of British forces East of Suez.

There is no reason to doubt the sincerity of Attlee's public explanation: that it made no sense to keep troops east of Suez once the Asian colonies had been abandoned, and that the large defence savings thus effected would enable the housing programme to reach its 1950 target of 350 000 houses a year (which it duly did). The American reaction was, however, strong and immediate. Furious that Britain should thus withdraw from the defence of the 'free world' in Asia, the Truman Administration withdrew its support from sterling, forcing Attlee to devalue the £ by 50 per cent to $2.00. In the long run, of course, this devaluation was to underwrite the massive export successes of the 1950s but it was not immediately understood as the positive move it undoubtedly was. Wilson and Bevan resigned in protest from the Cabinet, Wilson attacking the Chancellor (Gaitskell) with his famous 'pound in your pocket' speech, while Bevan demanded that 'the Germans pay the full cost of peace' (by a heavy rearmament programme) and that Britain secure its independence from the US by the construction of its own nuclear weapons.

Reeling under these American and intra-party pressures, Attlee had only one way to move. Announcing that 'Our future lies apart from America and beyond an empire', he took the initiative in forming the EEC. He swept in the dubious French, Danes and Norwegians along with the mere enthusiastic Irish, Italians and Benelux countries, largely on the promise of the immediate abolition of food rationing in the UK to enlarge the market for imported agricultural goods. From the start Britain inevitably dominated the EEC – she had by far the strongest industrial base, enjoyed the trading benefits of an under-valued currency and provided a general political leadership to her diverse and loosely knit partners.

Thereafter Attlee lost his magic touch. The abolition of the House of Lords (1949) was followed by an unseemly wrangle over the premier's rejection of the boundary commissioners' report (which had threatened to produce a Tory parliamentary majority despite a Labour electoral plurality). In the event Gaitskell's smooth succession and his victory in the 1951 election saw no real change of course. It did, however, prompt Churchill to resign at last: clearly, if the Conservatives were to compete they too needed a youthful leader. To Eden's chagrin the party passed over his claims and picked Macmillan.

The outbreak of the Korean War led to a dramatic worsening of Anglo-American relations. Gaitskell's determined policy of non-involvement – it being absurd to go to war in Asia now that Britain had retreated from east of Suez – was broadly popular at home but Eisenhower, under pressure from Senator McCarthy, let slip the phrase that Britain was 'not only pink but yellow'. Gaitskell followed Attlee's example and again played the European card. Announcing that 'our future lies neither in Korea nor Wisconsin; a thousand years of history bind us to Europe', he led a successful campaign for EEC enlargement. His claim that only a 'bigger Europe' could stand up against Russia on its own was, perhaps, somewhat spurious – the Russians welcomed the formation of a neutral bloc in Europe, after all, and tensions between the eastern and western halves of Europe noticeably relaxed. It was, none the less, a popular selling point at home and among the new EEC members (Greece, Turkey, Sweden and Iceland).

The year 1954 saw the granting of independence to all the remaining African colonies except Rhodesia. It was none too soon – in Kenya, for example, the newly independent government had to move quickly to head off the so-called 'Mau Mau' movement. Even so, Kenyan independence was achieved only despite a fierce (though brief) settler backlash – which was why Gaitskell backed away from the problem of Rhodesia. Lacking Attlee's cool nerve and moral certainties, Gaitskell recoiled with burnt fingers from the fuss over Kenya. It was thus that the seeds of his ill-fated Suez adventure (1956) and consequent electoral defeat were sown. Finding himself increasingly at odds with his own party, then with Nasser, and then with just about everyone, Gaitskell displayed a disastrous vein of stiff-necked stubbornness. On the day before he was finally forced to pull British troops back from the Canal Zone he made his ill-timed declaration that he would 'fight, fight, and fight again'. Nemesis followed and within three months Macmillan was in power.

Macmillan moved swiftly to repair relations with Washington by sponsoring the entry into the EEC of West Germany – America's European 'favourite son'. It was a shrewd gamble. Britain was by now so far the dominant industrial power in Europe that she could afford the risk of German competition. The Germans, on the other hand, were by now so anxious to enter the booming free-trade area that they were willing to pay Macmillan's price – a series of huge British takeovers (Morris Motors' takeover of Volkswagen, ICI's of Bayer, GEC's of Siemens, etc.). The result was an accelerating European boom led by the new Anglo-German partners. Inevitably, this caused trouble with the French who found themselves badly squeezed between the joint power of London and Bonn.

Meanwhile Macmillan had weathered his first major crisis – the Rhodesian rebellion led by Ian Smith. The Colonial Secretary, McLeod, dealt brusquely with Smith (whom he described, dismissively, as 'too clever by half') who surrendered within hours of the arrival of the first British battallions ferried in from Kenya. With Nkomo's victory in the ensuing election Britain granted independence to her last colony. The whole incident – 'a little local difficulty' as Macmillan called it – had taken only a few months but its longer-term significance was that Macmillan now felt free to lend mild support to the cause of Algerian independence.

This brought matters to a head with France. De Gaulle railed furiously at the 'perfidy' of the British, who, he claimed, had eyes only for Algeria's oil and gas. (It is only fair to admit that Britain's earlier support for their cause may indeed have weighed with the post-independence FLN government. Shell and BP certainly got the lion's share of the oil and gas concessions.)

De Gaulle also angrily reasserted the French demand for a common agricultural policy for the EEC, claiming that France was being ground between 'the Saxons and the Anglo-Saxons'. Macmillan loftily turned de Gaulle down with the famous remark that the French 'had never had it so good'. The speech did little for Anglo-French relations, but it helped Macmillan sweep the country in the 1960 election.

Macmillan's eclipse under the weight of an unlucky series of scandals a few years later brought to power a determined new Labour government under Crosland. The achievements of the ensuing ten years are perhaps too recent for proper historical judgement to be possible. Undoubtedly, though, Britain would be coping far less well with today's recession and energy crisis had Crosland not pushed through so vigorously his programmes of regional development, railway expansion and the huge buildup of the coal industry. In retrospect his government towers in stature above its ill-fated (but blissfully short-lived) Labour successors under Wilson and Benn. Their collapse in the wake of the Thorpe trial and the Concorde fiasco respectively ushered in the present Conservative Administration under Chataway. It is still too soon to know how far this government will fulfil the promise of Macmillan's progressive Toryism at home (though its abolition of tax relief on mortgages and the ending of the charitable status of public schools are encouraging signs). Quite possibly, though, its main achievements will lie in the smoothing of Anglo-American relations. Certainly, Morris Motors' rescue takeover of Chrysler and ICL's promise to bolster IBM against Japanese competition have done much to earn transatlantic goodwill.

*   *   *

Any 'unfinished' history is, by definition, flawed and the account above is no doubt vulnerable to criticism in that it dwells too much on

the successes of the post-war period, too little on the many disappoint-
ments and wasted opportunities. No doubt one could construct a more
negative narrative centred on the 'what-ifs' and 'might-have-beens'.
But that, of course, would be quite a different sort of history.

11

What's Good for the Midland . . .*

The summer 'silly season' never had much chance this year in the face of the continuing spate of economic disaster news. With dole queues lengthening, bankruptcies up and profits down the economy is still visibly readying itself for worse to come, rather as a ship steadies itself just before its final dive toward the bottom. One welcome result has been the reopening of serious debate over what exactly is happening to the British economy and why so much of current government policy is, perversely, directed in a way which makes things worse rather than better.

There is, after all, no serious dispute over the latter point. It is a fact acknowledged on all sides that industry is being crucified by the murderous combination of high interest rates, a strong pound and a lack of effective protection against the flood of cheap imports. Nor does anyone doubt that the VAT increases have hit the retail trade hard at a time when it was on its knees anyway, or that the main brunt of public expenditure cuts is being felt by the (private) construction industry. Equally, fewer and fewer people are able to understand the government's staunch attachment to the Common Market which seems to have boiled down to a strange affair in which (even after the recent reduction) we pay a still hefty membership fee to belong to a club in which we enjoy the privilege of not being allowed the sell our lamb to the French in return for their being able to bury our farmers under a flood of cheap apples. 'Perverse' is Wynne Godley's word for all this and, in truth, it hardly seems exaggerated. But the question still remains: what on earth is going on and why?

There are several possible answers. A fast-diminishing group is still

---

* First published in *New Society*, 11 September 1980.

willing to accept the government's view which is, roughly, 'we're making things worse and worse so that later on they will get better. Sort of, well, automatically.' A far larger group, encompassing most of the Labour Party and not a few Conservatives too now, holds that Mrs Thatcher is invincibly stupid or – it's a thin line – invincibly mad.

Listening to Mrs Thatcher responding to the news of unemployment over the two million mark, one could understand the gathering strength of this school. 'You can't avoid the consequences of your own action', she said. 'If you pay yourselves more for producing less, there *will* be more unemployment.' One should prepare oneself now for similar statements every time unemployment reaches a new record notch. We are ruled by someone who sees the calamities her policies have helped to produce, not as failures or mistakes, but, incredibly, as self-vindication. The worse the news gets, the more self-righteous she feels and the more 'you' are to blame.

None the less, the madness school is, I think, wrong. The lady never gibbers. She seldom foams. And by no means always does she rave. Nor, in any trivial sense, is she stupid. We have frequently had rule by the stupid (Home, Callaghan and, in some respects, Churchill) and it's not all that bad: such men, knowing their limitations, often listen to advice. What is much worse in Mrs Thatcher's case is that she is, at once, invincibly ignorant and hugely self-important.

In a way you can't blame her. She trained in chemistry and then in law but she became an MP precisely by casting such book-learning to the winds and mouthing instead the rather tired platitudes which went down best with the Tory ladies of Finchley. The fact that these platitudes chimed exactly with her own gut prejudices and that she did her mouthing with an energy that was anything but tired, meant that she became quite a winner. She hammered on with the same backwoods truisms for a few years longer and, hey presto, found herself in the Cabinet. Much encouraged she mouthed on yet further and lo! she became the first woman prime minister. It is no good telling her *now* that her little warmed-over set of half-truths would not get her an A level. They have already passed trials and tests far more important than that, at each stage confirming her own large opinion of herself. One result is that she doesn't know her limitations – or even that she has any at all – and nor, accordingly, does she listen.

Reluctantly, then, one must discard the idea that one can understand what is happening in Britain now by studying what Mrs Thatcher says or thinks. For she is, in a sense, the perfect apparatchik. She doesn't *know* what interests are being advanced through the mediation of her actions. In a fundamental sense she doesn't know what she is doing and she doesn't know that she doesn't know.

A second line of interpretation, favoured by many on the Left, is that the government is deliberately creating mass unemployment in order to break the power and will of organised labour. This view is taken, naturally enough, by proponents of the Glyn and Sutcliffe thesis (propounded in their still seminal *British Capitalism, Workers and the Profits Squeeze*). According to this view British capitalism has been caught in a classically Marxist squeeze between the claims of labour on the one hand and the demands of capital investment on the other, resulting in a steadily falling rate of profit. This crisis can only be solved within the capitalist framework by a forcible diminution of the labour side of the equation. In practice this can only be achieved, as now, by the infliction of mass unemployment in order to produce a cowed, docile and thus, ultimately, cheaper labour force. (Glyn and Sutcliffe would, of course, prefer to solve the crisis by a socialist revolution – though it is not clear how this would, of itself, conjure away the stark contradiction between wage demands and capital investment needs. But that is another matter.)

This interpretation has several advantages. Phrased in only a slightly different vocabulary it commands wide support on the Right as well as the far Left. It is theoretically coherent and it corresponds to many of the known facts. What is more, it corresponds to the known prejudices of many within the government, Mrs Thatcher first and foremost. (Being a 'gut' politician her real dislikes are impossible to hide and it is tolerably clear that she enjoys her revenge for the great strikes of 1972 and 1974.)

But there are problems with such a view. Above all, the workplace power of labour means that unemployment is no longer produced in the classical way – by firms discarding some labour and exacting sharply higher productivity from the rest. Instead, firms keep their labour, or pay through the nose to make even a few redundant, while output and productivity sink. The firm contracts painfully in size and, in the end, simply goes bankrupt. Even many of those who discard labour fast frequently find that their neglect of capital investment in years gone by has left them too exposed to cut-throat international competition to survive once recession removes the easy pickings from the table. The result is the same.

In other words, the government can only wreak its wrath upon the
workers at the cost of ruining large numbers of capitalists – and it is
quite difficult to believe that Mrs Thatcher has deliberately set out to
procure the economic ruin of her own best supporters. In any case, to
pay too much attention to Mrs Thatcher's uninformed prejudices in
the matter is, we have argued, to head down a false trail. More
important, just because the crises of the retail trade and manufacturing industry stand at the centre both of nineteenth-century Marxism
and our current social concerns (because they are such large
employers of labour) does not in itself guarantee that they are
analytically central to what is happening. Indeed, a good case can be
made that these crises, awesome though they are, are still merely a by-
product of a larger process.

Perhaps one should begin by asking, simply, *cui bono?* Who is
actually doing well amidst all this mess? If you glance at the company
profit league tables the answer is deafeningly clear: the oil companies
and the banks. A little further thought suggests that one ought to
leave the former aside as a (very) special case: their position has been
bolstered by huge and repeated revaluations of their oil stocks; they
are the *only* industry to have achieved oligopolistic market control on
a world scale with which to protect their position; and they are just
about the only industry left which can generate all its own capital
investment and thus remain proudly independent of the banks. So it is
the latter we are really talking about – or, more precisely, the financial
sector and the various service industries parasitic upon it.

Who, after all, benefits from high interest rates? Who benefits from
a strong pound? The answer is the same – both these things help
generate large inflows of foreign capital for the banks to manage and
play with, so that even if the home financial market is depressed, their
business still expands. Once you start this litany you can just go on.
Our largest manufacturing company, ICI, has just reported profits
down by over half – but the Midland Bank, only our third largest, is
so flush with funds that it has just decided to buy up Crocker
National, the twelfth largest bank in America. Or compare the
multibillion pound rescue mounted in 1974–7 to save the banks from
the ruinous consequences of the property collapse with the decision to
allow large numbers of industrial lame ducks to go to the wall for the
lack of a fraction of that amount. Perhaps most striking of all, the
government has chosen now – of all possible moments – to give the
banks the thing they have dreamed of for forty years, the abolition of

exchange control. This move is, of course, a further disaster for industry, which desperately needs the funds now flowing happily abroad, but it was greeted, as the *Financial Times* put it, 'with almost hysterical enthusiasm' by the merchant banks. As well it might be when it allows one to go shopping for bargains as big as Crocker National – with over-valued pounds at that, to make your dollar purchases all the cheaper. It's an ill wind . . .

Some members of the government have recently come close to rationalising this situation by talking about industrial exports 'having' to fall in order to 'make room' for larger oil exports – as if there were some predetermined overall figure for exports. But it's not much good looking to the government to explain. It is doubtful if Mrs Thatcher more than very dimly descries the fact that what she lead is, *par excellence*, a bankers' government. Mentally, she's still talking to those Finchley ladies for whom Crocker National is a horse-race run at Aintree. She and they are good Conservatives and probably do think that what is happening is all about 'social discipline' or some such.

Equally, I would not argue that Glyn and Sutcliffe aren't good Marxists. The trouble is they don't seem to be Leninists. For the key perception is surely Lenin's – that of the inevitable long-run supremacy of financial over industrial capital. It's not that the banks *want* to destroy industry any more than Mrs Thatcher wants to. It's just that in hard times it's a matter of first things first. If the bankers can only survive and prosper by pushing industrialists out of the life-boats, well, they're awfully sorry about it but push they will. It's not necessary to believe they are at all hard-faced about this – some of my best friends, I hasten to add, are bankers. It's far more a matter of 'Really regret this, old chap. Nothing personal, y'know – sort of immanent logic of the system. It's all in Lenin, actually. You haven't read him? Look, here's a copy to look at when you make land. If you do make land, that is. What's that? Can't carry a book and swim? Of course all right, of course. I'd be the last one to want to add to your problems. . . .'

12

The Way Elections Work Now*

It has been interesting to watch the ambivalent reactions of British Conservatives to Reagan's triumph. Only the more simple-minded 'social democrats' of the hard Right (Lord Chalfont, Paul Johnson) and monetarist ideologues (Rees-Mogg) have sounded naïvely happy. It is no small tribute to the speed and thoroughness with which Mrs Thatcher has wrought havoc on our economy that, only eighteen months later, a majority of her party are downright fearful (à la Heath) of what an American Administration promising to repeat the Thatcher experience over there may do.

The manner of Reagan's victory, however, has given further encouragement to a much broader band of radical pessimists who regard the modern electoral process as the purest form of lottery. Whatever the case in the past, elections nowadays are, on this view, desperate, last-minute-fluke events, decided by bored and volatile electorates on the basis of capricious circumstance and media trivialisation. Once upon a time, the argument goes, elections really were about issues and principles – and, as such, had a certain dignified predictability about them. Now they don't: the opinion polls soar up and down in response to orchestrated non-events – and fail to get the result right in the end. Democratic decision-making has been overtaken – submerged, even – by the dynamics of advertising and popular fickleness.

There is, perhaps, nothing intrinsically Conservative about this sort of radical pessimism, but equally there is no doubting that its assumptions appeal powerfully to the Conservative mind. Conservatives of all kinds – Michael Foot libertarians or Quintin

---

* First published in *New Society*, 20 November 1980.

Hogg authoritarians – frequently feel an instinctive dislike for sociological investigation of any sort. They are delighted if it can be claimed that the pollsters 'got it wrong', for this seems to preserve the sovereign mysteriousness of human behaviour – their primal escape route from all manner of positivist arguments. Similarly, the notion of mass fickleness and triviality provokes, as any reader of the Crossman Diaries will recall, strong confirmatory feelings among those of self-elected mandarin status.

It is easy to see why the Reagan election is grist to the radical pessimist mill. All year long the polls yawed up and down, most violently in response to the pure media events of the conventions. With a week to go the pollsters were forecasting a close race. Some polls even, briefly, put Carter ahead. Then, in response to the entirely cardboard dramatics of the Great TV Debate and, apparently, the non-news that the Tehran hostages were still not free, Carter's support fell away like a stone in the last few days. The election was supposed to deliver a judgement on such matters as inflation, unemployment, economic decline, and war and peace. Instead – or so one is told – it all came down to Reagan's awesome folksiness and his well-packaged pieties about 'a land placed by God between two oceans' and a 'shining city on a hill'. Faced by this heavy rhetorical artillery Carter's voters simply wavered, broke and ran.

This trivialising view of the electoral process is, I would submit, just plain wrong. Indeed, it is possible to argue that voters now behave in more sophisticated fashion than ever before. Before putting this case, however, let us first admit that elections and election campaigns throughout the Western world have certainly changed. It is not just a matter of television now being central to everything so that nobody goes electioneering on the back of a train any more. It is simply that elections – in the US or Britain, in France or Australia – just ain't what they used to be.

Once upon a time in the 1950s the whole election business had a nice predictable shape. First of all, political opinion was in every sense more stable. Electoral swings were smaller, partisanship (and with it, electoral turnout) was higher, and there was no electoral one-way street in which governments suffered an almost automatic ebbing away of support as soon as they were elected. (It was even possible then to find governments winning seats in by-elections they had not managed to win in the preceding general election – an unheard-of monstrosity nowadays.) Opinion polls, though far more primitive then, were far more reliable. Indeed, what pundits insisted on regarding as the great 'upset' elections of the time – Labour's victory in 1945, Truman's triumph in 1948, de Gaulle's sweep in 1958 – would not have been regarded as upsets at all if people had bothered to notice the polls, which forecast them quite exactly. Moreover, movements of opinion between the contending parties tended to operate in a fairly predictable fashion. Typically, politicians in power contrived to manage a sustained inflationary boom, replete with give-away budgets, in the run-up period to elections. Although most voters remained too stolidly rooted in partisan prejudice to pay much attention to this, a fringe of 'good time' voters could be won over from every social group. Accordingly, this extra burst of affluence produced an across-the-board advantage to the government without affecting the basic partisanship structures within the wider electorate.

This whole arrangement worked markedly in favour of a sitting government getting itself voted back into power. One had to be notably stupid (the 1945–51 Labour government altering the electoral system to its own disadvantage) or notably wicked (the 1959–64 Tory government reeling from one scandal to another) to lose. But if a government was even modestly competent, it got re-elected. From 1932 to 1960 America was ruled unbrokenly by presidents who secured re-election. Tory governments in Britain were re-elected through the 1951–64 period. In Australia Menzies was endlessly re-elected from 1949 to 1966. For politicians in power it was a golden age; their leaders now seem like the great undefeated batsman of heroic cricketing memory. How, nowadays, could one imagine an Adenauer, re-elected endlessly, retiring at 87 as Chancellor and carrying his bat as party leader until the age of 90?

It was only around 1970 that it gradually became clear that the old model of the electoral process wasn't working properly any more. In that year Labour lost power in Britain despite a carefully orchestrated wage-explosion and against the tide of almost all the opinion polls. In February 1974 Heath went down to defeat despite an even larger lead in the opinion polls. In October 1974 Labour faced the electorate after seven continuous months of give-aways (the miners' strike settled, subsidies on food prices, job-subsidies galore, pension increases, etc.). In 1966 this sort of thing had brought Labour a landslide; now it failed to produce even a workable majority. In 1976 Carter beat Ford handily despite polls showing them neck and neck. In 1978 the Right won in France despite polls showing a Left majority. In 1979 Callaghan had all but closed the gap on Thatcher in the polls – but lost heavily all the same. Carter has now suffered an exactly similar fate at Reagan's hands – just a month after Fraser had been returned to power in Australia despite polls showing a Labour majority. Things like this simply did not happen before the 1970s. Since then they have happened all the time.

In retrospect it now seems clear that the 1950s model of the electoral process rested on two conditions that have now largely vanished: steady economic growth and strong political cleavages within the electorate. With the coming of stagflation governments have found that the old pump-priming tactics simply don't work. In all but the strongest economies a pre-election boom will either be unsustainable for the length of time required for it to have much political effect; or it may even have such disastrous consequences that it would be rational for a government to initiate one only if it was convinced that it was going to lose the election anyway, and that it was merely handicapping its opponents by leaving them to clear up the mess. Governments have accepted the logic of this unhappy situation with remarkable fortitude – in the past two years we have seen Messrs Fraser, Carter, Callaghan and Barre all steer head-on into adverse electoral winds, manfully refusing to tack away from harsh austerity policies even as the storm broke. This astonishing reversal of old electoral habits, radical pessimists should note, is clearly based on the assumption that today's electorate is more sophisticated than of yore and more prone to see a pre-election boom as the cynical financial irresponsibility which, in truth, it always was.

The second change – the diminishing power of political cleavages, whether of class, ethnicity, region or religion – is even more fundamental, and is also the key to why opinion polls so frequently get elections results 'wrong' nowadays. The truth is that they don't get them 'wrong', for it was never their job to get them 'right'. Polls are still photographs of moving pictures, after all. If, in the 1950s a poll showed one party with a 3 per cent lead a week before the election, the reason why this result was so often replicated in practice was the underlying stability of opinion. Now that electorates are so notoriously more volatile no still photograph, even one taken very shortly before 'impact', can predict the final trajectory. This is so despite great improvements in polling technique. In the 1950s we were taking excellent pictures of a stationary vehicle with a crude camera; in the

1980s we are using a perfected camera and getting blurred images of a runaway train.

The fact that political behaviour has so largely broken loose from its old sectional moorings does not, however, mean that it has thereby become less rational. Indeed, it would be asserted by some that only with the rise of the politics of issues in the place of the politics of group attachments, have we begun to be rational at all. The appearance of irrationality is, in fact, largely a product of the modern election campaign which flashes a succession of issues and images before the electorate in the hope of achieving as many positive refractions as possible.

Happily, though, all the evidence is that the gyrations of opinion thus produced in the course of a campaign have less and less to do with the actual result. For the best way to predict elections these days is to ignore the campaign-period polls and ask what the fundamental lie of the land was before this last-minute media blitz began. If you focused properly on the depths of unpopularity plumbed by Ford in 1975, Callaghan in 1978 and Carter in 1979, you would quite correctly have predicted the triumph of their respective opponents in all the succeeding elections. Everything suggests that the deep-seated and, dare one suggest, more mature, popular judgements of a government's long-run performance formed around the late-mid-term mark, are what counts nowadays.

To this extent, at least, the radical pessimist case fails: electorates are probably less capricious than ever before in the way they are judging issues on their merits and governments on their records. Unfortunately, that's as far as it goes, for under the rules of the New Model Election it has become truer than ever that oppositions don't win elections but that governments lose them. If there is irrationality in the present system it lies in the fact that electorates seem willing to vote for almost anybody to get rid of what they've had. At the moment the Right are happy because this effect has redounded to the benefit of neanderthal conservatives in a large number of countries. Those who are now rejoicing in the triumph of Thatcher, Fraser or Reagan would do well to remember that the new electoral ground-rules have merely established that hitherto unimaginable political wild men (and women) – of right or left – can now win. Thus a week which began with the triumph of Ronald Reagan has ended with Michael Foot's election as Labour leader here. It is safe to assume both men will perform appallingly, but that's another question . . .

13

How Soft at the Centre?*

It seems tolerably clear that 1981 will see some sort of answer to the political question which has taken up so many editorial inches: whither the Centre? At least (to put the matter bluntly), Roy Jenkins retired from his EEC job yesterday and it is almost universally believed that, with some degree of backing from David Steel, he will announce some large new centrist initiative within the next month or two.

In some senses this will be a great relief. It has been very difficult to maintain a receptive ear over the last year to the continual flow of non-items of no-news on this subject: that Roy Jenkins will not (yet) launch a Centre Party; that Shirley Williams will not (yet) leave the Labour Party; that David Owen will not run for the shadow cabinet; and so on. I long for the day when one of these men or women will stand up and announce, positively: 'I *am* the glittering alternative' or even, to coin a phrase, 'The time is now.'

On the face of it, the time seems yet extremely fair for a centrist initiative. For many years now, polls have shown pluralities, sometimes even majorities, of the electorate willing to plump for what are widely conceived of as centrist positions on a whole range of policies. The likely leaders of such an initiative not only enjoy a very high degree of political visibility, but a large measure of public popularity as well. Moreover (and the two things are linked, of course), they have very powerful backers in the media. Mrs Williams, for example, in order to gain front-page headline treatment in *The Times*, has only to announce that she will not accept the Labour nomination for her old

---

* First published in *New Society*, 18–25 December 1980.

seat – even when, as a matter of fact, it had not been offered to her. There is little doubt that there is a good deal of 'smart money' willing to back the centrists.

Most of all, of course, there is the considerable and probably growing potential of the Liberal vote. It has become almost an iron law of British politics that when Labour is in power the middle classes consolidate behind the Conservatives, but that when the latter are in power they drift disaffectedly towards the Liberals, taking a large fringe of floaters with them.

The result has been a continuous series of Liberal revivals – in 1958, 1962 and 1973. Each of these revivals has taken place under a Conservative government, and each has been magnified by a run of dramatic by-election results. In every case, the subsequent general election has seen some fall-off in Liberal support. But each time the Liberal tide laps a little higher up the beach, so that every next revival has started from a higher base.

At present, with the Conservative government only 18 months old and no by-elections to help, the Liberals already stand at 15 per cent in the polls. All recent history suggests that yet another Liberal revival should be under way by late 1981 or early 1982. The question is simply whether Jenkins *et al.* can catch the tide at the full and whether, this time, they can add a crucial fringe of extra ('social democratic') support to carry the re-formed Centre through the magic 30 per cent barrier needed to win a significant number of seats at an election in 1983 or 1984. And – so the scenario goes – the centrists will then use their crucial block of seats to force proportional representation on their coalition allies, ensuring their large-scale parliamentary presence in perpetuity.

This is all very promising. But the prospects for such an intiative get even better if one accepts that a Tory Party which has moved right under Thatcher and a Labour Party moving left under Foot may evacuate an unusually large space in the centre ground; that a shaving-off of the Labour right wing may further enlargen this space by leaving the Labour rump even more solidly in the hands of the left; that Roy Jenkins, Shirley Williams and the rest probably enjoy the private sympathy of several right-wing trade union leaders; and that the severity of the Thatcher recession is likely to produce a wider and deeper (and quicker?) Liberal revival than ever before. The time is now, all right.

The first problem with all this is that the centrist initiative, if it is to succeed, will have to defeat both history and the political system. Successful arrivals on the parliamentary scene in the past – Liberals, Labour, the ILP, the Communist Party, the Ulster Unionists, Plaid Cymru and the SNP – have all relied heavily or even exclusively on their bases within the Celtic fringes. It is difficult to see today's Centre getting off the ground there. If it's going to make it, I suspect it will have to change all the rules by conquering English suburbia first, and spreading outwards from there.

The Centre will have to start at the centre – and it will have to do so without the benefit of any hard-core 'natural' constituency. The Centre's potential electoral base is undeniably large, but its amorphousness makes it more fertile ground for 'flashflood' movements than for the sustained growth of organised political strength. All this means that the success of the centrist initiative will depend a great deal – unhealthily much – on such imponderable factors as mood, timing, and continuous media support.

This softness of the Centre extends, moreover, to its leadership. If you survey a list made up of Roy Jenkins, David Owen, William Rodgers, Shirley Williams, David Steel and (perhaps) Edward Heath, you realise that the chief-to-Indian ratio is uncomfortably high; or, to change metaphors, this is a team made up exclusively of would-be opening batsmen. Arranging an order of precedence or a consensus will be no easy business. Already the so-called gang of three has split three ways on tactics – Rodgers was elected to the shadow cabinet, but Owen refused to stand, Shirley Williams has refused even to contemplate joining him on the Labour backbenches.

And there could be something peculiarly fragile about the popularity of leaders like these. The one cause they have in common – their strong pro-EEC stance – is now regularly rejected by 70 : 30 majorities in poll after poll. They enjoy a wide but shallow 'good opinion', not the gut loyalty a Thatcher, Foot, Powell or Gwynfor Evans can provoke. In particular, they are only too frequently the Labour politician most favoured by Tories, or vice versa.

In a crunch, this sort of support is useless. No one should know this better than Roy Jenkins (witness the Stechford result after he quit, when the Tories nearly won). Or, *a fortiori*, Mrs Williams. Hertford and Stevenage was precisely the sort of seat – outer London, classless, new town, a large Liberal vote – where a centrist ought to thrive. No doubt many of those Tories and Liberals who voted her out in 1979 are among those telling the pollsters how well they think of her. The fact remains that she lost on one of the largest negative swings seen anywhere in the country.

Most important of all, of course, the new Centre cannot, by any amount of hocus-pocus, get round the fundamental obstacle the old Centre (i.e. the Liberals) have always faced: that in a two-party system, the real question about a third party is simply which of the two big parties it is going to hurt most. The thinly disguised hope of many who fan the flames of such a movement is that, aided by 'social democrat' breakaways, the Centre will hurt Labour most.

If this turned out to be true, so that the real point of a Centre Party was to return a Thatcher government with a majority of several hundred, the game might well be quickly over. The new party, lacking leverage, plausibility or anywhere to go, might collapse. No trade unionist would be seen within a mile of it.

But despite the complete lack of any major Tory adherents to such a centre grouping, the intriguing possibility exists that its effect might be just the opposite. If you examine Labour's postwar electoral successes you find that the party has rested quite heavily on the Trojan horse of Liberal votes. In 1950 Labour held on to power thanks to a high Liberal poll; in 1951 the Liberals collapsed, and the Tories won. In 1964 the Liberals achieved their three million vote target, at last – and Labour sneaked in, despite its own falling share of the vote. As the erosion of the solid Labour vote has progressed, so the party has become more and more dependent on Liberal revivals to steal the Tory vote. In the 1974 elections Labour's popular vote continued to decline but, with the Liberals now up around the six million mark, they still won twice. The ironic possibility exists that a powerful new centrist initiative is just what is needed to put a truly left-wing Labour government (shorn of its social democratic right) into power. Were this to be so, of course, the Centre would experience exactly the same speedy collapse as would be achieved in the alternative scenario.

The only way the Centre can avoid both Scylla and Charybidis is by a large breakthrough into parliament at its very first attempt. It really is double or quits. If it fails to hit this bull's-eye at the first attempt, it will very likely get no second chance. Thus the real oddity of the Centre. To achieve anything at all, this collection of ultra-moderates have to become successful anti-system radicals, overthrowing all the rules of the game – the working political constitution, in effect – at their first try.

Things will still be pretty odd if they *do* get up enough Poujadist steam to break through into parliament in large numbers. For they will be quite the strangest band of revolutionaries: their main aim will be that, in essence, nothing should be changed.

From 1945 to 1979, after all, Britain was ruled by a scarcely varying mix of the Butskellite consensus. Right-wing Labour Chancellors were followed by liberal Tories who accepted the welfare state. Until Thatcher, the Centre was *always* in power. It was the Centre which brought us the mixed economy: comprehensives *and* private schools; Concorde; the EEC; incomes policies galore; and so on. The new centrists talk bitterly as if they have somehow been prevented from having their way. But the truth is that nobody but them has had their way.

Perhaps that is the whole point. If Thatcher's election meant anything – or Foot's too, perhaps – it was that the political elite was, in its own way, acknowledging the bankruptcy of the old centrist mix. But the abandonment of Butskellism is proving a painful affair. Like Americans who look back wistfully to the balmy Eisenhower days – so tedious and wooden at the time – the new centrists are looking back nostalgically at the not-unhappy Britain of the 1950s and 1960s.

This is why, despite all the difficulties in its path and, despite the arguments above, the potential of the new centrist initiative should *not* be under-estimated, despite what I've said so far. Few revolutions are as radical, as appealing, or, of course, as impossible, as those which aim at putting the clock back. Nobody should lightly discount a movement which can muster moral fervour and anti-system disaffection, crusading zeal and sheer apoliticism, all in order to promise 'more of the same'.

14

Ireland and the Runcible Men*

Few British politicians are willing to say so openly, but it seems possible that Bobby Sands, first by his election, and then by his death, has at last begun the process which can end only in the termination of British rule in Ulster and thus in a united Ireland. On all sides the sound of political throat-clearing fills the air. The Labour Party is tiptoeing towards a united Ireland policy, provided (laughably) that 'working-class unity' can first be achieved. Tony Benn wants the United Nations in. David Owen wants a (non-existent) EEC peace-keeping force in. Even Conor Cruise O'Brien has suddenly veered round to the idea of a fresh partition of Ulster.

All these noises, it should be understood, are timid and preliminary. They are emphatically voiced, of course; but people are always emphatic about Ireland, even when, as in all the above cases, they are in the middle of changing their minds. And while Messrs Benn, Owen and O'Brien are a fairly various bunch of men, they have this in common: they are all acutely sensitive to tides of opinion and operate at the frontiers of opinion-formation for the various currents they represent. For this reason their statements are more worth listening to than the political muzak of such notorious opinion-followers as Archbishop Runcie ('the hooded men of violence' and so on).

While Bobby Sands was dying I was in Paris. Frenchmen of all political persuasions were, I found, utterly gripped by the hunger-strike drama. It was the *only* story which could drive their elections off the front page. I met no Frenchman from any party, Communists not excepted, who was not both fairly sympathetic to the British dilemma

---

* First published in *New Society*, 25 June 1981.

in Ulster and equally convinced that a united Ireland was the only right or possible solution.

This curious unanimity of sympathy on one side, and conviction on the other, derived from the single great fact that all these Frenchmen had lived through the agony of the Algerian war. Many of them had for years fought passionately for *Algérie Française*, for the myth that Algeria was not a colony but just an overseas 'province', an integral part of France. They had been, indeed, far more passionate about this than most British people are about the myth of Ulster as an overseas but integral 'province' of the UK.

This historical fact prevented Frenchmen – even those hardly known for their Anglophilia – from adopting any simple anti-British attitude. They knew too well the anguish of the mother country struggling to keep 'her' family together. Equally, though, no Frenchman alive today can regret for one moment that that struggle came to an end. It was inevitable that Algeria should divorce France, and rejoin her own Arab family. To Frenchmen it seemed just as inevitable (and right) that Ulster would before long divorce Britain and rejoin her Irish family.

This Algerian parallel is not easily accepted by most Britons, who are quick – too quick – to assert that their problems are unique.

But we've been in Ulster for centuries – it's part of our history, our tradition, even our literature. Generations of Protestants have been born there and it's their home. They're not like settlers in Kenya or Rhodesia. For one thing there's far more of them, and for another they're just across the water, a short boat-trip away. They couldn't all be repatriated, whatever happens.

Well, the French were in Algeria from 1830. Their settlement there lasted through three revolutions and five republics. Algeria was part of their history, their tradition, even their literature (Camus was an Algerian *colon,* after all). The *colons* indignantly denied they were settlers. Algeria (= France) was their home. And it wasn't a far-flung colony. It was just a short boat-ride across the Mediterranean. There were more than a million of these *colons.* In the end, almost all were repatriated.

But (the argument goes) *to concede a united Ireland would mean giving in to the* IRA *– bloodthirsty terrorists who blow up and maim innocent men, women and children. It would be tantamount to saying that Bobby Sands and his like were right. And it would mean admitting that many brave lads in the British army have died in vain. Everybody*

*agrees that that's impossible. It's not just the Conservatives and the
Ulster Unionists who say that. Look what a strong stand Michael Foot
took over* IRA *terrorism in the Commons a few weeks ago.*

Well, of course, the same arguments were heard in France twenty
years ago. Algerian independence would mean giving in to FLN
terrorists like Ali le Point – men who placed bombs in supermarkets
and discothèques, who used ambulances as armoured vehicles, who
killed and maimed innocent men, women and children. And it would
mean that the French army had wastèd the live of many brave young
Frenchmen fighting the inevitable.

Everybody agreed you couldn't do that. Not just conservatives,
but almost the whole Socialist Party. Men like Guy Mollet and Jules
Moch gloried in the tough stand they took in their parliament against
FLN terrorism. So did a younger François Mitterrand, waging the war
on the home front at the Ministry of the Interior.

There are always short-term political gains in doing that. When the
history of the reunification of Ireland comes to be written, Wilson,
Callaghan and Foot will look just like Mollet and Moch do now in
histories of the Algerian struggle. Foot and the rest would do well to
remember that it was Algeria which led Mollet to launch the Suez
expedition, which Foot, Wilson and Callaghan so righteously
opposed.

*But look, it isn't as simple as that. At present the people of Ulster
enjoy such civil rights as divorce and abortion. They would have to give
all that up if they became part of Ireland, which is a backward,
benighted and priest-ridden state.*

In Algeria the *colons* were even more aghast at the prospect of
becoming citizens of a backward state, where they would be subject to
the anti-feminist and obsolete morality of Muslim law. In the end,
however, the fact was that Algeria was part of the Muslim world;
staying there would mean bowing the knee to the hegemony of Islam.
For the few *colons* who stayed it didn't turn out as bad as they feared;
but that wasn't the point: they just had to choose what mattered to
them most.

Being part of Ireland *means* being part of a predominantly Roman
Catholic country. It's a matter of geography, not religion. You have
to choose where you want to be. And, by the way, please note that the
IRA will be just as insignificant within a united green fairly reactionary
Ireland as the FLN militants turned out to be within orthodox Muslim
Algeria.

Yes, but we've said over and over again that we won't do anything without the consent of the people of Ulster. We've even held referenda about it. There's a huge majority in Ulster for the status quo – and we can't go back on our promises.

The truthful answer to this is: yes we can; and no, the consent of the Ulster Protestants doesn't really matter. It's a matter of whose consent, after all?

The French could have conceded Algerian independence but kept the most developed part, Algiers, which was predominantly French, for themselves. They could then have held referenda galore in Algiers, with repeated massive votes for continuing integration with France. It wouldn't have solved anything. The Algerians would have remained second-class citizens in Algiers, and they would never have tolerated the situation.

Effectively, that's just what the British have done in Ireland – drawn a line around the most developed part which was predominantly Protestant and kept Catholics there in a state of second-class citizenship. If you wanted to hold a meaningful referendum over Algerian independence you had to ask all the people of Algeria or (less clearly) all the people of France what they wanted. If you want a meaningful referendum over Irish reunification, you have to ask all the people of Ireland or (less clearly) all the people of Britain.

Eventually, there was a 70 per cent majority for Algerian independence, even within France. The result in Britain might not be very different. And if you're going to ask what will the Welsh and Scots do then, the answer is just whatever they like – but probably that won't be much.

But the South doesn't really want a united Ireland. Conor Cruise O'Brien is always telling us that.

A minority of Algerians said they wanted continued French rule. For a while the French made considerable propaganda use of them – but in the end they counted for nothing. Dr O'Brien has had his propaganda uses too – particularly since the British gave him the editorship of one of their major papers.

Dr O'Brien once wrote that intellectuals, faced with situations they cannot change, vent their impotence in exposing the hypocrisy latent in those situations. This is what Dr O'Brien has been doing ever since he discovered that his colleagues in the Irish government privately did not want Irish unity. But in the end it doesn't matter what the Irish government – Haughey or Fitzgerald – privately want. Publicly, they, their voters, and their constitution demand a united Ireland. This is very fortunate for Britain – we would have a far greater problem if Dublin could say publicly that it doesn't want Ulster at any price. Happily, this is a political impossibility: we can drop Ulster in Dublin's lap any time we want. We may be handing them a bloody and costly horror, but they'll have to *sound* pleased.

You still haven't mentioned the crucial thing, which is that to proclaim a united Ireland means to risk a religious war on a scale as yet unimagined. As it is, only the British army keeps the sides apart. The Protestants are armed to the teeth, and they'll fight. It will be awful.

Quite possibly, but not certainly. In Algeria the *colons* were armed to the teeth too, and they formed the loathsome OAS to wreak a horrible vengeance on many innocent Algerians. But it didn't last that long, and it was never quite on the hideous scale feared by many. Once the OAS found ranged against it not only the Muslim majority but also the French Army, it died away. And then, at least, there was an end to all the bloodshed. Algerian independence brought an end to the struggle which would otherwise have gone on for ever.

It's possible that Ian Paisley and the UDF will behave like the OAS, and many innocent people will die. But once it's clear that they face a Catholic majority *and* the British Army, they'll give up surprisingly soon. And at least there'll be an end to the interminable bloodshed then. Without Irish unification it will go on for ever.

But it took a de Gaulle to do all that. Our politicians don't have his stature, and they've all invested a lot of their reputation in a British Ulster. How on earth will we muster the political will to do what you suggest?

It's because our politicians don't have any stature that we are now in our twelfth year of bloodshed in Ulster, whereas the French took only five years to settle the Algerian problem once the war had begun. De Gaulle was a great man not just because he wasn't willing to be bullied by the *colons* and the OAS and conservative opinion, but because he could see that ultimately the future of France was a far more important matter than anything which might happen in Algeria. The problem about having cowardly politicians is that the blood-letting goes on for longer, but in the end even they will get there.

For the rest, don't worry. A month or two after the issue is settled men like Archbishop Runcie – the runcible priests, if you like – will discover they were in favour of Irish unification all the time. Paisley is quite right to see him as a Vicar of Bray. If we're going to move on from the awful Irish imbroglio, we are going to need a lot of men like Runcie. Fortunately there's no shortage.

None the less, this last objection is the strongest of all. Perhaps the only politicians with the sort of determination required to carry through Irish unification are Thatcher and Powell – and they're both on the other side. While the issue is handled by men like Callaghan, Whitelaw or Foot there isn't much hope. They are, pre-eminently, runcible politicians.

To be sure, the political prize for a successful solution of the Irish problem is immense. De Gaulle's solution of the Algerian problem kept him in power for a decade, and changed the course of French politics. The same could be true here. But it took a coup to bring de Gaulle to power. At present a British Army which staged a coup in order to get itself extricated from Ulster would not be sure whom to place in power to achieve that object.

At the moment it looks like the choice would have to be between Benn or Owen (O'Brien being Irish). It seems doubtful that either are names to conjure with in the officers' mess.

One has to face even such outlandish possibilities as these, because it seems clear that the war over Ulster – fought to preserve the present political structure of the UK – has also been fought out as far as the present political structure can take it. Since the war cannot go on for ever, something, somewhere, has got to give.

In France the politicians only acted once it was clear that the army was planning a parachute drop on Paris. If Mrs Thatcher wasn't so busy bashing her wets, and Michael Foot wasn't similarly occupied in bashing Tony Benn, they might look up and notice the sky here was growing dark and threatening, too.

15

The Age of Powell and Benn*

In the furore which followed Mr Benn's recent 'nationalisation without compensation' speech one embittered Labour MP was quoted as saying that 'Now we [the PLP] will have to do to him what the Tories did with Powell, isolate him to the point where he excludes himself from the party.'

It is strange, amidst all the present talk of mould-breaking, that this parallel (of which, one hears, Mr Benn is himself deeply conscious) has not received more attention. The one thing that today's motley crew of mould-breakers (Muddites?) have in common, after all, is that they don't look as if they could collectively crush a grape. To date the only thing the SDP's most charismatic personality has broken is her own leg. (It is interesting, by the by, to compare the media's solicitude for Shirley's leg with their earlier derision at Foot's hurt.) Few Muddites, moreover, have the distant, staring eyes which mark out both Powell and Benn as true mould-breaking material.

But deeds, not words nor personal traits are the acid test. And if we are now about to witness a recrystallisation of British politics along new lines it seems certain that future historians will give chapter one of their account to Powell and Benn. If one wishes to trace the origins of the radical free-market Toryism with which Thatcher has so decisively broken from the post-war consensus, where else does one start but with Powell? And who has done more to shape the context of debate on race, immigration and the inner city than Powell? And who did more than he to rend the old fabric of traditional Conservatism and propel it towards starker, more populist solutions?

Similarly, the intense speculation as to Benn's political future tends

---

* First published in *New Society*, 28 January 1982.

to obscure the fact that his role has already been decisive. Who propelled Roy Jenkins out of the Labour Party by securing the adoption of an EEC referendum but Benn, way back in 1972? Who was most responsible for the adoption of Labour's most radical post-war programme back in 1973? For the reassertion of the NEC, which we were all taught had been put in its place for ever when Attlee publicly squashed Laski back in 1945? Who did more to win the day for reselection, for a new form of leadership election, for unilateralism, for the adoption of the Alternative Economic Strategy? All these things are effectively now irreversible. In achieving them Benn has driven three separate Labour leaders squawking in front of him like so many headless chickens. Each of them in turn has attempted to pass off their problems as just 'a little local difficulty with Tony', but two of them are finished and the third almost so, while Benn lives to fight another day. Whatever happens to him now he has already spear-headed the decade-long push which has transformed the Labour Party both ideologically and constitutionally. These men, Powell and Benn, are without a doubt the true mould-breakers. Next to them Jenkins, Williams and Steel are mere passive beneficiaries, the residuals in the equation.

Nowhere is this clearer than in the way that the new populist forms of politics initiated by Powell and Benn have gradually been adopted whole by those who originally resisted them most fiercely. The Conservatives vehemently resisted the whole concept of referenda back in 1972–5, but now they talk of referenda on strikes and even on rates. Williams, Rodgers and Owen fought to the death against parliamentary selection contests and extra-parliamentary election of party leaders. But who is now more involved in the politics of reselection than Rodgers, and who is keener than Williams and Owen that the SDP leader should be chosen on a one-member one-vote basis? Indeed, the SDP leaders who left Labour because they could not countenance the dictation of policies to the PLP by the party conference, now happily say that the SDP's policies will be whatever the SDP's mass membership will in future choose them to be. Yesterday's last-ditch defenders of the sovereignty of parliamentary elites have become – or so they say – the ultra-populists of today. It is no longer a matter of what Powell and Benn say we reject, but of what Enoch and Tony do we can do better. It is at this level that the success of Powell and Benn is, at once, at its most profound and most uncontested. An examination of how Powell and Benn achieved what they did is thus a study of the genesis of the changes now occurring within our political system.

Both men, it is worth noting, were socially somewhat marginal to the mainstream recruitment patterns of their parties. Powell, the son of two Welsh schoolteachers, was no more a typical Tory Cabinet member than was Benn, the son of a Viscount, typical Labour Cabinet material. Despite this both rose, against considerable odds, to become leading – though not pre-eminent – members of the Cabinet elite. Although their careers and views were conventional enough up to this point, both were held back by reputations for being slightly 'oddball' characters. Thus when their parties lost power, in 1964 and 1970 respectively, both were positioned for only middle-rank leadership roles. Both had some support within their parliamentary parties – Powell even tried for the Tory leadership in 1965 – but both needed some more or less dramatic fillip in their career if they were to reach the real prizes at the top.

It was of some importance that the 'charge' which both men then mounted was made while they were only Shadow Cabinet members of parties in position, that is, when their respective party leaders, unprotected by the authority or patronage of office and wanting only to win the next election, were most vulnerable to populist electoral pressures. this made it hard for the party leaders to rein them in and gave them a space for manœuvre which both exploited to the full.

The first sign of their mounting 'charge' was that both men began to give speeches and take up positions in areas way beyond their Shadow briefs. Powell not only made economic speeches as if he was the Shadow Chancellor, but denounced the Commonwealth as a fiction and questioned Britain's (then sacrosanct) role east of Suez as if he were Shadow Foreign Secretary – and then took up the Home Affairs issue of race. Benn, after 1970, similarly began to develop strong views not just on technology, but on industry, the EEC, the Labour Party constitution and (later) even defence. In part, this development of, effectively, alternative party programmes was just a matter of signalling ambition, but there was, too, a persistent search for issues left unrepresented by the smug little world of the Westminster consensus.

With his 1968 race speech Powell found such an issue with a vengeance. Voters responded massively to someone who so powerfully evoked concerns they felt the parties were brushing under the carpet. Polls straight after the speech found no less than 82 per cent of voters agreeing with his views and 73 per cent critical of Heath for having sacked him from the Shadow Cabinet for his outburst. This popular support was, moreover, slow to ebb. In 1972 Powell not only won a BBC 'Man of the Year' poll by 2:1 against his nearest challenger (Heath), but Powell was by far the top popular choice as 'the MP who best understands the problems facing the country'. In mid-1973 the polls were still showing him running neck-and-neck with Wilson and Heath as the popular choice for prime minister, and even after his 1974 endorsement of Labour and his peregrination into Ulster his popular following has never entirely ebbed away.

Benn never found an issue with equivalent power to that of race. Like Powell (both men had been early EEC supporters) he was ineluctably drawn towards the anti-EEC cause in the 1970. To all appearances it seemed a classic populist cause, with all three party leaderships committed to the EEC and public opinion ranged overwhelmingly against it. Here, surely, was scope for a popular tribune, particularly since the public were particularly resentful that their 'full-hearted consent' had never been obtained. Benn made the cause of a referendum all his own and forced the Shadow Cabinet into a humiliating somersault on the issue. It was no good – in the end only 48 per cent of Labour voters voted No. This 48 per cent did, however, include virtually all the real Labour activists and henceforth it was to this group that Benn addressed all his attention. Just how effective this alliance came to be – on reselection, the form of leadership election, unilateralism and the alternative economic strategy – needs little further emphasis. The fruit of this campaign was to be found in the astounding pro-Benn vote of over 80 per cent of constituency associations in the 1981 deputy leadership election. No Labour leader in history had ever commanded such monolithic allegiance from party activists before, and certainly not one who opposed the official leadership. It is doubtful if Nye Bevan ever got more than half-way towards such a figure.

It is often said that Powell and Benn owed their striking success simply to the fact that they echoed what the man in the street was saying about race or the EEC. This is to miss the whole point. There were other Tory and Labour MPs who made virulent anti-immigrant and anti-EEC speeches long before Powell or Benn did – and got precisely nowhere. And when the man in the street talks about race he quite certainly does not use words such as 'Like the Roman, I seem to

194   *Britain: The Eye of the Storm*

see "the River Tiber foaming with much blood".' The whole point of such language, the whole reason why Powell's and Benn's interventions were so explosive, was that they, as acknowledged members of that inner patrician elite of Privy Councillors, were able to dignify and legitimate, even to add a classical Gladstonian stamp to, populist issues in a way that no plebeian backbencher ever could. A Cyril Osborne fulminating about race or a Dennis Skinner threatening nationalisation without compensation were just part of the landscape. In a political system which is parliamentarist rather than democratic, and in which the hierarchies of power are overlaid with a class significance, nobody could mistake the dramatic attempt to erect a lightning conductor which ran all the way down from the patrician summit to the proletarian depths, entirely by-passing the parliamentary elite in between.

Thus the strange symmetry of Powell's and Benn's careers. The minute the lighting flashed down the conductor, the threatened parliamentary elite acted to punish and exclude these men. No sooner had Powell raised a tidal wave of support on race than he was evicted from the Shadow Cabinet and virtually sent to Coventry at Westminster. No sooner had Benn won his way on a referendum than Jenkins departed, and when Benn committed the cardinal sin of exposing MPs and even Leaders to a broader electoral franchise, the parliamentarist reaction was strong enough to trigger wholesale defections from the PLP and bitter hostility from those who remained. Even many Tribunites shrank from real tribunitial politics when they found out what they actually were.

The current centrist wave, despite the populist clothes it too has been forced to don, is rooted essentially in this parliamentarist reaction, the revolt of the middle and upper levels of our political system. Given the class conceptions overlying the hierarchy of power, it is not surprising that the chief support for this reaction comes from the middle and upper levels of the social structure, encompassing, inevitably, the media.

One by-product of this overwhelming reaction is the virtual public crucifixion of those who would play the role of tribune. A Benn or a Powell has to become used to living in a Westminster club which execrates them, to travelling round the country addressing the faithful in draughty halls. (Powell, in his hey-day, faced riotous hostility at almost every train stop.) Every newspaper they open, every broadcast they see or hear, carries the same deafening roar of opprobrium. It is not surprising that both men begin to act erratically, to develop those rolling, distant eyes.

The symmetry is not perfect, of course. Powell had a real mass following, which Benn has never had. In part this was just luck – the EEC never 'caught fire' as an issue. But it was also a case of each man mobilising the electorate relevant to his strategy.

Second, Powell has ended up excluded from his party, even from England itself. This seems unlikely to happen to Benn, who is, in an old-fashioned sense, less purely a man of principle than Powell. When Powell's party adopted a policy with which he disagreed he denounced it and called for a Labour vote. It is difficult to imagine any matter of policy being so important to Benn that he calls for a vote for Mrs Thatcher. He is a party man, first and last; his specialised appeal is to *party* activists. His dilemma is simply whether to press forward his campaign so that he one day heads a Labour Party with only 20–25 per cent of the the vote. It is worth noting that the 48 per cent of the Labour electorate who followed Benn in voting No to the EEC in 1975 already constitute a potential electorate of exactly that size.

In the end, of course, personalities do not explain history. What gave both Powell and Benn their opportunity was not just the fact that the parliamentarist elite exists in a cosy little world of its own. While that elite seemed successful the electorate was hardly susceptible to the appeal of the tribune. It is the repeated failure of that elite which has opened the floodgates of populist pressure. The fact that it is the old parliamentarist elite, the very politicians whose failures have created the present impasse, who now stand poised to exploit this opening, is not without a certain irony. If they do succeed in regaining power few things seem more certain than that they will fail again. In which case the scope for populist and tribunitial politics will widen further still. Then the age of Powell and Benn – perhaps later Powells, later Benns – will really have begun.

16

My Country Right or Left?*

England is at war again. A fascist regime, guilty of the most barbarous crimes against its own people, has committed a clear act of aggression – covering itself, of course, with the usual rhetoric about historical claims to the disputed *lebensraum*. The prime minister, who decides to stand up against this is a ferociously Right-wing Tory, given to biting criticism not only óf the Labour Opposition but of the softness of previous Conservative governments as well. The old white Commonwealth is solid with Britain, as are the French, but the Americans are playing a more neutral game while both Irish and Afrikaner nationalists are flirting with Britain's enemy. The Russians, hitherto so loud in their condemnation of the fascist regime, have suddenly veered right round and are trying hard to befriend it, denouncing Britain for its 'imperialist war'. As usual the outcome of the war depends squarely on the Royal Navy. June 1940? Yes, and June 1982 as well.

It is a pity Orwell is not with us to witness the Falklands war, for it is not merely the geometry of international alignments which is so perfectly replicated. Once again the crisis has served to throw into sharp relief all the most stereotypical aspects of British life, of which Orwell was the most penetrating commentator. It is a sobering thought that Orwell's usual platform, *Tribune*, might well have refused to publish him in 1982.

The trouble starts, as usual, with the benign patricians of the Foreign Office. First, concluding that the Falklands was, like Czechoslovakia, a little country far away of which we knew little, the FO made the fatal concession that yes, perhaps it might be possible to

---

* First published in *New Society*, 17 June 1982.

hand it over to the hungry fascist regime next door. This time it was even worse: the Falklands are a lot further away from Argentina than Czechoslovakia or even Poland was from Germany and there is no equivalent group to the Sudeten Germans to bolster the puff of historical claim this time. On this occasion it was actually British subjects that the FO was contemplating handing over to the sort of regime which tortures nuns, drops people into the sea with their feet set in concrete or puts them into gas ovens, as the case may be. This initial grotesque appeasement is then compounded by the sheer professional incompetence of failing to realise, despite all the signs, that Galtieri really was going to take Port Stanley, just as Hitler really had marched into Prague. A country pays in blood for having a foreign office like this.

The next group on stage are the hard Left. They have always proclaimed their hatred of military aggression and of Fascism, so this ought to be an easy issue for them. But when one gets to the crunch they find, parochially, that they hate a Right-wing Tory prime minister even more. They simply can't bear to find themselves on the same side as their old class enemy even if the old class enemy is doing the right thing for once. It is just easier, in the end, to parrot what the Russians are saying about an imperialist war in which British and Argentinian/German workers are going to get killed. Last time the hard Left kept this sort of nonsense up for two whole years (until Russia got attacked), even dismissing stories of Nazi crimes as so much atrocity propaganda. (It is an awesome thought that had Hitler not attacked Russia the hard Left might well have ended up trying to dismiss accounts of the Holocaust as propaganda exaggerations. Pacifists like Vera Brittain ended up doing exactly this – she wrote of 'the discoveries in the camps being "played up" by news-reel and radio to prevent the development of a growing sense of (our own) guilt'.) Once again, over the Falklands, the far Left has, fantastically, got itself into a position where it finds itself discomfited by the publication of news of fascist atrocities. It would do well to remember that forty years of rewriting the history books have still not removed the embarrassment of the Nazi–Soviet pact period. If, as seems perfectly possible, Argentina tries to regain American favour after the Falklands war by seeking to topple Left-wing regimes in Cuba or Nicaragua, no doubt the far Left will quickly rediscover its hatred of fascist aggression. As in 1941 there will then be a lot of red-faced 'explaining' to do. . . .

These contradictions lap over inevitably on to the soft Left. In the 1930s this group spent its time campaigning against Fascism *and* rearmament, vacuously ignoring Churchill's persistent demand that if we were really going to stop Hitler we were going to need the guns and planes to do it. Michael Foot, very much a product of this era of Labour Party silliness, later came thundering out with denunciations of the appeasers, the 'guilty men', blithely disregarding the fact that Labour had supported anything, including appeasement, in the cause of peace.

At the onset of the Falklands crisis Labour MPS managed to remember the 1930s for about one day. Many of them were, indeed, quite visibly wishing their mothers had christened them 'Arthur' so that they could 'speak for England' at this hour. This quickly gave way to all manner of protestation once the task force was dispatched. The sight of real ships predictably induced an acute attack of moral collywobbles. Collywobbles, not scruples, it was clear because criticism was always expressed in logistical, not moral terms. It was wrong for us to extend ourselves at such a distance. (On that argument we would never have gone to war over Poland, which our troops couldn't get to at all.) The fact that the islands were nearer to Argentina was suddenly seen to have some moral weight, though on these grounds we could take over Iceland or the Americans Cuba, and all claims to *lebensraum* are justified. This was accompanied by the quite inspired silliness of which E. P. Thompson made himself the leading spokesman: the government was hypocritical because it had 'no interest in liberating the Argentine people', and had only recently discovered that the government there was fascist. It was just the same in 1939, of course – Conservatives often had a soft spot for Nazis till then, but this in no way lessened the value of Churchill's stand against Nazism when it was made. Moreover, governments do not go to war with one another to change their internal policies, and quite rightly so. Had we launched an unprovoked attack on Argentina in order to liberate its people E. P. Thompson would no doubt have been the first to protest, again rightly so.

This sort of posturing gave way in turn to a pleading that the UN should settle the matter. In the 1930s the soft Left had attempted to treat the League of Nations in the same way, long after it had become clear that this leads nowhere at all, faced with the happy disregard of its charter by a Hitler or a Galtieri, unless a major power somewhere is willing to stand up. There would, after all, have been no majority in either the League or the UN to deal with Hitler in 1939. The US, Ireland, Sweden and Latin and Central America all took a neutral stance then, after all, and the Russians would clearly have used their veto on the German side. Most of the Third World would have felt the same – Nehru denounced it as an imperialist war at the time and there were strong sympathies for Germany in much of the Middle East. As now, Italy and Japan would hardly have been in our hot support and nor would the German client states of Austria and Czechoslovakia. The very best we could have hoped from a UN in 1939 was a draw and quite likely we would have been in a minority. Happily, although conscious, then as now, of the heavy price we would have to pay, such mouthing was ignored.

Just as the attitudes of the hard Left lapped over the soft Left, so the latter's views fed into the world of conventional liberal opinion. In the weeks when the task force was at sea the commentators of the quality press regaled us with all manner of confident wrong-headedness. The whole thing was quixotic *qua* impracticable (geography as the queen of the moral sciences again). Military action was unnecessary because economic sanctions were a far more powerful weapon (remember Abyssinia?). Most of all, while public opinion was strongly behind the task-force mission while it was *en route*, once there began to be serious casualties there would be a wave of pacifist revulsion. Behind this last, colossal misjudgement there lay something even more profound: the natural defeatism of liberal intellectuals. Orwell waxed with particular ire against this class, finding there the only ones who were sure Hitler would defeat us. Once again it was E. P. Thompson who gave clearest voice to this almost hopeful defeatism: 'Will 500 years of imperial naval history end in a tragic encounter in Falkland Sound? And how will the land forces be rescued and brought back? How, across those 8,000 miles, can we mount another Dunkirk?' What made such talk so grotesque was not just its whopping practical misjudgement of affairs, but the gravity of the distance between such an attitude and the profound popular determination to beat a Hitler or a Galtieri whatever it took.

Thompson wrote as he did on 31 May. A whole seventeen days earlier (and this was a war in which days counted) Enoch Powell had taken the measure of the situation far more surely: 'The British are never so formidable as when they are in this mood. It is a mood which, almost irrespective of any outcome, will leave nothing unchanged.' The fact that Powell had got it right and Thompson had got it wrong was not without a wider significance. Regrettably, no doubt, the British electorate was presented with the apparent fact that when it comes to a real crunch the only group one can rely on to show real backbone are Tory Right-wingers. Specifically Right-wingers, for when things reach a crisis the Tory wets, in 1982 as in 1940, simply collapse. In that sense the departure of Carrington and the sudden, deep popular suspicion of Pym have a more than personal importance. It is no real answer to this to say that Labour would have behaved differently had it been in government, that Foot would have been pushed round as effortlessly by the chiefs of staff as he was by trade union bosses in the past. The question is quite precisely about standing up out of backbone, not because one is too weak to resist the pressure to stand up.

Orwell would no doubt have been penetrating on the Newspeak of Ian McDonald, the Ministry of Information's television spokesmen, and blunt enough to say that the Falklands crisis has been an immensely enjoyable affair for most. (We were really happy during the war, calls the voice of 1940 again.) He would have known what a long and odious class history lies behind the greater nerve and backbone of the Tory right. But he, more than anyone else, would have known how profound a fact it was that this truth had been glimpsed once again by the British popular classes. He would not have been surprised (though he would have been angry) at the way the Left has undermined its own moral credentials. (CND could have grasped the Falklands cause as showing the irrelevance, as well as the obscenity of nuclear weapons. Instead it has, fatally, tried to gloss over the distinctions it sought so long to make clear.)

Most of all, Orwell would have understood, even, in a sense, sympathised, with the fact that workers, trade unionists, even the unemployed, are flocking over to Thatcher in droves. It would, no doubt, have stuck in his throat to say she deserves their votes. But Orwell did feel, to his very marrow, that socialist intellectuals and their parties had no presumptive right to the workers' votes: they had to deserve that trust. If they behaved as badly as he always believed they might, he would not contest the moral justice of their losing. He was, after all, the man who wrote, in *My Country Right or Left* in 1940 of 'the spiritual need for patriotism and the military virtues, for which, however little the boiled rabbits of the Left may like them, no substitute has yet been found'.

17

Not Cricket, Old Chap*

Assisted, no doubt, by the marked variations in their annual climate, the English have always had a strong sense of 'season'. No one can read English literature without becoming conscious of how thoroughly the life of the middle and upper classes was organised around the 'season'. Memories of the last one, anticipations of the next, helped get one through those bleak, featureless winters in the provinces. This seems quaint now, partly because we have been taught by marketing men to be intolerant of pursuits which do not have mass appeal, but mainly because we don't expect our ritual stimuli to be so brief and so infrequent. Getting through the year is not supposed to be the problem any more. John Lennon caught the mood of the 60s and 70s more accurately with one of his last songs, *Whatever Gets You Through The Night*. To a generation demanding constant highs, even eight hours can be a problem.

But people do still need a way of getting through the year and for many, even most perhaps, the rituals and stimuli which structure, excite and anaesthetise are now provided by seasons of a different sort – those of the sporting calendar. Late winter brings the climactic stages of all manner of soccer competitions, giving way to the Grand National, the Boat Race, the start of the cricket season, Henley, Wimbledon, the Test Matches, the Emsley Carr Mile, the Derby, Ascot and the Open. In no time the new soccer season looms, with the rugger internationals, darts and snooker close behind.

Stimuli galore, clearly. But ritual too. In part the ritual element derives simply from the steady annual rotation of events, like planets swinging regularly through space. The rhythm is so sure it hardly

---

* First published in *New Society*, 22 July 1982.

seems man-made. But for a ritual really to succeed more than regularity is required – it must express and encapsulate things beyond itself in symbolic form. The most common symbolisms are, of course, those of combat (boxing, bull-fighting, most forms of rugby and football) and sex (gymnastics, swimming, some forms of athletics and winter sports). Sex, violence and individual competitive machismo are, indeed, such deeply and universally appreciated motifs that probably no game can hope to attract a mass following nowadays without them.

It doubtless says not a little of the British national character that we have been far and away the world's leaders in the invention and perfection of game forms through which to sublimate and indirectly express fundamental values and feelings. But we have gone even further, perfecting games whose symbolism bears on the social and political order itself, most notably golf, tennis and cricket. All of these were originally elite sports, developed downwards, as it were, rather than mass sports (like soccer) developed up. All display some form of master–servant relationship (tennis-players and ball-boys, golfers and caddies, batsmen and bowlers/fielders). And all have strong codes of gentlemanly conduct and the observation of unwritten rules (they had, after all, to be suitable spectacles for the upper-middle-class womenfolk who made up part of their audience from the outset). More than that, they had to be fit royal fare since all three games enjoyed strong aristocratic and royal patronage. To this day even Connors and McEnroe have to drop bows to royalty as they leave the Centre Court. When test teams play at Lord's (the name itself so richly redolent) they generally meet the Queen. And the Open is more than the golfers' cup final: it is the Royal Open.

What we celebrate through these games is, in part, the social order itself – or, rather, a romantic view of that order as idealised through upper-middle-class eyes. Probably in no other country of the world do games carry such heavy social symbolism. For that reason alone, even if we are not the most sports-mad nation, sport plays a greater social role than elsewhere, its general pressure being towards forms of social integration acceptable to those above.

The best example of this is cricket. This game has quite routinely and explicitly been held up as a symbol of the desirable social order, with (in its English form, anyway) its stress on captaincy ('leadership'), team spirit, fair play, not letting the side down and so on. What makes political and social appeals on the analogy of cricket so instinctively appropriate to those who voice them is the more material fact that the organisation of cricket itself replicated the sort of regional and class structure in which they believe they live in or would like to live in.

Originally the game was played in two quite separate arenas. There was village and local league cricket played by the rustics and proles (the terms 'rustic stroke' and 'cow shot' are still in use as deprecatory epithets) and there was the patrician game played by gentlemen from Oxford, Cambridge and exclusive clubs in the south of England. The County Championship was formed essentially by affixing the term 'first-class' to this latter group of socially and regionally exclusive clubs and ensuring that they played only against one another (no wonder the imagery of class came so naturally to those who did the labelling). When W. G. Grace first captained England in 1888 there was still no room in the first class for Derbyshire, Leicestershire, Warwickshire, Worcestershire, Northants or Glamorgan. The expansion which allowed in these northern and midlands clubs was part of the process whereby, thanks largely to Grace, cricket became probably the world's first mass spectator sport. In purely cricket terms it was nonsense, of course: each Riding of Yorkshire could have entered teams which would have thrashed most others, while the standard of play in the Lancashire League was far higher than anything known at Oxford or Cambridge. But the notion of 'first-class' corresponded with the relative weights of clubs in the broader social order. Being first-class was about class, not cricket.

But the county championship did bring the rustics and the gentlemen into the same arena. This uncomfortable reality was met by the erection of rigid class barriers within the game itself, though all within a framework of rules and conventions which 'proved' the feasibility of class co-operation under elite leadership. The most fundamental of these distinctions was, of course, that between Gentlemen and Players (whose fixture against one another – generally won by the Players – continued, amazingly, until 1962). But there were others. Gentlemen had lots of initials on the score-cords; Players didn't. The captain had, of course, to be a Gentleman. And, generally speaking, Gentlemen were batsmen – bowling and fielding were for the rustics (the phrase 'toiling' is still used of bowlers and fielders, never of batsmen). When Violet Butler surveyed *Social Conditions in Oxford* (1912) she found that a significant source of income for town lads in May and June each year was 'fielding cricket and tennis-balls on college grounds'. The young Gentlemen bashed the ball around; others bowled and ran and had to be paid for it.

Even today much of this survives in some form. The countries remain heavily weighted towards the south. *Wisden* finds room for the scores of the public school matches at the expense of first-class cricket elsewhere in the world. Even in the post-war period the England XI has been accustomed to rely for its bowling on a long line of players from the 'proletarian' counties of Yorkshire and Lancashire: Statham, Trueman, Greenough, Hilton, Tattersall, Wardle, Laker, Lever, Higgs, Shuttleworth, Appleyard, Illingworth, Allott. If at all possible the captaincy still goes to someone from Oxbridge: even since the war the list includes Yardley, May, Sheppard, Smith, Cowdrey, Dexter ('Lord Ted'), Lewis and Brearley. Finding such material isn't always easy, so young prospects from this stable are brought on by every means possible. (Would Pringle be in the present England side if he was studying at Loughborough?) When gaps in this royal line do appear we have what is known as 'a captaincy crisis', where a non-gent has to be the leader *pro tem*. This is always very worrying (as under Botham or, at present, under Willis) and such captains often rule only briefly before being discovered to be rotters (Close, Grieg). But there's always stability at the very top: even as he was being rejected by the electorate at large Sir Alec Douglas-Home was being elected MCC President. Today's President is P. B. H. May (the three initials are important) and Lord Cornwallis is Vice-President for Life. . . .

But just as cricket had led other sports into the era of mass spectatorship, so, ironically, this most traditional of games, was also the first electronic sport. As attendances declined, so radio and TV audiences grew. For decades now cricket has been a media game. Back in 1954 we were already hearing Tyson skittling out Australia in Brisbane over the harsh crackle of the Third Programme. Long ago TV, now assisted by satellite, became the standard forum of the game. Other sports have only recently followed this lead; the 1982 soccer World Cup was probably the first in which live attendance was adversely affected by TV.

But cricket is the old hand at this. It was immediately recognised that this phenomenon gave enormous importance to the Commentary Team. When John Arlott retired last summer he was, to use one critic's phrase the 'authentic voice of English summer'. No more powerful tribute to the ritual nature of sport could be paid. But, with the sadly missed exception of Arlott, the BBC has always assembled a commentary team which is True Blue in every sense. Brian Johnstone, with his Home Countries Right-wing views and public-school giggles, talking about his son at Eton. Fred Trueman, the worthy rustic who came good (at last) and is now the prototype Working-Class Tory. Trevor Bailey – a Cambridge Man, of course – talking about so-and-so being 'a class batsman' (there is no such thing as a 'class bowler'). Arthur Wrigley and Bill Frindall, the necessary statistical technicians who know their place and speak only when spoken to. Across the ether, via TelSat from outer space, beams this traditional High Tory little world with a whole radio channel allocated to it all day long. If you've got your Sony Walkman plugged in you can even listen to it literally as you stand in the dole queue.

But ritual is, all the same, losing out to stimulus. The need, even in cricket, is for Superstars, for speed and violence (hence the demise of the slow bowler), for six-hitting, for big money. Just as Wimbledon is less gentle and had to accommodate Jack Kramer's Circus, so cricket has had to bend to Kerry Packer and if Ian Botham didn't exist we'd have to invent him. After all, thanks to electronics, our calendar stretches wider every year. Darts and snooker were never spectator sports till TV found them. And now the ritual calendar includes the US Open and Masters, the French tennis championships, boxing in Las Vegas, and soccer in Madrid. Soon, every week of the year will be mapped out in the ritual sports calendar. We can have highs all the time, relive them with highlights and interviewers who ask 'How did you feel when you scored the winning goal/put the ball in your own net in extra time/hit that six/skewered yourself on your own stumps', etc. It seems inevitable that the symbolism of power, speed and violence will win out over rituals supporting merely local hierarchies. Even if he's not a gent, if Lillee bowls fast enough he's still a Superstar and that's what counts. Mind you, he'll never be a *class* bowler. . . .

18

Our Shirley in Exile*

To read the British – or even the American – press over the last few years is to imbibe the belief that there are really only two politicians of note in this country: the Prime Minister of the day and Mrs Shirley Williams. That foremost American writer on British politics, Samuel Beer, has recently gone so far as to annoint Mrs Williams with the word 'charisma'. At home even those who habitually write in more neutral vein are quick to concede her reasonableness, her ability ('a good minister') and, above all, her 'sheer niceness'. There has, simply, been no business like the Shirley Williams show business.

This is all distinctly odd. Even a cursory examination of the record reveals Mrs Williams as a petulant, wilful and, above all, a self-centred woman; a politician of poor political judgement; a minister with a record of fudge, muddle and failure; an intellect which, for all her honorary doctorates, falls far below the best that British politics has to offer; and a parliamentarian of no note at all. All that cannot be gainsaid her is her popularity, which is real, large – and puzzling.

To understand, one must start at the beginning. Shirley was the daughter of George Catlin, a professor at an American university, and Vera Brittain, the pacifist writer. The family's circumstances were unusual (Catlin and Brittain spent much of the time living separate lives on different continents), but always comfortable. Vera had, indeed, been one of the tiny elite of Edwardian women to make their way to Somerville College, Oxford. There were always several houses and housekeepers and, of course, a nanny for Shirley.

Both parents were, first and foremost, liberal internationalists with a somewhat lofty passion for the League of Nations, European unity

---

* First published in *New Society*, 4 November 1982.

and the like. It was typical of Shirley's mother that she should decide
to join the Labour, instead of the Liberal Party while on a tour of
eastern Europe, out of a belief that Labour's foreign policy might fit
better with the world she wanted. There is little sign in any of
Brittain's books of concern with the conditions of the lower orders at
home or, indeed, of much that resembled a democratic instinct at all.

She was a brave, formidable, though often muddled woman of
independent mind. Her pacifist views made her unusual and something of a radical, but in every other way she was of the mandarin
middle classes, with a strong and natural set of elitist assumptions.
For Shirley's brother the parents refused to consider any schools
other than Eton or Harrow while Shirley attended St Paul's private
school for girls.

Shirley, too, went to Somerville College. By the time she graduated
she was already quite effortlessly poised for a brilliant career in
Labour politics. Perhaps no one in her entire 'Labour Generation'
had advantages equal to hers: a famous, best-selling feminist-pacifist
mother; a father who was both a knight and former Labour
candidate; political contacts galore; the attractiveness of confident
feminine youth; and the best upper-middle-class education money
could buy. From the start she was, inevitably, chic; within the Labour
movement she was 'our Shirley'.

What more natural, then, than that she should quickly be offered a
job on the *Daily Mirror*. This at the age of 22. At 24 she had
gravitated to the *Financial Times* and accepted her first nomination as
a Labour parliamentary candidate.

By the age of 29 she was fighting her third election in a winnable
marginal, and at 30 she was General Secretary of the Fabian Society.

Rapid rise to power

As with others born with silver spoons in their mouths, the rapidity of
her ascent bred an enormous confidence in her own views. She
contributed chapters to books with titles such as *What the Human
Race is Up To* and *Christian Order and World Poverty*.

In 1964 Shirley was given a relatively safe seat and, at the age of 34,
she was an MP at last. The vagaries of electoral fortune meant this
had taken a little longer than anticipated and so the Labour
Establishment now brought on 'our Shirley' at breakneck speed. She
was spared even a single day on the backbenches and became,

immediately, a PPS. Within three years she was a Minister of State for Education, then at the Home Office. Labour lost power in 1970, Shirley along with the rest. Simultaneously, however, she joined the NEC, became a front-bench spokesman and also an Honorary Fellow of Somerville at the age of only 40.

In 1974 she assumed Cabinet rank as Minister for Prices and Consumer Protection, a post she held till 1976. It was hardly a great success. Between January 1974 and December 1976 prices rose a whopping 68 per cent – faster than ever before in British history. If one assumes that the Minister for Prices was not actually trying to make them go up, the kindest thing that can be said is that she simply failed to make any impact. Perhaps fortunately for her, more attention fastened on her role in the 1975 EEC referendum when she announced flatly that if the vote didn't go the way she wanted she'd resign.

In 1976 she became Minister of Education. With Crosland's comprehensive revolution now achieved, the question was what Labour would do about its long-standing commitment over private schools. Journalists immediately posed the obvious question: how come Shirley's own child was at a private school? Shirley defended hotly, saying it would be wrong to change the child's school half-way. This was an odd answer for someone who had been a Labour candidate for twenty years and already previously a Minister of State for Education. The real question was why the child was at a private school in the first place. Later, Shirley reversed herself and the child changed schools.

On the actual issue of private education she did nothing. Indeed, in three years her ministry did very little of anything. Instead she launched the smokescreen of a 'Great Debate' over education, modelled, no doubt on the similar 'great debate' smokescreen Harold Wilson had thrown up over the EEC. This involved a great deal of what Shirley, idiosyncratically, called 'participation'. That is, a series of regional conferences were called, to which she invited participants who listened while she explained *her* 'problems and priorities'.

A fascinating glimpse of both why Mrs Williams is so popular with those who have a fleeting impression of her but less so with those who have worked with her over time comes from a civil servant who worked both under her and her predecessor, Mrs Thatcher, at the DES. When he put his views to Mrs Thatcher, he reported, 'she'd sit behind her desk and harangue me. I'd only get the odd word in and

I'd come out totally depressed at the thought that I hadn't changed her mind on one single point. Shirley, on the other hand, always listened most sympathetically. Head to one side, understanding shining from her eyes – it's not a sophisticated technique and I can't understand why more politicians don't practise it. But here's the odd thing. At the end of the day Thatcher might actually have incorporated your point of view and changed her position. Shirley, the great listener, would not have moved an inch.'

Oddly, though, this apparent fixity of purpose did not mean that Mrs Williams had a clear idea of what she wanted to do. After three years of her stewardship of the DES – and even now, several years later – it is extremely difficult to say what the Great Debate of her ministry achieved. All else apart, she was famous for her chronic muddle and her habit of flying off to private engagements in the US (on one occasion Callaghan put his foot down and simply forbade her to go).

In 1979 Labour lost power and Shirley lost her seat in one of the biggest swings seen anywhere. She was deeply shocked and considered partial emigration to the US. Within a week of the election, however she announced that she was to 'return to academic life' (which she had never been in) and had accepted research grants to study 'unemployment resulting from technological innovations, public spending in the welfare state and the use of the world's dwindling energy resources'. Quite how the DES would have responded to an applicant for thousands of pounds wanting to study almost all the world's major problems at once, one can only guess.

It seems unlikely, in fact, that Shirley ever did any of this 'research' – within days she was off on a lucrative lecture tour of the US. She was furious at what Tony Benn was getting up on the NEC, but actually missed the crucial October 1979 NEC meeting (at which the attempt to inquire into entrist groups in the Labour Party was quashed): she was off in America.

She retained her NEC seat while actively organising the launch of the SDP. By January 1981 all was ready. Shirley suddenly produced a whole new set of conditions which had to be fulfilled before she'd go over. Confusion. Equally suddenly, she withdrew her conditions and agreed to a meeting of the Four on 18 January. The day arrived and Shirley suddenly decided she wasn't coming after all. The venue was changed. She came, but raged violently against Roy Jenkins, who was gently but comprehensively upstaging her. She demanded the excision from what was to be the Limehouse Declaration of Jenkins's phrase about 'a realignment of politics'. It was cut out – then put back in. She signed all the same. At last they were ready to meet the press. At the last moment Shirley refused – she couldn't 'go out to be photographed like *this*' (wearing old clothes). A crisis of several hours followed before she would go outside. It has gone on much like this ever since.

Then Warrington came up. Shirley turned it down flat: it wasn't winnable. Roy took it and engineered a triumph. Stung, Shirley immediately announced she'd take the next seat up, Croydon, blissfully ignoring the alternate electoral arrangement agreed with the Liberals. She had to back out and take a public rebuke from David Steel for her sheer wilfulness. She had now got herself into a position where she *had* to take whatever seat come up next. It was Crosby and she won it. Only slowly did it dawn that this was a major disaster. She is now locked into one of the safest Tory seats in the country which, barring miracles, she cannot hold for long, even if the SDP does well.

The broken mould

Meanwhile, Shirley had quixotically decided she was against private education after all. This greatly embarrassed ber colleagues who knew very well that the SDP appealed precisely to the sort of Labour voters who had children at private schools. She quickly found the heat too great and reversed herself on this issue yet again.

In terms of our old political conventions Shirley was clearly 'born to rule'. Dandled on Nehru's knee as a baby; a Labour candidate father; ıaken to tea in the Commons at the age of 13 by Herbert Morrison – the way was always signposted. The great Labour Establishment was always there behind her, like a following wind. Jobs, nominations, media attention, even ministries were all given to her, and she got used to having her way. Now, suddenly, she is bereft of all this.

Now when she goes to parliament there is no automatic front-bench position and she vanishes into anonymity. Now she needs to rely on her own sense of political judgement, tactics and strategy – Transport House doesn't provide the service any more. Rodgers, Jenkins and even Owen all seem able to cope with this – they are political pros. The evidence to date is that Mrs Williams can't.

Hence the irony of the Shirley Williams phenomenon. She is popularly identified, even abroad, as the prime mover in the 'breaking of the mould'. Yet it was that mould which provided her with political position, which guaranteed her success even when she didn't succeed. It was only through that mould that she was 'our Shirley'. She needed that mould more than most. Now that she's set out to break it we are threatened with a re-enactment of the story of Humpty Dumpty. They couldn't put him back together again.

19

Cambridge in Command*

During the late 1950s and early 1960s it seemed clear that the major British political parties were becoming steadily more alike not only in their organisational structure and their common mix of Butskellite policies, but even in the type of people who led them.

It has long been a truism that Tory cabinets were almost exclusively composed of public schoolboys who had been to Oxbridge, but by the early sixties more and more Labour ministers were being recruited from similar backgrounds. Indeed, of the thirty-seven ministers in the 1964–70 Labour government, no less than eleven had been to private schools and sixteen to Oxbridge. Moreover, an increasing proportion of these ministers were relatives of other Labour politicians and they were also increasingly likely to send their children in turn to private schools.

Not far in the future, it seemed, loomed the prospect of a single, unified political elite covering both parties but recruited from the same tight little circle of exclusive schools and universities and linked by a dense network of dynastic and kinship relationships.

Twenty years on, it is clear that quite the reverse has happened. As the major parties have diverged ideologically, so too has the composition of their elites – a process in which cause and effect are doubtless combined. A number of new trends have established themselves. Given the glacial rate of change to which elites are normally subject, the clarity and rapidity of the new trends are quite striking.

The first point to note is that if the trend of the fifties and sixties was *towards* convergence, the party elites never actually converged. This

---

* First published in *New Society*, 3 March 1983.

becomes clear if we compare the backgrounds of the thirty-three ministers who participated in the Tory governments of 1957–64 with their thirty-seven Labour counterparts of 1964–70. In retrospect it seems clear that this period represented the high point of convergence. But even then major differences remained. It was certainly notable that 30 per cent of the Labour ministers were privately educated – but a whole 90 per cent of the Tories were. The prominence of Etonians was a sort of shorthand for this. Well over a third of all the Tory ministers came from this school, and they were the men who dominated the cabinets – Macmillan, Home, Hailsham, Salisbury, Thorneycroft, Heathcoat Amory and so on. The Labour government had just one, marginal, Etonian member – Lord Longford.

Similarly, while it was striking that 43 per cent of the 1964–70 Labour ministers were Oxbridge graduates, this was still far short of the Tory proportion (79 per cent). A more curious fact was that, in Labour's case, Oxbridge really meant just 'Oxford'. Shore was the lone Cambridge graduate. In the case of the Tories, Oxford graduates outnumbered Cantabrians by better than two to one, but this still left a sizeable Cambridge minority, several of whose members were identified with more Right-wing economic policies (Selwyn Lloyd, Macleod, Powell).

It is worth noting this because recent trends make it clear that the easiest rule of thumb by which to judge how right-wing a government is is the number of Cambridge graduates it contains. A large Cambridge group infallibly implies a Tory government; and the greater the size of that group the more right wing that government will be. This is far more considerable political fact than any number of Cambridge-educated Communist spies.

Within Tory governments, the Oxford–Etonian patricians were strongly identified with what would now be known as 'wet' economic policies. In the Macmillan/Home years of 1957–64 this group was wholly in command. In the Tory palace revolution of 1965, however, this group lost power, perhaps for good. Remarkably, the new leader, Heath, was not only a non-Etonian but had not been privately educated at all. He promised, moreover, a new and more abrasive brand of free-market economic rigour.

In retrospect it is easy to see that the Heath government was a halfway house in elite terms as well as ideologically. In 1970–4 the proportion of Etonians in Heath's Tory government dropped slightly (from 36 per cent to 32 per cent), while state school products increased from 10 per cent to 16 per cent. The Cambridge group increased in size, and its members (Macleod, Barber, Carr, Whitelaw, Prior) had almost exclusive control of economic policy. Outside the cabinet, another state school Cambridge man – Powell – made all the running, and exerted enormous pressure on the government.

Meanwhile, within the Labour Party, the failures of the Wilson governments of 1964–70 had produced an analagous reaction towards the Left and away from the political style of the somewhat mandarin group which had dominated that administration. These shifts were mirrored in the composition of the 1974–9 Labour governments. The proportion of Oxford graduates among ministers fell back (from 40 per cent to 32 per cent) and in 1976, for the first time in over 40 years, Labour turned to a non-Oxford graduate (Callaghan) as its leader. The proportion of Labour ministers who had been privately educated also fell sharply, from 30 to 20 per cent.

As the split in the party widened, it was precisely the privately educated (Prentice, Williams, Owen) and the Oxford graduates (Rodgers, Jenkins, Dell) who were most prone to leave for the SDP. The dominance of Jack Jones and the trade unions over the early life of the 1974–9 government was symbolic indeed, for within the Labour elite those with working-class origins (Mellish, Varley, Mason, Orme, Booth) were more strongly represented than for decades past.

The Thatcher government elected in 1979 saw not only a continuation of the shift to the Right which the Heath government had begun, but also an accentuation of the elite-level strends already visible under Heath. Most remarkably, of course, the removal of Heath in 1975 had seen the leadership remain within the tiny group of the non-privately educated. The proportion of Etonians fell again (to 23 per cent) and, probably for the first time in any British Cabinet, Cambridge graduates outnumbered those from Oxford.

It quickly became apparent that these Cambridge men, who had almost complete control over economic policy were the driest of the dry: Howe, Nott, Biffen, Howell. Heath now stood for the Left of the party, while the reconciliation with the extreme Cambridge dry (Powell) proceeded apace.

By 1983 Thatcher had extended her control over the Cabinet, very much at the expense of the old, Whiggish Oxford–Eton group. Out went Etonians like Gilmour, Soames and Carrington – so that today there are only three Etonians left. Of these, Hailsham is 76 and can hardly continue much longer, while Pym is clearly under siege from a bitterly hostile Prime Minister. At the same time the Cambridge group has increased by leaps and bounds. In 1983 it outnumbers its Oxford counterpart by almost two to one. The new Cambridge entrants – King, Brittan and Parkinson – are all clearly super-dries and Thatcher men through and through.

Thatcher has greatly expanded the non-privately educated proportion of the Cabinet. At 27 per cent it is, by 1983, a Tory record. Of these the supreme example is, of course, Tebbit whose rise to the effective rank of Deputy Prime Minister suggests that the passing of the succession to a yet further state school populist is by no means impossible.

The Labour front bench (the Shadow Cabinet elected in 1982 plus Foot, Healey and Benn) has, meanwhile, continued to evolve away from the mould of 1964–70. There are now only three public schoolboys left (Foot, Benn and Silkin) and four Oxford graduates (Foot, Benn, Healey and Kaufman). This looks like a disappearing species. Foot is 70, Healey 66, Silkin 60 and even Benn is 58. (Shore, the other Oxbridge man, is 59.) The future succession would appear to lie between a Barnsley boy who graduated from the University of Hull (Hattersley) or the son of a labourer and a nurse who went to University College, Cardiff (Kinnock)

Only three members of the Labour front bench now sit for seats in the South of England. This is a sharp contrast with the Tories. Most of them sit for seats in a tight little circle of the South-East.

The key to understanding this complex pattern of evolution lies a long way back, in the early post-war era. The great Labour landslide of 1945 had the effect of swinging over to Labour's side a sizeable proportion of the middle-class vote for the first time. As part of this flood there came a whole generation of young middle-class leadership recruits. They were the best and the brightest of their day. They were impelled towards Labour by a happy combination of wartime idealism and straightforward ambition. The 1945 landslide had made the Labour Party a promising vehicle through which to achieve power. This group finally came into its inheritance in the 1960s, and a glittering galaxy it was: Wilson, Healey, Jenkins, Crosland, Crossman, Castle, Gordon-Walker, Gardiner, Soskice, Rodgers, Williams, Jay, Stewart, Greenwood, Shackleton and Benn: in a word, the Oxford group.

It was, though, a one-generation phenomenon. From the 1950s on, the middle-class vote of 1945 began to trickle away towards the Tories and the Liberals. In the 1970s the trickle became a flood, and the Oxford group within the Labour elite failed to renew itself. Some died, some retired, and some followed their voters towards the centre.

The result has been to re-create a Labour elite very much in the image of the pre-1975 period. Labour has simply gone back in time. Its leader is now a man who fought his first election in 1935. And, as in the 1930s, its front bench is shared between the Welsh and Scottish Nonconformist fringe and by elderly manual workers with limited education and safe seats in the north of England. It is very much a residual group. Its members have been around a long time (only three of the front bench are 50 or under) and they have inherited their positions largely by default.

The new Tories have their roots not in the wave of post-war social change but in the reaction to it. Traditional Conservatives never really adapted to the accommodation with the new power of labour (and Labour), which was the chief task of the Eton-and-Oxford Tory patricians of the 1950s. This posture of accommodation was uncomfortably tolerated only as long as it won elections. Once it lost – in 1964 – the knives were out, and an altogether harder nosed set of men of affairs seized the reins.

The dominance of Oxford had meant the rule of those schooled in Classics and PPE. The new dominance of Cambridge brought in a swathe of barristers, accountants and businessmen: those who, like the Prime Minister herself, found their lack of education in the humanities, social sciences and economics a strength rather than a handicap in their confident and doctrinaire approach to social and economic problems.

The new wave of lower-class Tories are equally the fruit of 1945. The Conservatives responded to that defeat by building what is now, without doubt, the most powerful mass party machine in the country. One unintended effect was to open paths to power to those willing to slog their way up that machine. A whole one-third of the present Cabinet have done so, including Norman Tebbit, who joined the party as a 16-year-old school-leaver.

The lower-class Tories are, of course, the most paradoxical of the elite groups. They are bent on their own self-abolition. With success they become privileged and their children go to private schools. But the paradox goes deeper than that. They are the super-hawks of rigour and austerity, though they themselves are the children of affluence. Only the post-war era of full employment could have created the expanding opportunities which gave the Thatchers, Biffens and Tebbits their chance. Yet it is an era they scorn.

When Norman Tebbit joined the Tory Party in 1946 he turned his back on Clement Attlee's England for good. It was, perhaps, an odd decision. If, after all, he were a 16-year-old school-leaver today Tebbit might find that the allure of Tory Party politics was less compelling than that of, say, cycling.

20

Marx's Ghosts*

As the Marx centenary celebrations gather pace one is faced increasingly with a sort of identikit speech or article which goes roughly as follows: 'Marx wrote and worked in England . . . his whole analysis based on 19th-century British capitalism . . . Engels up in Manchester . . . Marx in British Museum . . . used to go riding on donkeys on Hampstead Heath where Foot takes his dog today . . . Highgate cemetery . . . continuing relevance of Marxism . . . nobody doubts existence of classes . . . and so on . . . and so on . . .'.

Anyone can fill in the blanks. By the end there is no doubt that Marxism is about as English as fish and chips, and we move to the apparently obvious conclusion of 'the continuing vitality of the Marxist tradition'.

Now, in its way, this is all very well. If, as Henri IV put it, 'Paris is well worth a Mass', then Marx is surely worth a celebration. But the identikit speech/article above is also seriously misleading. The fact is that Marxism has never developed any deep English roots – in a hundred years England has still not produced a single leading Marxist theoretician. It has, instead, been a philosophy in exile on these shores, just as Marx himself was an exile.

An an intellectual tradition it has always depended on blood transfusions from abroad and, for this reason, far from having a secure future of 'continuing vitality' this tradition now stands on the verge of a precipitous decline. There have, over the century, been three generations of Marxism – that is, periods in which the strength of the tradition has depended on a particular historical milieu. The

---

* First published in *New Society*, 31 March 1983.

third of these is now fading fast and there is no sign of a successor milieu to take its place.

The first generational period saw Germany established as the major Marxist focus. Marx had hardly been laid to rest in Highgate before the centre of gravity moved away from London to Berlin. Even before the death of Engels it was clear that the rise of the German Social Democratic Party had created a forum of Marxist discussion against which all others paled. The intellectual power and sophistication of the debates between the great men of the SPD — Liebknecht, Bebel, Kautsky, Bernstein and Hilferding — acted as a magnet to the young socialist intellectuals of eastern Europe, drawing figures like Plekhanov and Rosa Luxemberg into this forum, too. In the end the power of this milieu rested on the prestige and weight of the SPD, easily the strongest (and richest) socialist party in the world.

Only faint echoes from this milieu reached England, backward by comparison, and with no socialist movement to speak of. It was symptomatic that the greatest radical text of the day in England — Hobson's *Imperialism* — should both have borrowed extensively from Hilferding and be written by someone who was not a socialist at all, but a Liberal.

This period ended with the first world war, the splitting of the SPD into three factions, and the crushing of the Spartakist revolt in Germany in 1919. This tragedy had, however, merely served to ease the passing of the torch to the second generation of the Marxist tradition — the new men in Moscow.

The prestige of the Russian revolution would probably by itself have guaranteed the pre-eminence of the Soviet theorists within the Marxist current. But to this was added the strength of the new Soviet state and the emergence, right round the world, of Communist parties which acted as relay stations for the dissemination of the ideas and writings of Russian Marxists. A large part of the effort of the CPS and their publishing houses went into the distribution of millions of copies of the works of Lenin and Stalin like so many Gideon bibles.

The result was a much greater penetration of the ideas of the Soviet Marxists than anything the SPD theorists had achieved. Indeed, the dominance of the Russian focus was so great that it provided not merely the key 'orthodox' texts (by Lenin and Stalin) but also the key 'dissident' ones as well (by Bukharin, Trotsky and Kondratiev).

In purely intellectual terms the impact of the Soviet current had probably peaked by the late 1930s. In part this loss of momentum was due simply to events – the defeat of the Spanish revolution, the purges and the Nazi–Soviet pact – but there was a more fundamental reason too. Stalin was regarded as the supreme font of all wisdom. No mere theorist or philosopher (save the dead Lenin) was allowed to share the limelight with him.

In his youth Stalin, under Lenin's tutelage, had written a notable essay, *On the National and Colonial Question*, but that was his sole contribution to Marxist theory. All else apart, he was a working politician and his voluminous *Works* consisted mainly of talks on the practical problems of the day – industrial production, agricultural organisation and the like, together with a host of exhortations, homilies and slogans. No philosophical tradition could long survive on a diet like this, particularly in the absence of all debate.

The decisive role of the Soviet Union in the allied victory, and the continuing efforts of the world's Communist parties, artificially prolonged the life of Stalinist Marxism after 1945; but it was a dead thing. The *coup de grâce* was given by Khrushchev in 1956. Khrushchev intended, no doubt, merely to dislodge Stalin from his pedestal, but what he actually did was to kill off Soviet State Marxism as a major intellectual influence.

Copies of Khrushchev's, Brezhnev's and now Andropov's works were still printed as if they were Holy Writ, but they were not much read or discussed even within pro-Soviet circles. The whole idea of taking one's ideological lead from whoever happened to be general secretary of the CPSU now appeared ridiculous; the notion has failed to survive Stalin. Even the Russians tacitly accepted this by separating off responsibility for ideology from the general secretary and handing it to Suslov instead. But this deliberate divorce of theory from practice hardly helped the situation.

The consequent void was filled by two unlikely sources. First, there was Third World Marxism. The sudden emergence of a whole new generation of revolutionary Marxist leaders in the Third World was an exciting development which captured imaginations in East and West alike. Their writings were eagerly poured over as part of the quest for the new Holy Grail. Quite minor figures like Kim II Sung in North Korea and Sekou Touré in Guinea had their short-lived band of devotees. But most attention fixed on just four voices: Franz Fanon in Algeria, Che Guevara (through the medium of Régis Debray) in Cuba, Giap in Vietnam, and, most of all, Mao in China.

The mechanism was essentially the same as with Lenin in 1917: the prestige of identification with a successful revolution guaranteed the amplification of the theory.

The second source was even more unlikely – the Paris Left Bank, where a remarkable collection of writers and academies, all benefiting from the extraordinary status accorded to intellectuals in France, created a forum of Marxist debate which was, without doubt, the most powerful and sophisticated the world had seen.

It was a pantheon of enormous talent – Sartre, Merleau-Ponty, Balibar, Glucksmann, Lefebvre, Gorz, Poulantzas, Castoriadis and Althusser, among many others. These theorists were introduced to an English audience (and thus to the English-speaking world) largely through the efforts of a single journal, *New Left Review*, and it was also through this French filter that *anglophone* audiences first discovered the writings of other continental Marxists, most notably Lukacs and Gramsci, but also (to a lesser extent) the Frankfurt School.

This flowering of French Marxism was an event of crucial importance. Its proponents were brilliant, sophisticated and rigorous. For the first time a major Marxist forum existed which did not depend on institutionalisation by a successful revolutionary regime or on a party apparatus. For the first time since the days of the SPD, Marxism was associated with passionate and open debate.

Anglo-Saxons were prone, stealthily, to share the view of the French that French intellectuals were somehow special. They were, indefinably but definitely, of higher caste than their English-language counterparts – the inevitable vanguard of world intellectual fashion. For intellectuals who wished to see Marxism as the wave of the future there was something very comforting and reinforcing in the fact that the best and the brightest of the brilliant French felt the same.

To an astonishing degree, English-speaking Marxists failed to place the phenomenon of post-war French Marxism in any sort of historical context. It was simply assumed that the best French intellectuals would always be left-wing. Just as racists on the Right had discovered a single compound noun, '*colouredimmigrant*', so Marxists, speaking of France, had another, '*leftwingintellectual*'. In fact, what French Marxism represented was the final domestication of Marxism into a mere intellectual 'school', on a level with, say, the *Annales* school of historians. Hence the writers and academics; hence the divorce from political power; hence the debate. And hence, in the end, a change of intellectual fashion.

This is now what has happened. French intellectuals have not always been left-wing. In the 1930s the prevailing mood was conservative and non-political (the young Sartre and de Beauvoir, in the era of the Popular Front, could not see that politics had anything to do with them). The boom in Marxism was almost wholly a post-war phenomenon, born of the Resistance on the one hand, and the emergence of the Communists as the largest French party on the other.

But as French Marxism waxed and became, in its final Althusserian version, increasingly hard-line, the political balance in France was moving consistently the other way. With the waning power of the Communists, and the capture of the high ground by Mitterand's new, reformist Socialist Party, French intellectual Marxism found itself by the late 1970s further and further out on a limb, increasingly detached from what was actually happening in French society.

The result was a sudden collapse. In the wake of the 1978 election, French intellectuals deserted the Communist Party in droves. Glucksmann has become a spokesman for the New Right. Gorz has become an ecologist. Poulantzas committed suicide. Althusser strangled his wife and pleaded the loss of his reason. Disarray is complete; and meanwhile the Communists go on losing votes with every fresh election.

Simultaneously the vogue for Third World Marxism has collapsed. Fanon's theories are hardly mirrored in the progress of the Algerian revolution. Elsewhere in Africa it is only his more pessimistic predictions which have come true. Guevara's theories failed in practice and Guevara himself was killed. Giap's theories of guerrilla war had less to do with the final triumph of the Vietnamese than did the conventional might of the North Vietnamese army. Most damaging of all, Mao is now openly discredited, even in China. His theories of autonomous development through the Great Leap and the Cultural Revolution are laid bare as utter disasters, arrived at only through the machinations of palace politics.

For a hundred years Marxism has provided a political analysis, a guide to political organisation and action and a major philosophical school. The ending of its third generation – with no fourth in sight – means that it will cease to be able to play all these roles. The fact that the Russians will continue to pay lip-service to Marxism will no doubt retain for it a certain currency, and Marx will continue to be studied in universities in the same way that Hobbes and Mill are. But the drive, the excitement, the political relevance will be gone.

There is no need for this to depress those who make the centenary pilgrimage to Highgate to gaze upon that awesome bust. The spectre which has haunted Europe these last hundred years deserves some rest. Marx would have been the first to scorn those who followed intellectual fashions beyond their point of exhaustion. And he quite emphatically did not believe in ghosts.

21
Pomp and Circumstance

British Conservatism in 1983 looked virtually impregnable. The government was not only returned in the election, but never really had to break sweat as it simply rolled over its opponents *en route* to a massive majority. Not since 1959 had this been achieved by a full-term government and then the trick had been performed on the back of a rising wave of affluence and full employment. Not only was the Tory parliamentary majority of 1983 far greater than that won in 1959, but it was achieved against the background of a deep and terrible depression for which the government bore a heavy responsibility. Although the government naturally tried to behave as if such an outcome was merely what any sensible person should have both wanted and expected, it was, on the face of it, an astonishing achievement. Throughout the Western world governments of all stripes had, until then, fallen like dominoes in the wake of recession and unemployment. Ford, Carter, the Spanish and Greek conservatives, Schmidt and Giscard had, at one time or another, looked as though they might buck the trend, but every one of them had succumbed in the end. Moreover, many of these leaders had worked hard to moderate unemployment but had still found their efforts unappreciated. The Thatcher government, on the other hand, had not only created a deeper depression than was suffered anywhere else, but had done so almost unapologetically on the basis of an unusually explicit monetarist rationale. So how on earth was it done?

Conventional answers to this conundrum varied. Some pointed to the unequalled wealth, sophistication and professionalism of the Tory election machine and its overwhelmingly favourable press. But Ford and Giscard had enjoyed a parallel advantage and it had availed them not. Others cynically pointed out that no matter how many of the wretched unemployed there were, there were still far more people in work and they had done very well. Again, this consideration had hardly saved other Western governments – and it was contradicted by polls showing that concern over unemployment was almost universally shared by the electorate, those in and out of work alike, and was many times as important as inflation as an issue. Others claimed that the Tories had not really won: they had lost 1 per cent of the vote from 1979 and had only been re-elected because the opposition had divided its vote. Leaving aside the fact that the opposition's willingness to act this way was in itself a testament to the lack of a galvanising anti-Tory mood, this argument was simply disingenuous. No one seriously pretended that the Tories would not have won one of the old two-horse races against Labour just as easily as it won the new three-horse race. In a multi-party system – such as we now have – a vote of over 40 per cent is a landslide and deserves to be called one. There were those who suggested that the Tories had been most helped by their leader's formidable personal popularity. Again, this doesn't wash. David Steel was more popular than her, as was Sir Alec Douglas-Home when he lost the 1964 election.

Most widespread of all was the explanation in terms of the 'Falklands factor': that the government, and particularly Mrs Thatcher, had won themselves lasting credit by the Falklands victory which had awakened echoes of 1940 and the old imperial glory beyond, showing the world (and a proud electorate) that Britain could not be kicked around any more. There was undoubtedly a great deal more to this explanation – certainly the polls showed that the Tories had, from the Falklands on, soared into a large lead which they never thereafter surrendered. But caution is required. The year 1983 was not a khaki election – the Falklands campaign was mentioned more often by Labour than the Tories. Foreign policy has seldom played much of a role in British elections, let alone won them. The echoes of 1940 were strong – but then they had been even stronger in 1945 and had, nevertheless, failed to save Churchill. Echoes of empire? It is as well to remember that the British electorate displayed a remarkable equanimity over the loss of empire – there was no reaction comparable to that in France – and have not seemed to miss it much since. True, there was some irritation at 'being pushed around' directed against the independent leaders of the new Commonwealth in the 1960s, but that had long been old hat by 1983. Indeed, with the demise of de Gaulle the British lost the only foreign hate-figure who 'pushed us around'. Since then the only country regularly to impose its will on Britain has been the US. But as the election showed yet again (over the Cruise/Pershing issue) the electorate was remarkably tolerant of such pressures. Mrs Thatcher was never made to suffer for her knee-jerk support of the US over defence policy, Central America or anything else Reagan wanted. Those who tried to rouse the British electorate on the issue of national sovereignty and the EEC have, similarly, found that this is a very difficult horse to get through the stable door. Without doubt the Falklands campaign touched deeper patriotic chords than that, and the polls show that *something* certainly happened to mass opinion at that time. But the polls also show that very few voters thought that the Falklands was or ought to be much of an issue in the election. At the very least, a certain caution is advisable before one accepts the 'Falklands factor' at face value.

It is, in fact, a somewhat unprofitable exercise to search around for purely short-term explanations of the 1983 Tory victory. One should in any case be put rather on one's guard by the fact that the same pundits who urge the centrality of this or that short-term factor feel no embarrassment at simultaneously offering long-term, sociologically determinist arguments for the collapse of Labour and the rise of Alliance centrism, even though these are merely the opposite sides of the same coin. It is more sensible to realise that the Tory success of 1983 cannot be divorced from a wider explanation of the persistence of Conservative strength in the modern period as a whole.

And it should be realised that this *does* take some explaining. Everywhere else in Western Europe large Conservative parties have only polled regularly over the 35 per cent mark when they have been able to rely either on a basically religious core vote (as in Italy and Germany), or, in the special case of 1960s Gaullism in France, on the essentially personal appeal of a charismatic leader. Without these advantages (and sometimes even with them) European conservatives have always performed more weakly, splitting into rural/urban, regional/linguistic or liberal/conservative fragments. British Conservatism alone defies this iron law: it has never been just the tail attached to a charismatic leader, and at least since 1945 it has not been possible to explain its performance by reference to a religious core vote. Indeed, such a confessional base is quite beyond the Tories, for Britain is by far the most secular society in the entire Western world. To some extent one can try to explain the continued strength and cohesion of the Tory bloc by reference to the electoral system and to the high post-war degree of class polarisation, which gave anti-socialists little option but to rally round the Tories, but the enigma remains. A satisfactory explanation can be found only in the peculiar British political culture, characterised on the one hand by the imprint of a uniquely powerful and successful state and, on the other, by its non-inclusive conception of the popular interest.

The authoritative state

The history of the British state is like that of no other, for it has succeeded in a way no other state in the world has done. For nearly a thousand years it has successfully protected the nation against invasion. It created not one but two vast colonial empires, each in their time the biggest humankind has ever seen. It has, since 1066, been successful in all wars where its national sovereignty was at stake and has won almost all of its lesser wars too. Other states have Established Churches, but these have resulted either from the church taking over the state, or from a concordat between equals; only in England did the state simply take over the church, prescribing it new doctrines in the interest of the state. This state fathered the world's first industrial revolution. Despite its small size it became the greatest power in the world, both economically and militarily, for a century. (Neither the US nor the USSR has ever known so long or so uncontested a supremacy.) At home this state was immune to revolution, even while all others succumbed. Naturally it never tolerated notions of federalism or even allowed any real forum for local initiatives which might have trespassed on its authority. For it knew that it was not just 'the authorities', but Authority itself. It even refused, uniquely, to subject its absolute sovereignty to a constitution. It developed an immense conception of its own dignity and solemnity. And, of course, so majestic a state required nothing less than a monarchy at its head, even in an age of republics.

The impact of such a state on its people was, inevitably, massive; indeed, a large part of what is taken to be the timeless British 'national character' is actually the historical product of that impact. The knowledge that such a state was at their backs gave Englishmen a self-confidence, indeed an arrogance and cool disdain, which became famous the world over. British sang-froid, the notion of 'effortless superiority', a confident and insular philistinism ('English empiricism') and a cultural and social parochialism all derived from this source. Britain was, unsurprisingly, the great originator of doctrines of racial supremacy throughout the world.

Quite frequently such attitudes fed on their own success. In 1940 Britain faced such overwhelming odds that the only 'rational' settlement was a negotiated peace. The country fought on simply because its people were secure in the certainty that the British state, when once engaged, was not beaten. Italians or Frenchmen who knew only too well that their states could be beaten, could hardly have behaved the same way – or achieved the same result.

At the same time this state was, to its own people, awesome and overwhelming. If Authority ordained that this government in Latin America should fall or that this tribe in Africa or Asia should be subjugated, so it happened. It was the same at home. True, the state felt so secure that it was sometimes willing to envisage compromise and the British 'genius for compromise' owed something to that, but more to the fact that this was the best one could hope for – the state could not be *beaten*. And once its mind was made up it was not to be brooked, lightly or otherwise. The British penchant for fortitude, patience, 'grin-and-bear-it' long-suffering owed much to this reality. The most famous exemplar of such traits is the much-remarked phenomenon of the orderly queue.

Such an all-powerful state was too overwhelming, too authoritative to be truly lovable. The fear that its strength might be used to intrude yet further on the lives of its people gave rise to a powerful protective cult of privacy, with the Englishman's home his castle. Many covered their insecurity in the face of the state and its Establishment with an all-pervasive deference. Attempts to make this behemoth more open, democratic and responsive met a fairly predictable end. Historians have often observed that the fate of German liberalism was sealed by the way in which the rock-like Bismarck, while refusing its demands, beat it repeatedly over the head with his military, diplomatic and economic successes until the demands all but ceased. It is strange that this observation is made of Germany for it was far truer for far longer of Britain. In the end British liberalism was neutralised, even neutered, by the sheer might and success of the British state.

The same dilemmas have faced the Left and the Labour movement in twentieth-century Britain. Deep down the Left has never believed it could overthrow this unbeatable state and its Establishment, or even radically change it. Hence, time and again, the Left went into battle defensively, preparing for defeat, full of windy expletives but in the end happier to lose and remain in opposition. The recent jargon for this is that the Left lacked a 'hegemonic consciousness'. Typically, those who criticised the Left for failing to develop such a consciousness were themselves its main victims.

The power of the state and its near-hypnotic impact also lay behind the general tendency of Left leaders to 'sell out': the temptation to posture briefly on so majestic a stage, to talk imperially, as Wilson did, of the 'smack of firm government' or of having Labour MPs on a 'dog-collar'. Within the trade union movement the deep assumption that the state could never really be made to answer to working-class needs provided a fatal encouragement to an inward-growing sectionalism. Deep down, the labour movement was defeatist, was sure it was always a likely loser where real political power was concerned – 'knowing its place' while hating the whole concept of 'knowing one's place' – then it was free to devote itself wholeheartedly to the unending scrabble over differentials. The habit became ingrained, an oblique tribute to the power and prestige of the British state.

Underlying these deep-seated attitudes is an even deeper loyalty to and reverence for the state. Governments may come and go and may be more or less popular but the devotion to the state is lasting and all-pervasive; indeed, almost the shortest route to governmental unpopularity is for a government to give the impression that it is failing to maintain the dignity and authority of the state. It is not just that the state has made Britain safe, rich and strong – the feeling goes beyond any such instrumentalities. It is more that the state, its Establishment and its institutions have come to be regarded as synonymous with the nation itself. Without its monarchy, peerage, Houses of Parliament, Britain would literally not be Britain at all for many of its people. This is a confusion the French, for example, could never make: the Third, Fourth and Fifth Republics and their institutions are one thing, France quite another.

In Britain one can commonly hear people say that they 'like tradition'; not this or that particular tradition but tradition in general. This does not mean that they have any view as to whether, say, the Zulus or the Trobriand Islanders should change their way of doing things or stick to the old ways. It reflects, rather, an affection for the sheer continuity of the British state, for its weird panoply of ritual, and the continuous celebration of the state through ceremonial. For the British actively celebrate their state in a way that would make C. Wright Mills blush that he had ever written of 'the American celebration'. Typically, a great deal of this celebration is conducted through the medium of the monarchy, whose social and psychological importance far outruns its slight constitutional role. The monarchy was – and is – immensely popular not just because it makes the state seem a little more human, but, far more, because it exemplifies and embodies the majesty of the state. Royal births, weddings and deaths are celebrated not just as incidents in the royal personal life but as 'state occasions'. And there is virtually no end to such occasions – the royal birthday, the opening of parliament, the Christmas message, the parades at the Cenotaph, the visits of foreign dignitaries and so on. To these have been added a whole list of quasi-state occasions, with the royal attendance at Wimbledon, the FA Cup Final, the Lord's Test and so on. Every such occasion is marked by large spontaneous displays of excitement and popular expressions of awe, love and reverence. In a nation not noted for unreserved displays of public emotion the capital political importance of such effusions is hardly to be missed.

In the end what the British are so endlessly celebrating is the continuity of their state and the feelings of confidence, self-belief and security it enables them to have. The feeling that 'there'll always be an England' is less a matter of patriotism than of personal reassurance. The notion of the state and its institutions as providing an unbroken and, indeed, unbreakable link between past and future is thus of a directly personal importance to most British people. And it is why the Civil War and the Cromwell period – the one clear break in the state's continuity – is hushed over still in the popular historical imagination. For the state, by providing an image of Authority by which they may order their lives in security, has actually entered into the personal identity of British people. They would, literally, be lost without it.

A public without citizens

The British political culture is unique among modern democratic nations in another way – it lacks any notion of popular sovereignty. In part, of course, this is merely the obverse side of the dominance of the state: it is unthinkable that a state like the British one can be 'possessed' by its people. The very institution of the monarchy makes this plain. The head of state is neither elected nor responsible and no ordinary member of the population may ever aspire to this supreme office. Palmerston was able to thrill his Victorian audience by boasting that a Briton should feel able to be secure in any part of the globe under the formula 'civis Britannicus sum', but perhaps it was no accident that he arrived at such a formula only by borrowing from Latin, or that he should apply it only to Britons abroad, for no Briton could, or can, be a citizen at home – only a subject.

The fact of the monarchy is again critical to this strand of the culture. Technically, at least, all the highest offices in the land – the Prime Minister, the supreme judiciary, one whole house of the legislature, all honours and decorations, and literally thousands of other offices are distributed only at the grace and favour of the monarch. The people have no rights in such matters. The monarch and her family are effectively above the law. Indeed, the monarch could even commit murder with impunity for there could be no criminal prosecution of the Crown by the Crown. The royal family, though immeasurably wealthy, pays no income tax, wealth tax, death duties or capital transfer tax. In practice the royal family is even immune from prosecution for dangerous driving. In addition to their large incomes from rents and investments each member of royal family enjoys a further annual tribune voted by parliament. These days one has to look as far afield as Saudi Arabia to find any analogy.

Faced with these facts Britons will somewhat defensively argue that foreigners flock to see this royal pageantry and would clearly like something similar for themselves. This is, of course, nonsense. The Americans or French enjoy the pageantry as a piece of real-life Disneyland, precisely because the actual assumptions of a monarchical state are now so unreal to them. The merest hint of monarchical behaviour by a Nixon or Giscard causes violent offence. Similarly, the British will somewhat shamefacedly claim that the monarchical state is merely a technical or legal fact, not a real one. This is patently not so. The fact of monarchy and of subject status beneath it are not disregarded as mere icing on the cake. They are, as we have seen, enthusiastically accepted and have major psychic and social importance. Traditions of politeness, deference and passivity are all heavily derived from subject status, and they too are real enough.

There is little room in such a culture for any strong sense of popular sovereignty, of 'we the people'. Lord Hugh Thomas has chided the British for not having the same sense of historical pride and fierce national consciousness as the French, but this is to miss the whole point. The French are able to feel deeply that their state, their institutions and their laws belong to them. They have made them the way they want by successfully asserting themselves against established authority, overthrowing three monarchies, four republics and countless governments in the process. Any Frenchman, like any American, can aspire to become head of state, and will then address his compatriots as 'Francaises, Francais' or 'my fellow Americans'. One cannot imagine a British head of state using such terms without sounding utterly bogus. The national pride and consciousness of the French, like the Americans, is based on an assertive and intrinsically egalitarian notion of citizenship, for which there is no British equivalent. The British political culture is quite actively anti-egalitarian and, indeed, in some ways almost anti-democratic. This fact permeates British behaviour and thought at every level. The British 'know their place' and that can often mean taking what's handed down and keeping one's feelings to oneself. As even so Tory a writer as Chesterton put it:

'Smile at us, pay us, pass us; but do not quite forget.
For we are the people of England, that never have spoken yet.'

Any notion of 'the sovereign people' is, however, undermined in Britain from another, more subtle direction: the conception of 'the people' on which the polity operates is a not necessarily inclusive term. Indeed, the terms 'people' and 'popular' are not often found in English in their European sense; instead, the curious word 'public' is extensively employed. Inevitably, a certain imprecision attaches to the term but even a rudimentary philological analysis quickly establishes that the entity thus described is not coterminous with 'the people' but is rather 'a particular section, group or portion of the community', and that the word is inextricably tied up with the notion of service to the state.

The root of this term is *not* 'res publica' (= republic), as is often thought, but 'pubes' (= adult males only). Murray's *English Dictionary on Historical Principles* reveals that a publican was originally nothing to do with drink – he was a tax-gatherer or state official concerned with the collection of tribute or duties. A public thing was something to be shared 'by all persons legally or properly qualified'. When Napoleon was declared a 'public enemy' this meant that he was an enemy of *the state*. Murray tells us that the term was sometimes also used in an international sense, but then always only of 'the European, Christian or civilised nations'. A 'public office' was one where the town council, police and magistrates were housed; public service referred to 'service of the State'. Early in the nineteenth century *The Times* began to use the phrase 'The Nobility, the Gentry and the Public' – clearly intending what one might call the respectable Third Estate only. A 'public man' was one in a high professional or official position, who was active in 'public life' which was the world of those in responsible positions of authority. When that glory of British civilisation, the public library, was created it was not necessarily for everyone – by no means the whole of the population were literate at the time.

Something of these connotations lingers on even today in the term. Implicitly excluded, at least, are those at the bottom end of society – the poor, those wearing ragged clothes, lumpen elements of any kind, the unemployed and all those who are not 'respectable' or 'responsible' (to mention two other key words of British discourse). Perhaps the clearest sense of its non-inclusive quality is found in the still-current usage of 'public schools' – meaning schools exclusively reserved for the progeny of the well-to-do. The view is very much one of the population from the top down rather than the bottom up: the public is all those people whom the state and its Establishment wish to address or acknowledge as their own. This sense of state agency is perhaps most explicit in 'public prosecution', which is a prosecution by the Crown. In a social sense 'the public' is clearly coterminous with something like 'polite society'. Whether or not one is one of the elect of the polite, responsible, or respectable is, of course, a matter for judgement by one's betters.

This restrictive conception of 'the public' is, of course, the historical product of the uniquely slow and gradual process of democratisation in a society which remained, even at the end of that process, rigidly stratified by class and acutely conscious of that fact. In most other democratic nations the concession of manhood suffrage was a relatively speedy affair: not long after the kings of France or America were overthrown every male had the vote. The franchise certainly remained for long restricted by sex, but not by class. In Britain, however, although a vigorous form of (oligarchic) electoralism had taken root by the early eighteenth century, it was more than two centuries later that manhood suffrage was finally conceded, and only in 1948 that a truly uniform system of 'one person, one vote' was adopted. During this period of more than two centuries those classes who had the vote became habituated, as a matter of stable reality, to the fact that they (and they alone) were part of 'public life' and that more or less large groups stood permanently outside this 'public'. This long historical period of oligarchy has, inevitably, affected the term 'public' with connotations which linger on today.

It is difficult to be precise as to where the boundary between public and non-public is drawn in this restricted conception. Until 1884 the non-public included virtually the whole of the working class, and up till 1918 it included the bottom half of the working class. Probably the most sensible place to draw the line in this lingering, restrictive notion of the public was somewhere just below the skilled, 'respectable' working class. It has always been fairly clear in Tory usages of the term 'public', for example, that trade unions belong to the non-public and that a natural opposition exists between 'trade unions and the public'.

The coming of universal suffrage inevitably blurred this meaning, but the connotations linger on pervasively. This is often true even in the usage of Labour politicians. A Labour MP who is leading a petition or protest will claim to speak on behalf of 'working people'; when explaining why people can't have what they want he or she will say that 'the public will not stand for it'. Among Conservatives, and within the Tory culture in general, the more restrictive nineteenth-century cadences are usually far more pronounced. The story is told of the Tory lady in 1945 exclaiming, on hearing of the Labour landslide: 'They have elected a Socialist government! The public will never stand for it.' But this restrictive usage is still also found in the theoretically more neutral world of the media. Even in the 1980s one can be sure that if the television news wishes to interview an outraged 'member of the public' during, say, a train strike, we will find a visibly professional and pin-striped figure on our screen.

The Tory Party within the Tory culture

It goes almost without saying that this is a political culture in which Conservatism swims like a fish in the sea, and in which a Labour vote has always been a deviant one. The national culture *is* a Tory culture. This is not to say that the values of this culture are equally shared throughout society. It makes sense, rather, to view British society as a series of concentric circles which are both social and geographical in their nature. To be at the epicentre – in the royal enclosure at Ascot or on the boards of the great merchant banks – is not just a matter of being socially and economically more upper class, but also, in a sense, more English. The real outer groups are not just the poor, the black or the working class, but those furthest from the geographical epicentre of the South-East. Thus the suburban professional from the South-East stands rather closer to this centre than, say, a Welsh, Scottish or North-Eastern entrepreneur, even if the latter is somewhat wealthier than the former. The Tory culture tends to follow these complex fault-lines. It pervades the whole society, but its influence is stronger the nearer the centre one goes, weakest on the periphery. This is why both Liberals and Labour have always done better in the Celtic outer regions than mere social class factors can explain.

This peculiar socio-cultural configuration is the secret of the Conservative Party's unique strength and cohesion, even in the absence of a solid confessional base. The Conservative Party is the *necessary* embodiment of the central core of this Tory culture. Indeed, there are some ways in which it exists more as this embodiment than it does as a political party. No other Western conservative party could possibly countenance such a grossly undemocratic internal structure as the Tories exhibit (the only real analogies are to be found in fascist parties) – but this is because the loyalty of the Tories is to the authority principle of the historic state rather than to the more mundane requirements of normal political party organisation.

Similarly, political activists of other persuasions are prone to mock the Tories for the fact that their gigantic membership spends most of its time on purely social activities. Again, this is to misunderstand: *some* organisation is required to fulfil this sociological function of bringing together of middle- and upper-class elites. The Anglican Church can no longer do it, so the Tory Party does. The sort of conflicts which have split European conservatives will always be less likely to occur among the Tories while it can perform this function.

For example, Mrs Thatcher was reportedly furious that Archbishop Runcie had insisted on including prayers for the Argentinian dead as well as that British in the Falklands Commemmoration Service. In other countries where there is a real communication gap between political and ecclesiastical elites this rift could have developed a threatening momentum. But in Britain a thousand little social overlaps – many of them within the Tory Party and its ancillary organisations (Mrs Thatcher and Archbishop Runcie were, for example, student members of the same Tory branch) – mean that quarrels like this are always settled 'within the family'.

The key to understanding the Tory Party, its peculiar strength and cohesion, is that in many ways it exists less as a political party than as a corporate social bloc whose members can normally recognise one another without ever discussing politics. Its members and many of its voters are not like (say) French conservatives who have voted for Peasant Independents, supported Vichy, de Gaulle, Giscard and then Chirac. Tories assume that their party, the social bloc it embodies, and the underlying culture and institutions which support it are all timeless and unchanging. Loyalty to the social bloc is partly class loyalty and economic interest, but it goes beyond that: in the 1980s one could frequently meet small businessmen being pushed to – and over – the verge of bankruptcy by the government's economic policies, who none the less expressed firm loyalty to the government and what is was doing. Similarly the Tory bloc has contained all the possible poujadist, racialist, free-market, regionalist and anti-EEC breakaway movements with which it has been threatened. The only failure of this almost miraculous cohesion was the secession of the Ulster Unionists – and it took several years of local civil war to produce that.

The crisis of the Tory culture

The story of the last two decades is very largely one of how this Tory culture came under pressure from almost every direction. First, there was the simple fact that the invincible British state underwent a series of dramatic threats to its authority or actual defeats. Generally, too much is made in this connection of the trauma of loss of empire and economic decline. Neither event was, actually, traumatic. Both phenomena were gradual and relative – the British got steadily more prosperous in absolute terms and Britain continued quite visibly to be the dominant power in many of the ex-colonies. Above all, the British state always seemed to be in fairly firm control of both processes. What mattered far more psychologically were the succession of sharp, clear defeats in battles the state had vowed to win: Suez, de

Gaulle's veto of British EEC membership, the devaluation of 1967, the failure to bring Rhodesia to heel and the dénouement over *In Place of Strife* at the hands of the unions in 1969.

These defeats were bad enough in themselves, but quite equally damaging was the apparent loss of authority by the state. Despite his boasts of the 'smack of firm government' Harold Wilson gave the impression that the state was humbled and knew it. Wilson recurrently sought compromises with Smith over Rhodesia which Smith contemptuously spurned. Wilson would clearly do whatever he was told to do by Lyndon Johnson over Vietnam; George Brown was dispatched on a further humiliating tour of Europe in order to have the EEC door slammed in his face again; Wilson couldn't make his pay freeze and incomes policy stick with the unions; and when unions went on strike the strike leaders were invited for beer and sandwiches as if 10 Downing Street was a transport café. This last was powerfully symbolic: Labour rule was resented as essentially ignoble within the Tory culture because it let the barbarians in at the gate. If one group was clearly outside the 'public' it was trade unionists and, *a fortiori*, strikers. If there was any point in Labour rule at all it was that now the unions might more easily listen to (i.e. obey) the government. But lo! the reverse was happening. The government was crawling to the unions and *still* getting humiliated by them.

Worse was to follow under the Heath government of 1970 4; further rebuffs over Rhodesia; a complete U-turn on economic policy when the government ran into too much trouble; the bringing into ridicule of the new Industrial Relations court, with a Crown Justice, no less, made a public fool of; the humbling of the government by the Pentonville Five – including the crowning humiliation of the government's invention of the Official Solicitor to get itself off the hook; a traumatic public trouncing of the government in the 1972 miners' strike; a further trouncing by the Clydeside shipworkers led by Jimmy Reid; and then, worst of all, the utter rout of the government in the 1973–4 miners' strike. Nor was even this all – the actual territorial integrity of the state was seriously challenged for the first time in hundreds of years, not just by the civil war in Ireland, but by the rising nationalist wave in Scotland and Wales. This was almost beyond belief. The barbarians were not only in at the gate, they were eating grapes in the Senate. For it was quite clear that neither the Pentonville Five, nor the miners, nor the IRA, nor the Celtic nationalists were members of 'the public'. Yet when the Heath government finally took a stand against the barbarians in 1974 it was evicted.

The year 1974 was by far the greatest national trauma since the Blitz. Its shock-waves reached far into the years ahead – we feel them powerfully still. The events also provided a real vision of *Götterdämmerung* in the shape of the massed crowds of burly proletarians, Arthur Scargill at their head, who overwhelmed the police at Saltley coal depot, and the flying pickets, a virtual private army against which the forces of law and order could not prevail. Even the great symbolic guardian of the public, the British bobby, was brushed aside. This was the barbarian invasion indeed. And the barbarians had won.

At the same time traditional Toryism was under threat from more subtle forces. The diminution of the old electoral class polarisation meant that an increasing section of the old middle ground was willing to desert the Tories for the Liberals, even at general elections. The Left naturally, and with a striking lack of discrimination or tactical sense, rallied joyfully behind each new sectional group to defy the authority of the state. The miners and Clydesiders, and particularly Arthur Scargill, Jimmy Reid and Mick McGahey, were its heroes, but so were the Pentonville Five and the Clay Cross councillors. Some Left-wing intellectuals swiftly overcame a lifetime commitment to a centralised Socialist state to advocate the cause of the Welsh or Scottish nationalists (Tom Nairn is a symbolic figure here) – or even the IRA.

For the Left, usually without having worked it out, sensed the importance of the dominant state to the Tory ethos; sensed too that the state was groggy, on the ropes; and threw itself into every possible avenue which might help deliver the final *coup de grâce*. The fact that this gave one some very strange bedfellows was unimportant. Interestingly, it was at this time that the Left as a whole began suddenly, after three hundred years, to take a strong interest in the history of the Civil War, the Levellers, the Diggers and so on. This popularisation of the one great and absolute defeat of the state and the only real break in its historic continuity, was partly a reflection of how far the mask of state authority had already been torn away. But it also reflected a deep though often quite unconscious longing that a truly decisive and lasting defeat – something comparable to the Battle of Naseby – could again be inflicted on the hated Tory state, its culture and all its works. The denizens of the Tory culture sensed this mood too. They too would have been hard-pressed to define their anxieties rationally and exactly – ignorant armies were clashing by night. But they could sniff the air, feel furious – and scared.

Finally, the Tory culture came under pressure from a more unexpected direction and from a force potentially more powerful than all the others – the market. The always increasing social penetration of market forces gradually created a new popular ethos which was actively hostile to the old Tory aristocratic order, which eroded deference and which demanded greater openness, modernity and managerial competence. And, above all, the market insistently pushed forward the notion of consumer sovereignty. The result was a real internal crisis for the Tory culture – one which it seems incapable of ever overcoming. For the fatal contradiction is that while Conservatism is committed to the promotion and encouragement of market forces, a Tory culture based upon the absence of any notion of popular sovereignty can never really accommodate the notion of consumer sovereignty. If there really is no free lunch – if the market is the one great fundamental – and the people's choices and wishes are ultimately sovereign in that market, how can the people fail to be sovereign in the political and every other field? Moreover, the philosophy of the market is anarchic. It is hostile to the strong state. It respects only what is powerful in the market. It is antagonistic to monopoly, let alone a hereditary monopoly such as the monarchy. It vulgarises and commercialises and in the end de-mystifies whatever it touches.

Already this process has, indeed, powerfully affected the monarchy itself. In the homeland of the market – the USA – consumer sovereignty now extends all the way to making popular idols – astronauts or movie stars – head of state. The younger scions of the royal family have clearly already accepted the same logic, that they are now part of the show business/celebrity world. They are an essential celebrity presence at big sporting and business events, invite popular comedians to their weddings, live the life of the Hollywood rich in Caribbean resorts, sponsor fund-raising campaigns, become fashionable photographers and have well-publicised entanglements with blue-movie starlets. Already one hears seriously intentioned argument that spectacular royal occasions are 'good for the tourist industry', while Lady Di's face on the cover of *Woman's Own* sells an extra 50,000 copies. Perhaps we shall come to see Trooping the Colour sponsored by Kodak, a royal wedding by Mothercare? A topless Koo Stark on our stamps would no doubt trigger a philatelic boom. . . . The monarchy has hitherto had major sacral importance and is still the head of the Church of England, but clearly neither it nor, *a fortiori*, anything else, is sacred any more. If market forces can wreak this sort of change on even the monarchy in less than twenty years, then clearly none of the shibboleths of the Tory culture are safe for long.

The growth of 'market consciousness' and the diffusion of the notion of consumer sovereignty have impacted heavily and repeatedly on the Tory bloc in the last two decades. Its first effect was to make the old 'magic circle' of the Macmillan–Home years seem archaic and pernicious. When the Powell–Macleod revolt in 1963 failed to prevent the Home succession Labour actually won the next election by appearing more modern and managerial than the Tories. This was simply impermissible for the party which was supposed to represent management. In future younger, more meritocratic leaders had to be found (not an easy thing to do on the Tory parliamentary benches): Labour must not be allowed to play the anti-feudal card again. Home was brutally ditched, a leadership election system devised and Heath elected. When Heath disappointed, a means of de-electing the leader and then a new electoral system were devised, and Heath ditched.

The leadership of the Tory Party had, until this point, operated very much as a reflection of the monarchical state. The leader had complete power over the party organisation, but was aloof, unelected, not directly responsible to anyone. Given that Tory conferences were heavily stage-managed to the point of being rigged, party members were anyway in a poor position to make leaders responsible. But it was a major symbolic point that the leader did not even attend the conference, arriving only on its last day to emit rallying cries and receive the statutory standing ovation. The leader had to pay some attention to the views of Tory backbench MPs. But not much: Macmillan was able to treat his backbenchers with scarcely disguised contempt and got away with it time and again. The only real check on the leader's authority lay in the small oligarchy of party grandees at the party's summit. But their influence could be tenuous and was almost always invisible so that the face the Tory leader presented to the world was not only untrammelled by any formal mechanism of responsibility, but was scarcely less monarchical than that of the Crown itself. Again, the only analogies with this sort of extreme leadership principle to be found outside Britain were in fascist parties (even Communist leaders are always formally elected). But it was 'natural' that it should be so – what should better reflect the Tory culture than the Tory Party itself?

The abolition of the old non-elected leadership was thus a major sign that the old equilibrium had gone. Immediately, it became the rule that the leader attended the whole of the party conference and sat there taking any knocks that might come from the floor. The conference itself became more assertive. Even so great a grandee as Lord Hailsham found himself howled down over divorce law reform; in 1972 Enoch Powell carried a whole 30 per cent of the delegate vote against the platform over immigration; and there were persistent and growing rumbles from the floor over the stage-managing of debates. A party report on candidate selection raised the suggestion that sitting Tory MPS should be subject to periodic reselection procedures. This was angrily kicked out, but it was another straw in the wind – the same wind of change which was blowing through the other parties as well.

The changes of 1965–75 in the leadership structure meant that Humpty Dumpty was off the wall at last. There is no chance at all now that the old leadership principle can be formally resurrected. Thus far, at least, the great gainers have been Tory backbenchers. A Tory leader is now their creation and they can, and if they feel like it, will bring him or her down too. It was the weakning of the leadership that pushed Heath into a risky snap election to regain mastery of the party which in turn produced the utter débâcle of February 1974 – the greatest crisis of the Tory culture has yet known.

The building of the backlash

The vote which disposed of the Heath government in February 1974 was, on the face of it, distinctly odd. Poll after poll showed large majorities taking the government's side not only against the miners, but on every major policy area as well. Labour was distinctly unpopular – indeed, the polls showed that the party was likely to be trounced. When Labour won and the polling entrails re-examined it was found that the only question on which Labour had enjoyed an advantage over the Tories – its ability to 'deal with the unions' – was also the one which had in the end been decisive. Faced with the horrid reality of a three-day week and the certainty of continuing crisis if the

Tories won, voters had overcome their dislike of Labour policies because in the end what they wanted most was social peace. The reasons that made Labour more able to 'deal with the unions' – its links with the unions and its promise to give them more power via a new 'social contract' – were not popular at all. It was, in other words, exactly the same decision of despair taken by Rome in decline when it entrusted the defence of its crumbling frontiers to barbarian leaders with whom it had struck a deal. Doubtless the Senate neither liked nor trusted such barbarian 'trusties': it was too much to hope that the old imperium could be re-established through them and it was quite likely that they'd either fail to stop the invading hordes or do a deal of their own with them. But you never knew; and it would buy time; and something had to be done.

The vote of February 1974 hung over the rest of the 1970s like a smothering cloud. The 'public' was uncomfortably aware of what it had done and had something of a guilty conscience about it. The commitment to Labour was so shallow and conditional that even after eight months of massive give-aways and election bribes the new government was still only returned by a whisker in October 1974. And Heath, as soon as he had been stripped of power and could do no more harm, became extremely popular. There was a growing rumble of indignation as the TGWU leader, Jack Jones, was seen to be making government economic policy, the unions getting their pickings in the shape of job-protection legislation and the closed shop. Actually union power was extremely transient – within two years the unions had seen their alternative economic policy and their anti-EEC views rejected, falling real wages, mounting unemployment, and the IMF-sponsored round of public spending cuts. None of this prevented a quite extraordinary display of hysteria within the Tory culture. Private armies were organised, the government castigated for leading Britain towards an East European type of people's democracy and the clearly weakened unions denounced as 'the new barons'. What this was really all about was that the implications of 1974 were still sinking in. The parrot cries of 'adversary politics' and 'elective dictatorship' reflected only too clearly the fact that the commitment of the Tory culture was to a strong state first, to the 'public' against the unions second and to democracy only a distant third. It was really just 'They've elected the Socialists and the public will never stand for it' dressed up in new clothes. But the mood was ferocious and pervasive and many hitherto neutral or even Leftish pundits (Paul

Johnson was a representative figure) were entirely carried away by it, revealing, not for the first time, that the deep undertow of the Tory culture reached far beyond the formally Tory ranks.

The government trudged on. There was no disguising its weakness. It had no majority to speak of and had to depend on the odd SNP or Plaid Cymru MP (barbarians both) to struggle through. It was clearly unable to preside over any great reassertion of state authority which was what the Tory culture wanted. Inflation hit 25 per cent and the pound went through the floor. Wilson jumped ship. The government was so little able to make authoritative decisions even on the future of the state itself that it threw the questions of EEC membership and devolution to popular referendum. With this innovation the issue of popular sovereignty was placed squarely on the table.

None the less, the government trudged on. Under the reassuring figure of Callaghan calm slowly returned. Inflation fell steadily, North Sea oil came on stream, the weather was good, the government's popularity began to rise. Above all, Callaghan seemed to have tamed the unions. Jack Jones had been dispatched by the Treasury and the IMF, and Callaghan slowly but steadily winched down every next round of pay settlements, ignoring the protests of the unions. By autumn 1978 Labour again reached 40 per cent in the polls and led the Tories by a clear 5 per cent. The calm was fragile – the panic and hysteria of 1974–6 had not really gone away, but, however tenuously, the state seemed to have regained command, which meant 'the public' was safe.

All this was dissipated in a trice by the 'winter of discontent' of 1978–9 as NUPE led the hospital workers, the grave-diggers and the garbage-collectors into a series of strikes. If the trade unions had wanted to resurrect the union-versus-policy polarity in the most vivid possible terms, they could hardly have done better than they did. The government, unwilling to go in for strike-breaking (which was exactly what the electorate wanted), sat on its hands. Every echo of 1974–6 was reawakened, but this time hysteria was replaced by a colder but at least equally ferocious hatred of trade union sectionalism. Labour's 5 per cent lead in November 1978 became a Tory lead of 18 per cent by February 1979. This piece of barbarian hara-kiri was followed two months later by another when the SNP withdrew its support from the government. The election was almost a formality. Hatred for what NUPE had done was so pervasive that it reached far into the ranks of trade union members themselves. While only 21 per cent of them had

244 Britain: The Eye of the Storm

voted Tory in 1974, in 1979 33 per cent did. It was the biggest pro-Conservative swing of any group in Britain.

Thatcherism, 1979–83

It is widely believed, and certainly by Mrs Thatcher, that the Thatcher government came to power with a clear blueprint for action which it simply rammed through and then persisted with thereafter. This is not entirely true. Mrs Thatcher is uneducated in economics and has never been renowned as a shrewd or subtle political strategist. Her impact on the British economy was very much that of an ignorant but unabashed child being let loose on, say, the Houston Space Centre, playing the rows of computers as if they were fruit machines. She immediately cut income tax because she believed her own campaign propaganda that this would produce greater effort through higher incentives and also greater investment. There was no sign of greater effort and investment fell. She doubled VAT charges and was then appalled to find that by putting up prices she had caused inflation to take off again. She abolished exchange controls on the grounds that freer exchanges were beneficent in themselves and then watched a gigantic haemorrhage of national resources. She took positive pride in a strong pound and refused to intervene to push its value down and then watched the over-valued currency decimate industry. She suggested that she would put another miners' strike to a referendum, but when the miners turned on the heat she quickly gave way. At first she talked cheerfully about bringing 'supply side economics' to bear, but soon lost interest in that phrase. Equally, there was a great deal of earnest talk about monetarism until it was found that the money supply figures weren't behaving as they should. She insisted that public expenditure had to be cut, and cuts a-plenty there were, only to find that public expenditure was still rising due to the ever-mounting bill for unemployment which her other policies had caused. She said that she was determined above all to cut taxes and then found that the tax take was actually increasing. Having announced that she would set free the productive dynamism of the private sector she found that her policies were causing great chunks of the private sector to go bankrupt.

At the end of two years of this Mrs Thatcher had produced plummeting investment and production, a massive outflow of resources, record interest rates and business bankruptcies, a ruinously strong pound, higher inflation, soaring unemployment and riots in the streets. Not surprisingly, she was often in a minority in her own Cabinet, but she was wholly unworried; 'my blue bunnies' was her term for her colleagues. Her party was aghast: nothing that the trade union barbarians had achieved in power remotely compared with this display of vandalism. The image of barbarism was clearly strong in Tory minds, hence Mrs Thatcher's nickname at this time, 'Attila the hen'. Tory cabals met in almost continuous private session wondering how on earth to get rid of this political King Kong they had so incautiously unleashed.

Mrs Thatcher's own response to all this was to assert that whatever the intellectual arguments against what she was doing, she was confident it would all come out right in the end. She could be so confident because she was 'a gut politician': she wasn't relying on intellectual reasons at all but on instinct. It was observed that despite the crumbling of her backbench base this instinct was clearly appreciated by the blue-rinsed hangers and floggers of the Tory conference who greeted her with wild acclaim.

Political writers generally make fun of the Tory conference delegates, and indeed it is an easy thing to do for they are usually both the most privileged and most backward elements of society. On this occasion it is important to give them credit, however, for they recognised and comprehended the true consistency of Thatcherism before the whole of the rest of the country, which only gradually came to echo their acclaim. What the conferees realised was that here at last they had a true child of 'the public' as leader, one of their own in a way not even Heath (let alone his aristocratic predecessors) had ever been. Her instincts were the instincts of the Tory culture and her energetic reliance on those instincts implied nothing less than a massive counter-revolution: the reassertion of state power in the defence of the 'public' in its old sense.

It is important to give the Tory conferees credit for this early appreciation of what Thatcherism was, for it was by no means clear. Mrs Thatcher herself did not spell it out that way. On the contrary, she went on at great length about the need to curtail the powers of the state and rejoiced that she was 'getting the state off people's backs'. There was, indeed, an important sense in which she herself did not know what she was doing – she was, as she said, acting on instinct. The situation was in any case confusing – the electorate and its major pundits were used to rating governments on a pragmatic economic basis. In those terms the government clearly was a disaster and things were not turning out at all as it had confidently predicted. Finding themselves at sea in this wholly new sort of politics many commentators evinced sheer disbelief that the government could long continue in its chosen course and every journalist competed with his colleagues in spotting the first sign of the 'inevitable' U-turn, rather like *Times* readers spotting the first cuckoo of spring. The reason that the Tory conference delegates grasped the situation better was not due to their superior intellect. Their comparative advantage over all others lay, rather, in their instinct. Like Mrs Thatcher they operated on instinct and they had the same instincts as her. They would have been hard pressed to explain exactly what they understood but understand they did. And they were in raptures: for like was calling to like from the podium of the conference hall to its floor. They were used to conference circus turns where a Hailsham or a Heseltine played to the instinctual gallery, but they'd never had it from a leader before. In its own peculiar way the Tory conference was entering the age of popular sovereignty. This leader might own them, as Tory leaders always had, but they owned her too. It was quite new – and very exciting.

There were clues even then as to what was going on. Mrs Thatcher clearly inhabited a world in which the 'public' still existed in its old sense. You could tell it from the way she spoke about the unemployed. She was willing to offer ritual expressions of pity for them, but her heart was visibly not in it and there was no hint of real compassion for them, let alone apology. She was openly dismissive of the old 'two nations' Tory philosophy, and the unemployed were part of the second nation. When she asked, indignantly, why 'they' didn't do more to help themselves, it was quite clear that 'they' were not part of the 'public'. (One could not speak of 'the unemployed public' – let alone 'the black public' – without making a joke.) And it was not just words but deeds. The 'public' was being given back its old Victorian social contours as this second nation (not just the unemployed but trade unionists in general, blacks, single parents, etc.) was thrown back by joblessness and welfare cuts into a larger and larger lumpen group. These groups clearly did not belong in polite society and now they were being thrust outside it again in much the same way as the inhabitants of 'outcast London' a century before. It was all quite open – right down to Mrs Thatcher's public nostalgia for that Victorian world.

This was grasped, at least in outline, by the Tory faithful. They realised, too, that Mrs Thatcher, despite all the nasty things in the newspapers, was not without compassion. She really cared about 'the public' and was determined to restore to them what was rightfully theirs – higher incomes, lower taxes, cheaper and more docile labour, more help for private health, overseas outlets for their investments and so on. And even in an era of swingeing education cuts she would find the money for more assisted places at private schools despite the open horror of the by no means radical civil servants at the DES. Similarly, even when Sir Geoffrey Howe pleaded against the wasteful irrationality of extending tax relief to those with £30,000 mortgages, she was not to be swayed and, once again, had her way. She knew what was important and she really did care.

Most of all, though, the Tory conference delegates had grasped the secret of the thing which had baffled all the commentators who had watched the electorate greet the advent of mass unemployment with glacial calm. This was that while mass unemployment could never be popular, its effects certainly could be. For in the wake of 1974 and the winter of discontent what the public yearned for above all was to see trade union sectionalism broken on the wheel – and this was just what was happening. Each new defeat for the Leyland workers, Arthur Scargill or ASLEF was greeted with a deep purr of pleasure. The electorate as a whole shared many of these feelings but, in these early days, were more likely to give the credit to tough employers like Sir Michael Edwardes. The conferees, more wisely, gave credit where it was due. Any misgivings at the immense human suffering caused by the creation of an environment in which all strikes failed were quickly submerged in the wrathful indignation felt at each new piece of bombast from Scargill, Benn, Livingstone or Buckton. The disastrously ill-judged political tactics of such figures were, indeed, a crucial support to the government which was able repeatedly to polarise opinion between themselves and this highly visible Left. What the government always had most to fear was that mass unemployment would affront the electorate's feelings of 'fairness' sufficiently to cause a deep revulsion. By being able to hold up the figures of Scargill, Benn *et al.*, they were able to counter this with an even stronger revulsion. One effect of this was to push large numbers of voters, repelled on both sides, towards the Alliance, which was harmless enough from the government's point of view. The more significant effect was to make mass unemployment politically tolerable to an even larger number of Tory voters. Once the 1983 election was out of the way Mr Tebbit was heard jocularly to remark that he hoped Mr Scargill would not change or moderate his views for he was far too valuable to the government just as he was. Like many of Mr Tebbit's jokes, this was not a joke at all.

Finally, the Tory conferees grasped instinctively – and long before the rest of the electorate did – that beneath all the rhetoric about weakening the powers of the over-intrusive state, what was actually going on was an immense reassertion of the power and authority of the state. This was immediately visible in the large pay increases recurrently granted to the key armature of the state – the armed forces, the police and the judiciary; and in the massive increases in the defence budget thereafter. It was evident, too, in the willingness to cut back on civil liberties to increase police powers; in the unprecedented moves to reduce the powers of local authorities to the advantage of an ever more dominant central state; and in the way that a whole range of public service appointments were politicised for the first time. The central impetus here came undeniably from Mrs Thatcher herself, with her repeated query as to whether a candidate was really 'one of us'. Equally striking was the brusque dismissal of all the other traditional claimants for influence within society – not just the trade unions but the CBI, the civil service and the great departments of state were brushed aside or even publicly humiliated. Mrs Thatcher's presumption was so thoroughly presidential, indeed, monarchical, that any government department thought to have an independence of view was regarded virtually as the fifth column of a hostile state. At the end of two years only the Foreign Office and the Bank of England held out, essentially because both were headed by strong-minded men who were also unsackable.

At the end of 1981 it seemed unlikely that the wider electorate would come to share the enthusiasm of Tory activists. It shared many of the instinctual responses of the activists – the Tory culture *is*, after all, the national political culture – but only as a rather pale reflection. It shared the repulsion from Labour and a degree of equanimity over unemployment and a certain grudging respect for Thatcher's personal determination. But it was well aware that the government was no success in the old pragmatic terms and it was not fired with any clear vision of the colossal reassertion Thatcher was attempting. 'Making Britain great again' (as Thatcher put it) was popular, and the cartoonist had picked up the theme – Thatcher as Britannia, as the Iron Lady or clambering over tanks in battle fatigues (as she was much wont to do) – but the tone of such cartoons – mocking and sceptical – had caught the public mood too. If it had been for real . . . well that would be one thing. But the electorate was too hard-bitten by the ghosts of politicians past, promising to 'put the Great back into Great Britain' or appealing to the Dunkirk spirit, while *en route* to the next shabby compromise or climb-down.

The Falklands factor and the 1983 election

It was only against this political background that the significance and meaning of the 'Falklands factor' can be judged. For the Falklands crisis was like a lightning sheet in an electrical storm which causes circuits to jump points, connecting up energy fields which had hitherto existed only potentially. The reassertion of state power was now witnessed in the clearest and most dramatic way possible: its armed might was deployed at a range of thousands of miles with all the *élan*, majesty and derring-do of old. It mattered not at all that the government had brought the crisis on itself, nor that the action taken left Britain with no future policy for the Falklands which was not both implausible and expensive. The assertion of state power itself was the glorious thing. The more the Americans, the UN or the Labour Party carped or dragged their feet, and the riskier the operation was seen to be, the more glorious that assertion was.

It is important to see that the 'Falklands factor' was not just a matter of a wave of military nationalism – indeed, perhaps no war ever has such simple effects. The lightning flash of the war served to illuminate the whole Thatcherite vision and to connect – almost to fuse – large sections of the electorate into it. Those who exulted at the sight of the Union Jack being run up over Port Stanley were not merely pleased that the crisis with the Argentinians had been resolved; indeed, they were aware that it hadn't really been solved at all. They were exulting at the reassertion of a strong state, a state which would protect 'the public', which would break trade union power, which would, in a word, restore the whole pantheon of the Tory culture. For with the Falklands crisis much of the wider electorate came to share, temporarily at least, the same mental world as the Tory activists, their enthusiasms and their certainties.

The Falklands war had two major political results. First, it made Mrs Thatcher unchallengeable within the Tory party and enabled her further to increase the personal concentrations of executive power in her own hands. It has been common, since Crossman first wrote about it, to refer to this phenomenon as the presidentialisation of British politics, but this is a misnomer. Presidents belong in republics. Similarly, Thatcher's happy willingness to embrace the personalist implications of popular sovereignty has led some to use the term 'authoritarian populism', but this too is a misnomer. Historically, populists have drawn their strength and distinctive style from the way they have been willing to include even those with bare feet and ragged clothes, the lumpen elements of street and prairie, into their broad cross-class coalitions. But Mrs Thatcher quite consciously appealed to a more restricted 'public', often *against* precisely that lumpen class. The fact that she none the less gained some support from such elements – always the most demoralised and easily swayed groups – does not contradict this proposition.

These formulae shy away, in fact, from recognising the full extent of Thatcher's personal assertion. As the upward push of popular sovereignty is felt within a monarchical Tory culture what it produces is not populism or presidentialism but a sort of popular monarchsim. Again, the cartoonists provide the clue with pictures of Thatcher actually displacing the Queen, of Thatcher as Boadicea, with the British state personified not by the monarch but by Thatcher. It was clear, moreover, that Thatcher herself instinctively accepted this mode. Returning from one summit conference, she spoke of how Reagan and she had talked together as 'two Heads of State' – a slip no previous British prime minister could possibly have made. During the election campaign she actually spoke of 'I as a government' – a slip no mere president could make, nor even an English monarch at least since Victoria. She claimed that 'I [not 'we'; or even 'this government'] can handle a big majority'. She showed no embarrassment in asserting that she trusted to instinct and that her (personal) instincts should thus provide the basis of the country's rule. When she intervened at an election press conference publicly to correct – and indeed, humiliate – her Foreign Secretary, her style was quite unself-consciously regal. Both in this and in her later attempt to promise away the Speakership (an office over which she has no authority) she went, indeed, considerably further than constitutional monarchs in Britain have felt it prudent to go for several centuries past. In a more practical sense her unashamedly personalist campaign ('The Issue *is* Thatcher', as *The Economist* put it) was climaxed by her final reduction of the two redoubts which had hitherto eluded her. She flatly dismissed her (still new) Foreign Secretary, filling his Cabinet place – and several others – with more compliant yes-men; and took advantage of the retirement of the Governor of the Bank of England to push in there a personal nominee, who, for all the scandal created by his lack of formal qualification, was clearly 'one of us'. Such an exclusivist phrase, it goes almost without saying, could never be found on the lips of a real populist.

The second major result of the Falklands war was that it made the electorate take a different view of issues quite unrelated to the war. The reassertion of the state it betokened placed a general premium on qualities of strength, firmness and capability. This redounded to the enormous disadvantage of the Labour party, and not just because the Tories under Thatcher were presumed to have all these qualities. The Labour Party's internal divisions would never have helped it, but now they were viewed as disqualifying almost in themselves. Similarly, Michael Foot would never have been an electoral asset, but now he became an unqualified disaster. Labour's candidate for prime minister and presumptive guardian of the strong State, was an old, frail, half-blind man of 70, white hair all over the place and needing a stick to walk. Arrayed against the always immaculate self-presentation of Mrs Thatcher was a man whose popular image was that of a scarecrow (Worzel Gummidge), unable even to keep his clothes in place. He didn't answer straight questions and he didn't finish his sentences. To speak of popular reaction in terms of a 'credibility gap' was insufficient: the notion of Foot as premier was greeted with sheer, gasping incredulity. The early election poll showing a Labour Party led by Denis Healey dead-heating with the Tories at 42 per cent each needs to be seen in this light. No doubt Healey's more centrist image was partly responsible, but his reputation for tough-minded capability was probably even more important.

What was worse was that Mrs Thatcher had irreversibly personalised and presidentialised the choice – the leader's gloss was seen on everything. In the case of Foot this meant that he had a sort of reverse Midas Touch with issues he took up. He was Incapability Foot and he simply spread incapability about. The awesome result was that as Foot and Labour took up one issue after another, on each one the polls showed a strengthening popular belief that the Tories would deal better with it. And Labour could afford a weak leadership

image less than anyone. In every elecion since 1959 the party's
sagging vote had been propped up by the fact that its leader ran ahead
of both the party and his Tory rival in the polls. Now the reverse was
true: even Labour's final 28 per cent was more than twice as high as
Foot's 13 per cent rating as 'best prime minister'. After the election, in
typically sentimental fashion, Labour's NEC announced that no blame
attached to Foot for the party's poor performance. Even Goebbels
might have recoiled at the sheer audacity of this untruth.

The unspoken but dominant theme of the strong state pushed the
issue of defence to the front. The Tories, who had done their market
research well, rejoiced at this. Labour, who had done no such
research, were lured on by polls showing popular majorities opposed
to both Trident and Cruise. The issue simply came apart in Labour's
hands, particularly when Labour indecison over the existing Polaris
armament became clear. Theoretically the debate was over detailed
questions of missile costs and capabilities: in reality it was about
Labour's general ability to defend the strong state. On the first
question Labour had a sympathetic audience, on the second – and far
more fundamental – question, it received a resounding vote of no
confidence. Hence the peculiar, and otherwise inexplicable, poll
findings that while large majorities thought the Tories had a better
defence policy, Cruise and Trident remained unpopular with a
majority of voters even at campaign's end.

Much the same occurred over the key question of the economy, on
which Labour's advantage should have been overwhelming.
Labour's proposal for a National Economic Assessment had always
lacked plausibility but it was now taken as a further damaging sign of
Labour weakness in the face of trade union pressure. Again, the
Tories' superior market research enabled them to exploit this opening
to devastating effect. The key Tory TV commercial panned across the
desolation of 1978–9 'winter of discontent' and began 'Do you
remember what it was like before 1979?' It was an extremely
audacious tactic, given the Tory record, to draw attention to a scene
of economic dereliction; more audacious still to use material from
before even the preceding election; and remarkably open in admitting
the revolutionary nature of the post-1979 change. But it was
brilliantly effective. The Tories had realised how enduring were the
images of earlier trade union bloody-mindedness, how the ghost of
1974 still walked. A Labour return to power meant going back to the
bad old days, the sort of antics which had got BL into a mess, to a fresh

lease of life for ASLEF, Arthur Scargill and other leaders of declining industries determined to use industrial muscle to halt the modernisation and rationalisation of Britain's industrial base. The Tories were now the party identified with the scientific revolution, Labour with economic Canute-ism.

The prospects for Thatcherism

Writing in the hour of Thatcherism triumphant it takes a certain boldness to predict its impending collapse. It is difficult to know how much that has changed has done so permanently. The mood of aggressive Toryism – of hero-worshipping the military, of a special spot for royalty every night on the TV evening news and so on – will probably not last. On the other hand it is difficult to believe that the British electorate will come at all quickly to tolerate again a government which, like those of 1945–79, is visibly in hock to mere pressure groups. In part this is simply because the ethic of the strong state is so enduring and now again so strongly reawakened. Mrs Thatcher's brutal toughness has been much admired and the electorate will not easily displace her for any leader who is not equally tough-minded, clear-eyed and determined. But in part this stems simply from the increasing atomisation of society which tolerates less and less the presence of powerful intermediaries between the sovereign electorate and its leaders. In this context Labour's relationship with the trade unions is not a stable handicap but an increasing one.

On the other hand it seems clear that the mock heroics of 1979–83 will give way soon enough to the reality – and the realisation – that, whatever its achievements on small islands in the South Atlantic, the British state has failed calamitously in its attempt to act as a ruthless midwife to a new era of ultra-capitalist prosperity. Mrs Thatcher's economic policies got through 1983 partly through a sense of a great experiment which was, as yet, only half-way complete. It is unlikely that the suspension of disbelief can last beyond the next election – there will be no excuses then. The mere fact that North Sea oil production will plateau and then fall will be enough to remove the underpinnings of Thatcherism. As this happens and the balance of payments worsens, the government will either have to admit defeat and make a prodigious U-turn; or it will engage in further endless rounds of deflation, which, coming on top of an already terrible economic depression, will inevitably be electorally suicidal in the end. The only hope for Thatcherism in such a scenario lies in a degree of division and incompetence on the part of the Opposition parties which is quite difficult (though not impossible) to believe in.

Long before that occurs, however, it is safe to predict that Mrs Thatcher's personal position within the Tory Party will come under threat. There is, though, an almost insuperable problem here. Never much given to intellectual self-doubt, Mrs Thatcher was, in the wake of the 1983 election, clearly riding a dangerously euphoric personal 'high'. Perhaps the clearest sign of this was her claim that she felt she almost communicated with Churchill in reverie, that she 'felt very close to Winnie' now. In the Tory pantheon of Mrs Thatcher's dreams that means 'close to God', so that the sheer familiarity of that 'Winnie' implies an almost divine status for Mrs Thatcher herself. What this means politically, is that Mrs Thatcher will probably be the last person in Britain bar none to contemplate a change of course; and also that if the Tory chieftains attempt to dislodge her, she will not go quietly.

And that is the nub of the problem. In the early 1950s Churchill's Cabinet colleagues, desperate to retire their clearly comatose leader, deputed one of their number to deliver their ultimatum. Churchill's only words of reply were 'Bugger off.' It was all he needed to say. If he would not go quietly the Cabinet could hardly risk newspaper headlines of how a backstairs cabal had forced out the man not even Hitler could bring down. Mrs Thatcher, on a rather lower scale, has now achieved a somewhat similar position. Owing to a series of accidents and vagaries of fate she unexpectedly hi-jacked the leadership of British Conservatism in 1975. In some ways her reign has seen the apotheosis of the Tory culture, but, to a degree which is likely to un-nerve traditional Tories in the end, the fate of British Conservatism has become inextricably linked, indeed subordinated to, the new and unstable phenomenon of Thatcherism. Something very similar happened to the American Republicans under Nixon. Here too one found Conservatism biting deep into the blue-collar vote, with the second election (of 1972) providing not merely a bigger victory than the first, but a landslide more than comparable with what Mrs Thatcher achieved in 1983. Here too was a leader of clear monarchical tendencies, much given to wrapping himself in the flag and to visceral displays of military force. When, in the end, he over-reached himself, the collapse was total and his party went down with him, even though traditional Conservatives had long been alienated by the leader's personalist style. None of this is certain to happen in the Britain of the 1980s, but it should, at least, give one pause. It is quite possible that in the hour of Thatcherism's triumph the seeds of its destruction have already been sown.

22

Must Labour Lose?

Ever since 1959 the question 'must Labour lose?' has hovered over the Left in Britain. It is, though, a question which has a wider than just a parochially British interest. Britain was the first country in the · world to experience the industrial revolution. It was the first to have a working-class majority. Its working class is older than any other: many Britons are now in the third or fourth generation of continuous proletarian status. It was the country which provided the major empirical background for the work of Marx and Engels: *Das Kapital* was written in London. And in the post-1973 recession it is in Britain that the collapse of the old manufacturing industries – a trend evident throughout the capitalist West – has gone furthest. For all these reasons, and despite the shrinkage in Britain's world importance, Britain remains a model of global significance. It is from Britain that the world will learn what happens to a major industrial country which undergoes de-industrialisation, and what behaviour may be expected of a mature working class in such an environment. In this sense the British working-class movement and the British Left has a significance which the usually far stronger force of British Conservatism lacks.

The question 'must Labour lose?' itself has an interesting history. First raised after Labour's third successive election defeat in 1959, it then dropped from public sight as Labour went on to win four out of the next five elections. That these victories were achieved on a steadily diminishing vote and were due almost exclusively to the rising third party vote became a constant refrain of electoral analysts – but nobody on the Left paid much attention. Winning on any terms was quite good enough and most of the Left had a resolutely know-nothing attitude towards electoral analysis, opinion polls and so forth which were regarded, mysteriously, as a 'bourgeois' form of knowledge. The Left only woke up with a start twenty years later, after the crushing Labour defeat of 1979.

This reawakening occurred in a curious fashion. The 'new' recognition of Labour's plight was led principally by Eric Hobsbawm, the distinguished Communist social historian, in the pages of *Marxism Today* (an official Communist Party journal) and in the collection of essays he edited on the subject, *The Forward March of Labour Halted?* The general thesis to emerge from the extensive discussion this triggered was that Labour had failed to win the support of the 'new' working or middle classes; that its old industrial working-class constituency was shrinking rapidly in size; and that even the Labour loyalties of this latter group were a great deal less firm than they once had been. As a result Labour faced an apparently inevitable slide: it was being reduced to the support of a residual and shrinking electorate concentrated mainly in declining regions and industries and on old-style council estates. The only way out, it was suggested, was for Labour to seek, instead, to put together a coalition of radical interest groups – its remaining working-class constituency plus women's groups, gays, animal rights and peace campaigners and so on.

What made this all so curious was not just the extremely belated nature of the recognition that Labour was in trouble. It was also clear that none of the contributors to this debate had bothered to become acquainted with the large body of electoral research which had accumulated on these topics: they still all had twenty years' reading to catch up on, and the new strategy they proposed was put forward without any supporting data based on opinion poll or other electoral analysis to suggest that it might actually work. Hobsbawm himself, despite his undoubted talents as an eighteenth- and nineteenth-century historian, was a complete stranger to the world of the sample survey, cohort analysis, electoral marketing and the like. It was strange indeed to think that Labour needed to take instruction in such areas from someone who was a lifetime member of quite another political party, one whose regular and vertiginous decline had in no way been stemmed by the wise counsel Professor Hobsbawm had been able to offer its leadership on such matters.

Despite these oddities the Hobsbawm theses quickly entered the bloodstream both of the Labour Party and the media. One result was that the Labour manifesto drawn up for the 1983 election bid wildly for the support of every radical pressure group in sight. The section on defence was simply an adoption of the CND platform. Radical women's groups inserted their platforms whole. The same thing happened with the animal rights lobby and not a few others. At the end the manifesto was like an old-time warship decked out in signal flags of every colour, each of them flapping its terse and detailed little message into the wind. Labour earned the dubious distinction, for example, of being probably the only major party in the world to enter a campaign with an explicit pledge to abolish value-added tax on sanitary towels. . . .

The second result was to be found in the media's analysis of Labour's defeat in 1983. Labour's plight in the wake of that election was so clearly catastrophic that even the press found itself casting around for longer-term causes than the usual calamitous tally of a poor campaign poorly managed, threadbare organisation, endless factional infighting and laughable leadership. All these things were truer than ever in 1983 – in terms of professionalism and plausibility Labour tailed the Ecology Party by some distance in 1983, and was only just ahead of such newcomers as the Raving Looney Monster and Green Chicken Alliance – and for them the election was *meant* to be a joke. Inevitably the media picked up the basic outlines of the Hobsbawm theses and extended them deterministically into the future. The old class alignment was eroding and Labour was corralled into a shriking ghetto. This ghetto could only shrink further, bringing with it the complete foundering of the Labour Party.

It is always well to display a certain caution when the British press selectively and on occasion discovers subjects like sociology or economic theory. Which major paper, the *Guardian* honourably apart, was not Keynesian until at least 1976 and was not Friedmanite thereafter? Which paper failed to tell us over and over again in the 1960s that Labour was now 'the natural party of government'? Which paper has not continued to repeat the quite verifiable falsehood that Mrs Thatcher has particularly attracted the 'house-wives' vote'? (I well remember the *Observer*'s political editor, John Cole, in 1976 chiding me for 'ivory tower nonsense' in believing that a woman could ever win at all: men would never vote for one. Actually men swung far more heavily than women to Mrs Thatcher in 1979, a trend not reversed in 1983.) Indeed, which newspaper has not forgotten that 'the housewives' vote' was simply a hustings invention of Harold Macmillan, that there is no evidence for the existence of such a thing at all, separate from the general feminine vote? It was the same now with Labour's decline. The press had reduced the matter to a formula which it authoritatively repeated over and over again in the wake of the 1983 election. It was all a bit too pat. By autumn 1983 Labour had shot back up from 28 per cent in the polls to around 37 per cent and suddenly the media lost interest in the question of Labour's irreversible decline.

Given that Labour was back to its inter-war levels of support, it is sensible to start the story there. In terms of votes (though not in seats) the 1983 result was an almost exact replica of the 1923 one, when the Tories took 38.1 per cent of the vote (43.9 per cent in 1983), with Labour next at 30.5 per cent (28.2 per cent in 1983), closely followed by the Liberals with 29.6 per cent (against the Alliance's 25.8 per cent in 1983). The electoral map was decidedly similar too, with Labour support concentrated in its Midland, Northern and Celtic heartlands and, inner London apart, Labour winning almost no seats in the south of England. This remained the basic physiognomy of the Labour vote throughout the inter-war period. It was not just that Labour could not break out beyond the working-class ghetto into the ranks of the middle classes, though this was indeed far beyond its powers. (The phenomenon of the left-wing intellectual was far more shocking to middle-class sensibilities then than later, for it was far rarer.) But nor could Labour capture even half of its 'natural' constituency, the working class. Even in 1935, which saw Labour's record inter-war vote of 37.9 per cent after four years of mass unemployment under the Tories, this remained true. In that election even some Scottish mining areas remained beyond its grasp; Labour failed to win many Tyneside seats – even ones it had won in 1922 – despite the record unemployment in that region; and the Tories only failed by 2000 votes to hold Jarrow. Despite four more years of mass unemployment, the picture had not changed by the outbreak of war. The last Gallup poll published before polls were forbidden as a possible danger to morale, showed the Tories at 51 per cent in February 1940, against only 27 per cent for the combined opposition parties.

Some time in the three years that followed a great seismic shift silently took place within British politics. It is impossible to date this event exactly but scattered by-election evidence suggests it began in 1942. By June 1943, when the Gallup polls resumed, Labour led the Tories 38 per cent to 31 per cent. Thereafter this lead grew steadily to

13 per cent by the end of 1943 and to 18 per cent by February 1945, when Labour led the Tories by 42 per cent to 24 per cent, with the Liberals and Others taking 22 per cent. Only the fact that nobody at the time paid the slightest attention to polls prevented Churchill from realising that, far from being on the brink of a great khaki victory, the Conservatives were in some danger of becoming the third party. In fact the Tories recovered strongly by the time of the election (largely by squeezing the Liberal vote) but still went down to crushing defeat, with a final Labour lead of 8 per cent. Despite the late Tory recovery a full 10 per cent of the electorate had moved to Labour. The result was treated as a sensational surprise on all sides, but it had, in fact, been a foregone conclusion at least since about the time of the battle of Stalingrad. Almost immediately after the election the Labour lead soared back to 19 per cent, with the Tory vote collapsing back to 30 per cent. The sea-change had taken place.

It is important to realise that the Labour vote of 1945 was in some ways a conservative one. Along with radical plans for a brave new post-war world and leftish sympathies induced by the heroic Russian war effort, there was above all the simple fact that the Tories were identified with the mass unemployment of the 1930s and that the working population, having just experienced four years of full employment, were no longer inclined to see unemployment as 'natural' or 'inevitable'. In retrospect the 1930s were remembered with even more bitterness than they were experienced at the time. People wanted above all to hang on to full employment – to keep the gains they had made – and they did not feel they could trust the Tories in that respect. There was, in other words, no real radicalisation. The triumph of Labour took place in a climate where the monarchy, the nobility and the Empire were still popular – as indeed was Churchill. The 'traditional British way of life' – the myth of the idyllic rural past, Beefeaters, cricket on the village green, and all the rest of it, was hardly put in question – indeed people wanted only to return in war-weary relief to enjoy a lot more of it. It had been a 'people's war', with rationing and conscription and cockney good humour through the blitz, but it had also been a deeply patriotic war in which the British bulldog had fought under the full panoply of the old cultural symbols. The workers voted Labour as never before, but the old cultural hegemony of the upper classes, though diluted, was not displaced. The Left had won but Britain had hardly become a Left-wing society. The cry – often heard in 1983 – that Labour must somehow 'recapture the spirit of 1945' ignored all of this, for Labour never bothered to understand quite what had happened in 1945: indeed, the very focus on 1945 suggested that it had all been something to do with a mere election campaign, not with a quite elemental change which had taken place two and three years before that.

The 1945 landslide saw Labour capture a significant number of middle-class votes for the first time, but its gains were far greater among the workers. Something like two-thirds of the entire working class voted Labour. Although this meant that a whole one-third still didn't, the net effect was an enormous strengthening of the class alignment. The election also saw Labour move into southern England in real strength for the first time. While the pro-Labour swing was as low as 2.5 per cent in Glasgow and was 12 per cent nationally, throughout the South-East, the West Midlands and East Anglia the swing was a gigantic 17 per cent to 22 per cent. For the first – and only – time in its history, Labour actually had a majority within England and won a whole clutch of rural seats.

This new class alignment actually became more clear-cut until 1951 as large-scale desertions of middle-class Labour voters were largely compensated for by fresh gains within the working class. In terms of seats won this relatively minor shift was, though, a disaster: by 1951 Labour's three-seat lead in the South of England had become a 107-sead deficit, far outstripping the small further Labour gains in Wales and Scotland and costing Labour power. Even in 1966 Labour never came within a mile of recouping these southern losses.

It is instructive to follow the fortunes of the major parties in the opinion polls through the post-war period – in many ways a better guide than the election results as a steady indicator of the distribution of partisan support, unaffected by short-term pre-election economic booms. The first point to note is that the war years saw potential third-party support (Liberals, Others and Don't Knows) at record levels (over a third of the electorate). This was then sharply compressed by the need for real electoral choice and, no doubt, by the starkness of the class polarisation of 1945–51. The second point is that the data virtually organises itself into sharply contrasting periods of dominance by one of the major parties.

Between January 1947 and December 1951 Gallup took 49 polls in which the Tories averaged 40.2 per cent and Labour only 36.5 per cent: the 1945–51 government is generally popular in retrospect, but it was so unpopular at the time that Labour lost a whole quarter of its 1945 vote in this period. The next period (January 1952 to December 1957) saw an almost exact reversal with Labour averaging 41 per cent and the Tories 37.2 per cent over 65 polls. Then, remarkably, came the period between January 1958 and December 1962 in which the Tories, despite the burdens of office, ran ahead of Labour 35.8 per cent to 35.6 per cent over 58 polls. Riven by splits and immersed in controversies over nuclear disarmament, the party seemed in clear danger of losing its grip on a good portion of the skilled working class ('the affluent workers').

There then followed a sharp Labour recovery which extended from January 1963 to December 1966. In the 47 polls of this period Labour averaged 40.5 per cent, giving it the biggest lead over the Tories (with 34 per cent) since the war. This was achieved largely by a very successful exercise in image projection. Despite a wholly un-modernised Labour organisation and a unity achieved by drawing a veil over policy disputes rather than settling them, Labour put itself forward as a modernising, technocratic alternative to a decadent, aristocratic Conservatism. Harold Wilson was shrewd enough to understand that neither the party nor the country had the stomach for an anti-capitalist crusade but could be coaxed – just – into a preference for scientific managerialism over feudalism. Even so, the social content of the message was restricted to the odd disparaging remark about 'the 14th Earl' and was later wholly disavowed by Wilson once he too became a peer.

Having achieved power the Wilson government dissipated its popularity in quite unprecedented fashion. Over the period January 1967 to June 1970 Labour averaged only 30.2 per cent over 42 polls, with the Tories at 39.6 per cent. There seems little doubt that this was the period in which the quite decisive damage was done to Labour support, which was never to average over 40 per cent again for any period of time. Across the whole year of 1968 Labour support averaged only 25.2 per cent, a level touched by the Conservatives only in 1944–5. Ironically, it was just about this time that Butler and Stokes's *political Change in Britain* appeared, suggesting that Labour was about to become the dominant party for simple demographic reasons. Because children generally inherit their parents' political affiliations Labour would now draw major advantage from the fact that the children of the pro-Labour generation of '45 were now entering the electorate. One needed look no further than the opinion polls of the late 1960s to see that Labour was moving away from, not towards, a dominant party position, but for a while, at least, this helped to nourish a quite unreal Labour optimism – as did Goldthorpe and Lockwood's explosion of the 'affluent worker' hypothesis at much the same time.

After August 1970 Labour did recover – but never back to its old levels. In the period from then until January 1974 the party averaged 37.7 per cent over 42 polls, with the Tories falling sharply to 32.4 per cent. With Labour's return to power in 1974 the positions were reversed. Between March 1974 and March 1979 Labour averaged 33.5 per cent and the Tories 36 per cent. This period concluded with the Thatcher victory of May 1979, produced quite largely by the heavy defections among male skilled workers to the Conservatives, a movement which continued in June 1983.

The poll data for May 1979 to June 1983 was quite unlike anything which had gone before. From 1979 to 1981 Labour gradually rebuilt its lead over an extremely unpopular Tory government. With the formation of the SDP in March 1981 the SDP/Liberal Alliance soared into the lead with a regular 40–45 per cent in the polls. At first both Labour and Tories collapsed to 25–27 per cent, but by mid-1981 Labour had recovered to a steady 33 per cent while the Tories fell to under 25 per cent. At this stage it seemed clear that the Alliance was hurting the Tories more than it hurt Labour, but all this was changed quite dramatically by the 1982 Falklands war: the Tories soared back to a steady level over 40 per cent, the Alliance virtually collapsed and the votes it took were now clearly hurting Labour more. The 1983 election saw the Alliance regain some of its lost ground while Labour fell back during the campaign from about 35 per cent to 28 per cent. To find a similar example of such gross volatility and such a large potential third-party vote we have to go all the way back to the 1942–4 period.

The central fact to emerge from this data is that British politics has, until recently, been conducted in the shadow of the 'critical election' (as political scientists call it) of 1945, that is an election which registers a major sea-change within the body politic which is merely confirmed time and again in succeeding elections. Despite all the rhetoric about war-time unity, the experience of war was a profoundly divisive one which greatly increased the class polarisation of the electorate. Immediately, and largely, this worked to the advantage of

264 Britain: The Eye of the Storm

the Labour Party, but it helped the Tories too by making them the only possible bulwark against Labour power. Hence the fact that although quite large numbers of people were tempted towards a third-party choice in the 1940s and 1950s, they were invariably squeezed back towards the major parties at election time. Only this can explain why the major parties both performed within the 43 per cent to 49 per cent range in every election until 1974, although the combined major party vote was a good 15 per cent lower than that all the rest of the time.

This alignment of forces was always threatening to erode, partly because of the artificiality of the first-past-the-post electoral squeeze required to sustain it. But it was also vulnerable simply because Labour did not, when it had the chance, act to change or abolish the key social and cultural institutions which so powerfully biased the whole policy in a Conservative direction. Even after long periods of Labour government the country still endured the dominance of the public schools, Oxbridge, the City, an established church, the nobility, the monarchy and a vastly inflated military establishment. In such an environment, with its deep cultural bias towards a sort of Tory Merrie England, a Labour vote remained a deviant one. It is perhaps no accident that it was in the South and South-East – the geographical epicentre of this ruling culture – that Labour had lost its grip as early as 1951, nor that it was able to consolidate its position only in the socially and culturally outer regions. Given the limitations of the 1945 'revolution' it would not, of course, have been at all easy for Labour to mount an assault on the hegemonic institutions of the ruling culture, but it was not inevitable that it should not do so. Few things are as inevitable as many Marxists believe.

With the South and South-East already largely gone by 1951, the next groups to begin to tug away from the Labour coalition of 1945 were the somewhat fragile recruits it had gained amongst the middle and white-collar classes, together with some skilled workers. To a not inconsiderable extent this was due simply to an imaginative failure on Labour's part to sympathise with the energetic materialism of these groups. Given that the spread of home-ownership was one of the most effective means towards a more equal distribution of wealth, it was quite remarkable that it became a Tory rather than a Labour selling-point. Most threatening to Labour was the threatened desertion of skilled workers – historically the cutting edge and organising soul of the Labour movement. Without doubt this group began to tug away as early as 1958–62, but its migration only received unambiguous recognition after 1979.

The peeling away, like onion-skins, of Labour's marginal groups was not a unilinear, inevitable process. It was true that the 1945 alignment was ageing. That is, the generation which had come across to Labour stayed loyal on the whole, but was diminished by mortality. Butler and Stokes were quite right to point out that 'the children of '45' should have been a major Labour asset, but they failed to take into account the fact that an inherited allegiance is bound to be weaker than one that is reached by going through the fire oneself. The young Labour voter of 1966, who voted that way because his parents did, was inevitably a far more likely vote-switcher than were his parents who had themselves stood in the dole queues of the 1930s. Even so, it was open to Labour to consolidate its hold on the newer generations by political means. The best proof of this is that it was actually done by Wilson's wonderfully successful political marketing strategy in 1963–6. From an average poll standing of only 35.6 per cent across the give whole years, 1958–62, Labour went on to take 47.9 per cent of the vote in the 1966 election.

Similarly, no argument from sociological determinism will do unless it takes account of the essentially political collapse of Labour in 1967–70. There was nothing inevitable about this at all. Wilson had come to power with a promise to take economic planning away from the Treasury, to go for growth at all costs, without letting sterling crises push him back to stop–go, and to contain inflation with an incomes policy. The plan was perfectly feasible – and was instantly jettisoned in favour of maintaining the sterling rate, imposing a wage freeze, letting the Treasury have its way and returning to stop–go. It was a simple and complete failure of nerve, courage and commitment. The same was true of policy towards Rhodesia, Vietnam, defence and education. The result was cynicism, demoralisation and a haemorrhage of Labour support which was not equalled even in 1983. The experience enabled the naïve Left – an essential part of every Labour coalition – to argue that Labour reformism had definitively failed and had to be replaced by more fundamentalist policies which a leadership would be unable to 'sell out' because it would be tied hand and foot by new party constraints. Actually, Labour reformism had not been tried at all.

The dismal experience of 1967–70 still lies at the heart of most of Labour's problems today. A whole generation of Labour leadership had tarnished itself almost irretrievably and Labour's 'natural' new recruits, the children of '45, were repelled in droves. Some became revolutionary student activists. Others became rebellious Young Liberals, some Tories, some apoliticals. A large number devoted themselves to 'community politics' and single-issue groups. They avoided Labour like the plague, particularly the best and brightest of them. Much of the support shaken loose in this period was never wholly or whole-heartedly recaptured. It was many times bitten and many times shy. The historic low-point of individual Labour party membership was probably reached in 1968–9 and many constituency parties virtually collapsed. When revival took place it often did so because of an influx of former student radicals, who, though drifting back to Labour, continued to observe a deeper loyalty to their original commitment to more Utopian and ideological forms of socialism. This influx merely fuelled the civil war which simmered within Labour ranks throughout the 1970s, and which lingers still today.

This new Left, as it became more strongly rooted at constituency level, concentrated its energies on the twin objectives of pulling the party leftwards and achieving its internal democratisation. In the old Attlee–Gaitskell days such a campaign would have been easily defeated by the invincible combination of a strong parliamentary leadership backed by the big union bosses. Now it was quite different. The union bosses no longer stood unequivocally behind the parliamentary leadership and that leadership itself was split, weakened by defeat, and gradually disintegrating. Nothing is more remarkable in retrospect than the way in which the 1960s leadership team – the most talented Labour had ever had – simply fell apart. Quite a few (Marsh, Gunter, Brown) had jumped ship even by 1970. Some, like Jenkins, bailed out in the mid-70s and were later joined by the SDP wave at the end of the decade. Quite a few (Soskice, Crossman, Crosland) died. Some, like Wilson and then Callaghan, took the premature retirement route, while some simply became too old (Jay) or went to the Lords (Lever) or Europe (Castle) or went chasing will-of-the-whisps (Longford). Above all, this old Oxbridge generation, which had dominated the Labour leadership since the 1950s, simply failed to renew itself. The few remaining Oxbridge figures (Foot, Benn, Healey, Shore and Silkin) were by 1983 shrinking maidens with their careers largely behind them.

Against this gradually disintegrating leadership the constituency

Left scored gain after gain. It was, in classical fashion, fighting the last war – attempting to fasten on the party policies and procedures which, had they existed then, might have prevented the sell-outs of the Wilson years. Their campaign, when it began, was aimed at a strong, tactically cunning leadership, willing to sacrifice almost anything in the cause of winning elections (something it was distinctly good at). By the time the campaign triumphed the party had a weak, tactically naive leadership without the slightest idea about winning elections.

Moreover, by the time the constituency Left had won it had turned allegiance to its Cause into a touchstone of loyalty to the whole Labour movement – it became Holy Writ. But, more or less by definition, the policies it advocated, however reasonable in the first place, had by then become hideously out of date. The alternative economic strategy dreamt up in 1973 was put into deep-freeze in order to surface as official party policy in 1983. Opposition to joining the EEC in 1971 became 1983's pledge to get out regardless of the irreversible shift in trade flows in the intervening twelve years. A leadership election now meant that the party could be paralysed by internal jockeying for the best part of a year. And so on. Facing opponents who were capable of great flexibility and fleetness of foot, Labour now decided in effect to run the contest as a sack-race. All this to exorcise the dread ghost of Wilson.

Labour's problems had been compounded, ironically, by its surprise victory in the February 1974 election. Indeed, it is clear in retrospect that it would have been far better for Labour to have lost. The flukish Labour victory not only meant more years of Wilsonism. It brought Cabinet rank for the first time for Messrs Prentice, Rodgers, Owen and Mrs Williams, providing them with an essential base from which to launch their later attacks on Labour: it is difficult to believe that the SDP could have acquired the same momentum if it had been led by a few backbenchers and former junior ministers. The 1974 election was also widely understood as the victory of a muscular militantism over a somewhat irresolute Toryism. On the Left this promoted Scargill and Scargillism – that is to say, displays of blustering which do not convince one's allies, which alienate the middle and which infuriate opponents against whom one is not, in fact, strong enough to stand. On the Right 1974 produced a grinding of teeth in determination to the tougher next time and a thin-lipped thirst for social revenge. These currents quickly disposed of Heath, promoted the otherwise inconceivable rise of Mrs Thatcher, and by 1979 eventuated in Thatcherism itself.

Most of all, though, 1974 encouraged Labour to sweep its problems under the carpet and to feel that the arts of political persuasion and political organisation were not so important after all. After 1970 Labour had been riven by factional conflict, had moved sharply to the Left, had done nothing to reform and revivify its antiquated and atrophied structure, and still less to pull back the deserting voters of 1970. And 1970 had seen Labour lose half of all its remaining southern seats as well as become the minority party in the Midlands for the first time since 1935. Despite all this, power had simply fallen into Labour's lap in 1974 like a ripe apple. This fatally encouraged the notion that Labour didn't really need to work or win its victories. The inevitability of continuing national decline meant that all governments would become unpopular quite quickly enough for the old pendulum effect to work. One just had to sit there and wait in the right place. Since this was so, there was no reason not to engage in factional conflict within the party and every reason to do so. For whoever came out on top in that conflict would inherit the corpus of the party so that when the pendulum swung power would drop into their lap. Only this absurd sense of false security can explain the blithely apolitical style of factional conflict which rent the party from then on. Equally, only a party which took an extremely light-hearted view of the need to woo an external electorate could conceivably have elected Michael Foot as leader.

And it was a false security. Labour had won in February 1974 with only 37.1 per cent of the vote. This not merely represented a steep fall from 1970, when Labour had, after all, lost, but was actually the very same percentage that Labour had scored in 1929 and fractionally less than it had achieved in 1935. With this result the last traces of the great sea-change of 1942–5 had at last been wiped out. Labour had won partly due to the miscalculation of their opponents in calling the election when they did and under the conditions they did, and more heavily still to the spoiling effect of the Liberals on the Tory vote. No betting man would have offered serious odds on this combination of factors recurring again any time before the next century, but Labour behaved as if it was a sure thing.

The sharp rise in the Liberal vote, helpful though it had been in 1974, was a major warning signal, for it showed that the mechanics of the electoral system were ceasing to deter the always numerous potential supporters of a third party from becoming actual ones. This trend was even more pronounced in 1983. Ironically, behind a smokescreen of talk about tactical voting the Alliance achieved what success it did by persuading large numbers of people to *stop* voting tactically, indeed to behave as if the proportional representation system they preferred was already in operation. Had tactical voting taken place one would have expected markedly different swings in marginal seats compared to the rest. Of this there was no sign. Instead there were 158 seats which the Conservatives won with less than 50 per cent of the vote. Had Labour and Alliance supporters all voted tactically against the Tories the Opposition would have won all these seats, producing a parliament with 314 Labour and 76 Alliance MPS, with, presumably, a Labour–Alliance coalition government.

The major point to grasp about Labour's electoral evolution is thus not so much that it now enjoys support only on council estates and in declining regions and industries. There is nothing intrinsic to the fact that one works in a declining industry that predisposes a Labour vote. The thousands of business bankruptcies in the South of England in 1979–83 did not produce a new flood of Labour votes there. It is that Labour's electoral profile now again mirrors its inter-war pattern of support prior to the great transformation of 1945. This support is concentrated in the socially and geographically outer regions of the country – where, not surprisingly, much low-quality public rented housing has been put and where investment in new industries has not been put. It is, moreover, misleading to talk simply of the 'erosion of the class alignment', for this erosion has been extremely one-sided. The rich still vote overwhelmingly for the Conservatives. Eton, Oxbridge, the City and the nobility stand as they were. The world of Royal Ascot is quite intact. In almost every sphere – in health, education, employment, housing and wealth – even in mortality rates – class differences have been greatly deepened and rigidified by the impact of Thatcherism and without doubt these trends will continue.

Labour's reversion to its old inter-war pattern of support has happened in two stages. In bad election years during that period Labour took only 30 per cent of the vote or slightly less; in 'good' years, such as 1929 or 1935 it could hope for up to 38 per cent. By the early 1970s it had clearly fallen back from the 43 per cent–49 per cent range typical of the 1945–70 period to around the 38 per cent mark. As we have seen, from August 1970 to January 1974 Labour averaged

37.7 per cent in the opinion polls, and in the next three elections (February and October 1974 and 1979) it won 37.1 per cent, 39.2 per cent and 36.9 per cent respectively. So throughout the 1970s the party performed steadily at the top of the inter-war range, so to speak. In 1983 it fell to the bottom of that inter-war range of results: that is, Michael Foot's leadership seems to have been an incubus almost exactly equivalent to that of Ramsay MacDonald in 1931. Relieved of that incubus, Labour swiftly moved back up to the 37 per cent mark in late 1983.

But was Labour's loss of its 1945 legacy inevitable? It is only partly true to say that this happened through an 'inevitable' process of generational change. Labour could and should have adapted to that – and the experience of 1963–6 shows that this *was* possible. It would be truer to say that Labour has largely squandered its legacy. In part this was because of the inherent limitations of the 1945 transformation itself; in part it was due to the fact that Labour never bothered to understand that legacy properly; and partly it was due to a failure of political nerve and then of political instinct. If one is looking for a personal culprit for all this there is no doubt that Harold Wilson's prints are all over the murder weapon.

On the other hand, the failings of Harold Wilson were not a purely personal phenomenon. He exemplified, albeit in heightened form, the traditional weaknesses of Left leadership in Britain. His timidity and irresolution merely reflected the Left's lack of hegemonic consciousness, even of any real sense of its own historic legitimacy. His relegation of such issues as the abolition of the public schools, reform of parliament and the Lords, and his failure to deliver on his promise of more open government all reflected the Left's longer-term failure to grasp that in Britain the completion of the democratic revolution must needs precede any hopes of Socialist transformation. Or again, his exaggerated respect for powerful vested interests and the way in which he endlessly reshuffled his Cabinet so that Ministers seldom had time to gain real control over their departments reflected the low priority the Left has always accorded in practice to real managerial competence. One only has to compare Wilson's 'artful dodger' style with the calm, competent self-assurance of a Helmut Schmidt or the passionate sense of history of a Mitterrand to realise how Labour's failings stemmed from a deep sense of self-subordination which Wilson exemplified but did not invent.

On the other hand, comparison with the French Socialists does suggest that a Labour recovery from the débâcle of 1983 is hardly impossible, The French Socialists reached their nadir just twenty years before in the early 1960s. Side-swiped by the tidal wave of Gaullism, discredited by the antics of the French Wilson, Guy Mollet, rendered irrelevant in parliament and facing serious internal splits, the party appeared to be in a state of terminal decline. It could look to no help from the unions (the biggest union federation was Communist) and had lost all the great gains it had made in 1945. Its support was reduced to a dwindling band of ageing voters in declining industries and regions. It retained only two real assets. It was able – just – to cling on to its old municipal bastions in Lille, Marseille and elsewhere. And it was clear that if there was ever to be democratic alternative to the monotonously victorious Gaullists, that alternative had to be based upon the Socialists: the Communists were strong but too unpopular to play such a role, while the centrists were popular but too disadvantaged by the electoral system to manage it. That the Socialists managed to rise from the ashes to sweep to power with an overwhelming majority in 1981 was due to the masterful and long-term strategy – it took sixteen years to achieve – of François Mitterrand. True, behind Mitterrand's presidential figure and that presidentialism was part of the strategy stood a whole new generation of Socialist leaders, untarnished by Molletism. But it was Mitterrand, above all, who provided the patience, the cool nerve, who simply out-thought and out-planned his opponents.

Labour's position in the wake of 1983 was weak – but still far stronger than that of their French analogues twenty years before. It is still the main opposition party in the country and overwhelmingly so in parliament. It enjoys (the admittedly mixed blessing of) the support of a united and far larger trade union movement. Even after allowing for its recent erosion, this union base still provides Labour with a more considerable organisational and financial base than the French Socialists possess even today. Labour still also retains its municipal bastions. Indeed, one of the most striking though least remarked phenomena of 1983 was the way in which Labour roughly held its own in municipal elections only a month before it dramatically failed to do so in the parliamentary elections. The discrepancies between the two outcomes were often very striking. In southern England, for example, Labour easily held on to large municipal majorities in both Oxford and Norwich – but then failed to win any parliamentary seat in these two cities. There is some reason to believe that one of Labour's major and unappreciated assets at the moment lies in its large store of locally well-rooted councillors enjoying what the French term the *prime du sortant*. The same may also apply in some degree at parliamentary level: although Labour lost 60 seats in 1983, only 26 of its sitting MPS lost their seats.

Moreover, Labour, like the French Socialists before them, still clearly provides the central core of any possible democratic alternative to Conservative rule. Even if Labour were to agree to stand down its own candidates and support those of the Alliance instead wherever the Alliance came second in 1983 this would, in 1983, have yielded only an extra 53 seats for the Alliance. Even if there should be a further large erosion of the Labour vote it will almost certainly remain true that no anti-Conservative majority can be assembled in which Labour does not play a crucial, probably preponderant part.

In terms of public support, Labour starts with a stronger base than the French Socialists ever had. Even with Labour reduced to its 28 per cent–37 per cent inter-war range of support this remains true. But in Britain's less than fully multi-party system 37 per cent is seldom likely to be enough to produce a parliamentary majority: to do that Labour needs to move back well over the 40 per cent mark. The formation of the Alliance has clearly made such a target more difficult of achievement, but it is hardly impossible. Even after four disastrous years of internecine Labour strife, opinion polls at the outset of the 1983 campaign suggested that Labour under the leadership of Denis Healey would receive 42 per cent of the vote. Apart from exemplifying the wholly new way in which British politics have been presidentialised, the poll showed that a large penumbra of former and potential Labour voters still exists.

None the less, Labour's results through the 1970s show that breaking back through the 40 per cent line is not going to be easy, particularly since many Labour policies are now distinctly unpopular with the electorate. What can be said with some certainty is that the strategy now urged upon Labour of putting together a coalition of radical pressure groups will not work. In part this strategy was tried in 1983 and it failed disastrously. This was hardly surprising: this strategy is usually propounded by those who are themselves members of one or other radical pressure groups and whose vote Labour is anyway fairly sure to get. So it gains no new votes. On the other hand the impression that Labour is controlled by such pressure groups (trade unions, CND, women's lib, etc.) repels large number of more marginal voters on the party's rightward flank. Thus, for example, the women's vote: despite – or because of – Labour's adoption of a strongly women's lib platform in 1983, the party lost a whole 28 per cent of its feminine vote, so that whereas Labour had a 30 per cent – 24 per cent majority over the Alliance among men, among women it was down to a 28 per cent – 28 per cent equality. Similarly, Labour's wholesale adoption of the CND platform did not prevent a large leakage of anti-nuclear voters across to the Alliance. It simply has to be accepted that today's mass electorate is increasingly antipathetic to political parties which appear to be in hock to pressure groups. Any strategy which counts on an even closer Labour identification with the more strident and noisier pressure groups runs exactly contrary to this dominant trend and is, accordingly, a recipe for disaster, particularly since all such pressure groups seem quite incapable of delivering a disciplined bloc vote of their own. This is true even of the trade unions: in 1983 voters who were members of white-collar unions were actually *more* likely to desert Labour than voters who weren't union members at all, while even blue-collar union leaders could not prevent a massive 27 per cent of their previously Labour-voting members from deserting the party.

Equally clearly, though, the old strategy – of mounting a reactive, defensive and populist tirade against the government in power and then waiting for the swing of the pendulum to drop victory in one's lap – will not do. In part this is because reliance on the pendulum effect, if it was ever sensible, is so no longer. The swing required to put Labour back into power is too big. Electoral volatility no longer works in such a tidy fashion anyway, especially since disenchanted Tory voters now have a third alternative place to go. More important, such a strategy depended on mobilising the defensive reflexes of a solidaristic working class. As Hobsbawm is only the latest to discover, one can no longer depend on that. A victorious Labour Party of the future is clearly likely to be more of a modern 'catch-all' mass party than the trade-union-centred 'party of the labour movement' of yore.

A third – and perhaps more likely possibility – is for Labour to overcome its distaste with the Wilson years sufficiently to ac-knowledge that whatever the disasters of Wilson-in-office, Wilson the campaigner was uniquely successful. Twenty years on, the 1963–6 period still stands out as the unique occasion when, by essentially political means, Labour made large enough gains to overturn a record Tory majority. This success rested on a number of factors: the papering over of party disunity; the downplaying of unpopular policies on nationalisation and defence; adroit use of the media; the projection of a youthful, dynamic and overtly presidential leadership; a firm commitment to planned growth ('and end to stop–go'); and, perhaps most of all, an aura of authoritative technical and intellectual competence. The fact that this turned out to be a fraudulent prospectus in office does not remove the fact that it was a winning one at the polls.

This strategy holds the greatest promise of success, but it is also the most difficult. The fact that it has been done once makes repetition harder, not easier: and conscious echo of Wilsonism would alone be disastrous. It will be harder to play down unpopular policies now. The media are far less friendly. The Tories are unlikely to put up such a bumbling performance as they did in 1963–6. And without a doubt the Labour leadership team of the middle-1980s is far less talented and has far less intellectual authority than its predecessors of twenty years ago. Finally, this time campaign style alone would not be enough. Labour would have actually to do what it said and carry through the political transformation it failed to effect before. All this would have to be done, moreover, on the basis of dramatically weaker party finances and in competition with a far more considerable third-party alternative. Clearly, Labour under Kinnock is unlikely to discard this strategy out of hand, but the obstacles to success are very great.

Finally, there is the Mitterrand strategy: open acknowledgement of one's initial weakness and thus a formal acceptance of an alliance with other Centre–Left partners; the art being to assume the leadership of such a coalition in such a way that one gradually fleeces one's partners of their voters, so that they are forced to tag along in an increasingly dependent fashion. In Labour's case this might involve an open offer of co-operation with the Liberals (though not the Social Democrats). Such a strategy would be a gamble. It would upset the local Labour parties which would have to stand down their own candidates to support Liberals. It might redound to greater Liberal than Labour advantage – though in terms of seats won that would be virtually impossible. It would be very difficult to operate such a strategy without conceding the possibility of a transition to proportional representation. And, finally, it is not clear that British politicians have sufficient flexibility or subtlety to play a winning game of coalition politics, particularly if the first move consists of an open admission of one's own weakness. Perhaps Labour needs a yet further electoral trouncing before it looks seriously at such an option. Against that stands the fact that this strategy is the most likely to defeat the Tories at the next election, and that a further Labour defeat could so weaken the party – and its leadership – that its options would then become very limited indeed.

In the past Labour's status as the only alternative to the Tories meant that strategic thinking was seldom necessary. In those bygone days party leadership was largely about tactical questions. Now all that has changed. Over the next few years the Labour leadership will have to choose quite consciously which of the above strategies it will follow. It is possible, of course, that the leadership will simply fail and will get pushed by intra-party pressures and the pace of events into making such choices unconsciously. None the less, choose it must. This gives a quite peculiar importance to the leadership itself in the period ahead.

Such an emphasis on the individual decisions of individual men will no doubt be resisted by those who have somersaulted from predicting the 'inevitable' forward march of Labour to projecting its equally 'inevitable' decline. The truth is that neither form of this sociological determinism will do – our survey of the evolution of the Labour vote shows well enough that this cannot be understood without reference to what politicians actually got up to, as well as the social categorisation of those who voted for them. The role of political leadership in all this cannot be denied: no de Gaulle, no Fifth Republic; no Mitterrand, no united Left in power in France today. All this is truer than ever in British politics now, with the increasing trend towards presidentialisation and the increasing room for political manœuvre created by the dramatic flux and volatility of the electorate. There is no 'must' about Labour's very survival as a mass party any more. *A fortiori* there is no 'must' about Labour winning any more than there is, yet, any 'must' in answer to the question 'must Labour lose?'